Ashes to Ashes

Also by Marcus Berkmann

Rain Men: The Madness of Cricket

Zimmer Men: The Trials and Tribulations
of the Ageing Cricketer

A Matter of Facts: The Insider's Guide to Quizzing

Ashes to Ashes

35 YEARS OF HUMILIATION (AND ABOUT 20 MINUTES OF ECSTASY) WATCHING ENGLAND v AUSTRALIA

MARCUS BERKMANN

Little, Brown

LITTLE, BROWN

First published in Great Britain in 2009 by Little, Brown

A CIP catalogue record for this book
is available from the British Library.

ISBN 978-1-4087-0179-9

Typeset in Bembo by M Rules
Printed and bound in Great Britain by
Clays Ltd, St Ives plc

Papers used by Little, Brown are natural, renewable and recyclable
products sourced from well-managed forests and certified
in accordance with the rules of the Forest Stewardship Council.

Little, Brown
An imprint of
Little, Brown Book Group
100 Victoria Embankment
London EC4Y 0DY

An Hachette UK Company
www.hachette.co.uk

www.littlebrown.co.uk

CONTENTS

	Introduction	1
One	1972	11
Two	1974/75	25
Three	1975	37
Four	1977	49
	Interlude	67
Five	1978/79	69
Six	1979/80	83
Seven	1981	95
	Interlude	114
Eight	1982/83	118
Nine	1985	136
Ten	1986/87	151
Eleven	1989	168
	Interlude	188
Twelve	1990/91	191
Thirteen	1993	201
	Interlude	213
Fourteen	1994/95	215
Fifteen	1997	229
Sixteen	1998/99	242
Seventeen	2001	255
Eighteen	2002/03	267
Nineteen	2005	277
	Interlude	302
Twenty	2006/07	307
	Acknowledgements	309
	Bibliography	311

INTRODUCTION

The cricket tragics . . . inhabitants of the interior land of Cricket where the stumps are never drawn. They know more history than the players and journalists; they love the game more; their stake is unattached to their own glory.

Malcolm Knox (in his novel *Adult Book*)

There's a lot in a name. Golf's favourite competition, the Ryder Cup, came into being in 1926 when a team of scratch American professionals played a British team at Wentworth (and lost 13½–1½). Watching the match was Samuel Ryder, a seed merchant from St Albans, who suggested afterwards that the event be made official, and offered to donate a trophy. The Calcutta Cup was instituted in 1878, when the only rugby club in Calcutta disbanded. Membership had plummeted after they discontinued the free bar. To perpetuate the name of the club, the remaining members withdrew all its funds from the bank in silver rupees and had them melted down and made into a cup, which they presented to the Rugby Football Union, on condition that it was competed for annually. The Super Bowl, which began in 1920, was a stopgap name until something better could be found. It did however supplant the original suggestion for a name: The Big One.

The Ashes, by contrast, may be the only significant sporting contest that acquired its name from the humiliating defeat of one of its regular participants. And who gave it that name? The

triumphalist winners? Or the ironic losers? Our national inclina-
tion towards self-deprecating humour is well known and utterly
confusing to most countries in the world, but I had assumed that
it developed only as our Empire dwindled and we suffered a
series of disappointing second places in the Eurovision Song
Contest. Obviously not. Followers of England cricket were
taking the mickey out of it almost before there was an England
cricket to follow. Our ancestors are to blame for the Ashes being
called the Ashes. More fool them, and indeed us.

In 1882, Australia toured England for the second time and
played a single Test at the Oval. The pitch was tricky, scores
were low and W. G. Grace set the tone for more than a century
of ill-feeling and mutual resentment when Australia were 110 for
six in their second innings, leading by only 72. The number-
eight batsman, Sammy Jones, left his crease to pat down a divot.
Grace immediately whipped off the bails and appealed. The
umpire, cringing at the sight of that enormous bristly beard,
gave the batsman out. Australia were all out for 122; England
needed 85 to win. Australia's great fast bowler, Fred 'the Demon'
Spofforth, thundered into England's dressing room between
innings and called Grace a cheat, which seems little more than a
statement of fact. 'This will lose you the match!' he promised.
And to his teammates, 'This thing can be done!' England looked
comfortable enough at 51 for two, but Grace hit an uppish drive
straight to mid-off for 32 and Spofforth blew away the rest with
seven for 44. The tension was so extreme that a spectator bit
through the handle of his rolled-up umbrella. Not for the last
time, the catering at an English Test ground had proved inadequate to requirements.

The shock was widespread and intense. It was England's first
ever Test defeat on home soil. A few days later a boozy old hack
called Reginald Brooks wrote a mock obituary for England
cricket in *The Sporting Times*:

In Affectionate Remembrance of English Cricket, which
died at The Oval, 29th August, 1882.
Deeply lamented by a large circle of sorrowing
friends and acquaintances. R.I.P.
N.B. The body will be cremated and the ashes
taken to Australia.

Note the lower case 'a'. It seems reasonable to assume that
Reginald wrote this in five minutes for a laugh, possibly before
disappearing to the pub. How could he have imagined that it
would be the most significant act of his life? Or that his words
would resound down the ages, to the extent that quite a few
cricket fans know them by heart? Nearly 130 years later we – you
and I and many of the people we know – are the 'large circle of
sorrowing friends and acquaintances', perpetually mourning the
death and re-death of English cricket. How can anything already
dead die again so many times? Maybe it's undead. Why are we
doing this? Why are we wasting our time?

Reginald's gag was taken up by the new England captain, the
Hon. Ivo Bligh, who, when setting sail for that winter's return
tour, promised to 'bring back the Ashes'. He repeated the line
when he landed in Melbourne two months later, to the mystification of everyone present. But the legend of 'the Ashes' quickly
caught on. After England had won the series 2–1 and 'regained'
them, a group of Melbourne ladies presented the Hon. Ivo with
a terracotta urn, filled with the ashes of, well, something. (No
one has ever known for sure.) 'What better way than to actually
present the English captain with the very object, albeit mythical,
he had come to Australia to retrieve?' said Mrs Ann Fletcher, as
that's the way Australian cricket fans talked in those days. Another
of the ladies, Miss Florence Morphy, of Beechworth, Victoria, hit
it off so well with the England captain that they were later mar-
ried, thus introducing to the contest an undercurrent of sexual
tension that, maybe thankfully, has been entirely absent ever since.

Nonetheless, versions of this story introduce every history of the Ashes, partly because it's a good story and partly because its absolute strangeness seems to set the tone for what follows. For the Ashes are a gift to a historian. There is an epic scope to this essentially ridiculous contest that has gripped cricket fans for more than a century. The intensity has never flagged for a moment. Only world wars could get in the way, and we fought those mainly to protect our way of life, a large part of which was the freedom to play the Ashes every four years.* During an Ashes series, we can think of nothing else. As soon as it's finished, we start looking forward to the next one. How irritating it must have been to be the West Indies in the 1970s and 1980s. They were one of the greatest sides cricket has ever produced, regularly beating England 5–0 with a grandeur we could only admire. At the same time, all we ever truly cared about was beating the Australians, however useless they happened to be. The Windies simply couldn't break in to that cosy mutual loathing England and Australia have enjoyed for so long, even if they were far stronger than either team and possibly both teams combined. My own theory is that this inspired them to thrash us even more comprehensively than they had previously intended. They wouldn't have minded being hated or despised, but to be marginalised was more than they could bear.

According to Matthew Engel, 'There are five major cricketing sub-cultures in the world: the traditional play-up-chaps MCC view; the hard-as-nails English professional version, centred on Yorkshire; the even tougher Australian way; the West Indian, carefree-seeming but with angry overtones; and the subtle Indian game. These are caricatures, of course, but fair ones. The last four

---

* The Germans' inability to appreciate cricket, it now becomes clear, was their severest weakness. Travelling through that now beautiful and peaceable nation, you can't help thinking that one thing and one thing only could improve it: large numbers of cricket pitches.

types all exist in opposition to the first.'* Australia need England to beat, rather more, I suspect, than England need Australia. Even now, almost half a century after amateur and professional definitions were swept away, Australians like to characterise visiting English cricketers as effete, upper class and liable to employ butlers. To an extent, the country defines itself by how much it hates us. To some, less developed Englishmen, who would probably be watching the football if it was on, this is all the provocation they ever needed: they return the hatred with interest, and pleasure. I don't really get this, but then I am probably a big softie who has always quite liked Australians.

'No, you can't quite like Australians,' said a friend of mine over a drink or two. 'I bloody hate them.'

'You're not going to believe this, but some of my best friends are Australian,' said I.

'They're bastards, Australians,' said my friend, hiccuping slightly. 'Whose round is it?'

As it happens, some of my best friends really are Australian. Admittedly, these are Australians who live in the UK, so it's possible that their Australianness has been tempered by years of hanging around with us lot. In my experience, though, most Britons have rather a high opinion of Australia and Australians. That so many of them really don't like us seems a bit strange. What have we ever done to them? 'Bodyline' and 'Gallipoli' are the usual responses, but that's like blaming German backpackers for the Second World War. We do laugh a little at them, it is true. *Neighbours* and *Home and Away* have supplied us with twenty years of exceptional comedy material, and Natalie Imbruglia's pop career didn't amount to much after a promising start. But we laugh at everyone, particularly ourselves. We mean no harm by it. Well, not much, anyway.

* *The Oldie*, January 2008.

So that will annoy Australians and the fact that we quite like them only seems to annoy them more. If we could only respond to them with lofty contempt, you sense they would be satisfied. Lord Harris and E. W. Swanton, where are you when we need you? But in the light of this, the Aussies' hatred ceases to look like a source of strength. In fact, to us it begins to look suspiciously like a weakness, a chippiness they really should have got over by now. Funny, because they see our liking them even though they don't like us, as a weakness on our part. Worse, a weakness they find patronising. Which it probably is if we think we have identified their own weakness, which they in fact believe to be their strength. And there's no telling them this, because they interpret it as lofty contempt (which of course is a weakness in itself). However you look at it, we just can't win – which, by astounding coincidence, is what usually happens on the cricket field too.

We are two nations divided by a common language, not wholly dissimilar cultures and an awful lot of miles. Over the years this curious relationship has made for some of the most compelling cricket ever played by anyone. No one, of course, actually compelled us to watch it; we just couldn't help ourselves. If we couldn't watch it, we listened to it, read about it, talked about it, thought about it, ground our teeth down to stumps over it. Has it been fun? In mental health terms, I'd suggest, most England fans would probably be better off if none of it had happened at all.

For if this book is about anything, it is about suffering. Recently I have discovered a simple pleasure that I had never imagined existed, that of watching Test cricket on television when the team you support isn't involved. It's fascinating, and relaxing, and it eats time as Greg 'Fat Cat' Ritchie eats buns. Instead of fretting about your team's performance, you just root for the team you dislike less. (If you are my six-year-old son, you root for whichever team is winning. He can swap allegiances three times an over.) It's pleasure without the pain. Admittedly there aren't the great surging feelings of triumph and joy when your own team wins, but at least you sleep better at night. Stress, anxiety, terrible crushing disappointment: these are words we know only too well. There have been a few good moments over the past 35 years, but in the main it has been a tough time for the England cricket fan to be alive. Not that we have a monopoly on suffering. When I told a couple of Australian friends I was writing this book, and just happened to drop the words 'Headingley 1981' into the conversation, they both flinched. I laughed, and said it again to see what happened. One of them admitted that while the 5–0 whitewash in 2006/07 was hugely enjoyable, it couldn't quite make up for the 2005 defeat. I could understand this, even though I couldn't stop grinning. The victories are wonderful and we love them, but the defeats seem to live longer in the mind. And in this, if in nothing else, England and Australia fans are united as one.

Do the players mind as much as we do? It's probably unfair to say this, but sometimes you suspect that they don't. After all, for them it's their career. If they lose a match but score a century, they are obviously disappointed, but they are going to play in the next Test. We all know the clichés: they outplayed us in every department, we are going to go away and work on our game, come back more strongly, hope to put them under more pressure. Whereas we, the spectators, want blood. We want one of the defeated team ritually slaughtered, maybe tortured first, something including killer bees and a number of very sharp spikes. We too will go away and work at our game, which happens to be murderous rage. In the bubble that is 'Team England', they obviously have no idea of this. They are young men, not always blessed with the sharpest minds or strongest imaginations. They are in the nets taking throwdowns from kindly coaching staff, or wondering whether it's too late at 28 to learn how to bowl one that goes the other way. The great shock for them will come after

they retire, and wander up to the commentary box, and start pronouncing on their successors. For gradually it will dawn on them
how awful this is, how much more fun it was to play than watch,
even when you're losing. Especially when you're losing. The ex-
players who write and commentate on the game slowly come to
realise how painful it is for us, and I'm sure some of them look at
us and wonder, Why do you do it? Why do you put yourselves
through this hell? By which time, of course, it's too late. They
could have got away. They had their chance. They could have
opened a pub or become postmen, as all sportspeople were once
obliged to do after retirement. Instead they take the televisual
shilling, and in their spare time they go out on the after-dinner
circuit and entertain fat men in suits with the same old stories for
the millionth time. No wonder they are all so bad-tempered
when they reach the mic.

The players and their performances tend to dominate most
histories of the Ashes – not entirely surprisingly, as without them
there would be no Ashes. But they aren't the whole story. We
matter too. Without the suffering spectators, the Ashes would
exist in a strange, silent, eerie vacuum, not unlike the third day of
a championship match at Derby. The spectators give context to
the contest. In fact I would suggest that the Ashes are as much
about our response to them as anything else. Reginald Brooks
and the ladies from Melbourne merely started that process. We
continue it, whether we want to or not.

So if this modest and highly selective history of the Ashes
adds anything to the familiar story, it's the spectator's angle. Most
histories aspire to objectivity, even authority. This one is subjec-
tive, personal, grossly tendentious. I would like to think that it is
the first ever emotional history of the Ashes. I'm sure we are on
safe ground here. Men who would struggle to shed a tear at the
funeral of a loved one have been known to blub like babies when
watching the DVD of the 2005 Edgbaston Test match for the
73rd time. I didn't actually watch it live, but I can remember

exactly where on the M40 I was when I heard we'd won. (Just passing the Polish War Memorial. Or the Kasprowicz Wicket Memorial, as I shall always now think of it.)

Cast objectivity aside. Give fair-mindedness the heave-ho. I certainly have and so have all the people I have interviewed. (They are all friends and acquaintances: people like us. I simply cast around for people with a deep psychological need to talk about the Ashes for an hour or more. They weren't hard to find.) Our judgements may, at times, seem harsh. In fact most of them are positively benevolent compared with what is yelled from the stands at players every day of their lives. And I have tried to avoid the simple crazed abuse that occupies the space where reasoned debate should be on the internet. But sometimes a harsh judgement can capture an important truth. Mick Jagger, for example, was once quoted thus: 'Glenn McGrath . . . what a bastard.' Now, everyone who knows him tells us that McGrath off the field is amusing, clever and excellent company, and if I met him I'm sure I would be as pitifully tongue-tied and awestruck as I always am whenever I meet famous cricketers. Nonetheless, Mick Jagger is right. Glenn McGrath . . . what a bastard.

A brief note about hindsight. I haven't avoided it altogether – that wouldn't be any fun at all – but I have tried to be sparing with it, because I know it can get irritating. Instead I have tried to write of these games in the present, in the moment if you like, just as we experienced them: we had no more idea of what was going to happen next than anyone does, ever, about anything. It's why we watch sport at all, because we don't know what is going to happen. (Which is why I didn't watch much Ashes cricket in the 1990s, because we all knew exactly what was going to happen.)

We start, then, in 1972 because that's where I start. I'd like to have something to say about the 1970/71 Ashes tour, in which Ray Illingworth's cracking side won 2–0 and regained the Ashes after twelve miserable years. But all I have to say is this: no Australian umpire gave out an Australian batsman lbw in the entire series. And I read that in a book. I can't write very much else about it because I was too young at the time and wasn't paying attention. My cricketing education began in 1971 when England entertained India in a three-Test series. At the time India were famous for their trio of spin bowlers, Venkataraghavan, Chandrasekhar and Bishen Bedi, and not at all famous for the dibbly-dobbly merchants, Abid Ali and Solkar, who opened the bowling purely to take the shine off the ball for the spinners. Before the second Test at Old Trafford, Illingworth's side had played 25 Tests without defeat: can you imagine that? I can't, because nothing like it has happened since. As Abid Ali and Solkar took the new ball on 5 August 1971, the BBC's commentators made it absolutely clear that they were not expected to take wickets or trouble the batsmen in any way at all. Within an hour or so Abid Ali had disposed of John Jameson (on debut), John Edrich, Keith Fletcher and Basil D'Oliveira to leave England 41 for four. I was captivated. Here was a sport in which reputations counted for nothing, where one tiny error could not be more cruelly punished, where expectations could constantly be overturned. Admittedly, England came back to score 386 (Illingworth 107, P. Lever 88 not out), and Abid Ali didn't take another wicket in the series, but I didn't care: cricket had found me, and I had found cricket. If we don't count parents, it has so far proved the most enduring relationship of my life.

The following summer, England entertained the Australians, who hadn't beaten them in ten Tests since Old Trafford in 1968. Incidentally, do you know how many Tests had been played around the world in the intervening winter? Five. One Test series, between West Indies and New Zealand, in which all five matches were drawn. England were to have toured South Africa, and South Africa were to have toured Australia, but apartheid saw off these arrangements, and nothing else was scheduled in their place. England's cricketers therefore had the whole winter off to tend their sideburns. Different times. Better times?

One

1972

He had everything: courage, variety, high morale, arrogance, supreme fitness and aggression.

Bob Willis on Dennis Lillee

Eleven–going–on–twelve is a susceptible age. You haven't lived long enough to know exactly what you are seeing all the time; in fact, as I remember it, you are so desperately short of information that you are constantly drawing completely incorrect conclusions from the little available evidence. When I first watched cricket on TV in summer 1971 it was all I could do to work out what was going on. That was a bat he was holding, am I right? The man wearing the tie was an umpire. Did Zaheer Abbas always score a double century? Wouldn't it be fairer if someone else had a go? By the following summer, though, I felt I was bedded in. I couldn't quite distinguish between fourth slip and gully, but I could already understand that five days for a Test match wasn't even half a day too long. A five-Test series, occasionally interrupted by the racing from Towcester, I could handle that. Growing up isn't a gentle incline; it's a series of shelves, and every so often you find the ladder that takes you up to the next level. The Australian series of 1972 was when I realised that cricket was ineradicably superior to football, my first love, and possibly to all other sports, not to mention school, employment, all the trappings of adulthood, and girls. I was wrong about girls, but otherwise I wasn't far off.

The Indians had been wily and unexpected, the Pakistanis stylish and aristocratic. The Australians, by contrast, were hairy and scary. It seems strange now, but in 1972 the single most important accoutrement for a prospective international fast bowler was a large, mobile mop of hair. Dennis Lillee had more hair than anyone, other than possibly John Snow. Soon Bob Willis would reemerge with the fiercest barnet of them all. In 1972 he was either injured or out of favour, maybe as a result of an inadvisable short-back-and-sides. The Australians, though, were generally hairier than the England players, mainly because they were younger. Ian Chappell, their captain, was 28, brother Greg was 23, Dennis Lillee was 22, Rodney Marsh was 24. Of the tourists who played in Tests, only two, opening batsman Keith Stackpole and mystery spinner John Gleeson, were over 30, and then not by much. Since the 1970/71 tour, Bill Lawry (35), Graham McKenzie (30) and Ian Redpath (30) had all been dropped. Only Redpath would play Test cricket again.

Compare with the England line-up. Captain Raymond Illingworth celebrated his fortieth birthday on the first day of the First Test. Basil D'Oliveira was staring 41 down the barrel, while M. J. K. Smith, recalled after several years' absence, was rising 39. The other specialist batsmen, Boycott, Edrich and Luckhurst, were 31, 34 and 33 respectively. Even John Snow was 30. In his book *The Ashes 1972*, John Arlott called them 'a capable – if elderly – team of known qualities'. It may have been their rather staid, schoolmasterly air – at least half the team you could imagine in cardigans, patiently filling pipes – or it may have been the fact that I was eleven going on twelve, but to me this particular batting order had a solidity about it, a permanence even, that no subsequent England batting order seems to have had.

1. G. Boycott
2. J. H. Edrich
3. B. W. Luckhurst
4. M. J. K. Smith
5. B. L. D'Oliveira
6. A. W. Greig
7. A. P. E. Knott
8. R. Illingworth
9. J. A. Snow
10. N. Gifford
11. G. G. Arnold

It may be that, when you are young and impressionable, a particular England batting order imprints itself on your mind, an Ur-batting order if you like, and every one after that is effectively a variant on that. For whatever reason, this one still makes me feel curiously warm and secure, as a late-night cup of cocoa might. But who knows? It could just be because cocoa is the drink you'd most easily associate with this team. (Although I can imagine Boycott insisting on Ovaltine in his cussed way.)

Illingworth, then, was captain, although only for the first two Tests. The selectors used the MCC vs Australians match as a Test trial. No one made serious runs, so for the Test they chose M. J. K. Smith, a man so old he had already retired once. Arnold had played only two Tests since his debut in 1967, but was now widely considered the best swing bowler in the country. Norman Gifford, chubby of face but receding of hairline, was preferred to Derek Underwood, supposedly because he was the better batsman but almost certainly because he looked older. It was the classic post-war bowling attack: genuine fast bowler (Snow), fast-medium swing bowler (Arnold), medium-fast (Greig), partnership-breaking dibbly-dobbly merchant (D'Oliveira), left-arm spinner (Gifford), off-spinner (Illingworth). This Ur-team of mine, the line-up I have never forgotten, lasted precisely one Test.

On a wet day at Old Trafford (the spiritual home of the umbrella), Illingworth won the toss and England scored 147 for five. The big news was Lillee. He only took one wicket, that of the ancient Smith, lbw for 10, but for an entire generation of cricket watchers he redefined (or in my case just defined) what it was to be a fast bowler. As well as the hair it was important to have an unfeasibly long run-up, a large number of limbs apparently flying in all directions, a terrifying black moustache, and an aggression so visceral that you could never doubt he wanted to do you physical harm. It was a mesmerising performance. At this stage Lillee didn't have the control he would later develop, but then batsmen didn't have the helmets they would later put on to counter the challenge of players like Lillee. Even his walk back to his mark – 44 paces – gave them the willies. On 16 August, Mr Richard Barry wrote to *The Times* on the issue: 'Sir, Commentators assess the run-up of Australian bowler Lillee to be 40 yards. Assuming them right and that Lillee bowls 25 overs to an innings means that in any match ten fielders, two umpires, two batsmen and countless thousands of spectators wait idly while this fellow runs in excess of six and a half miles . . .'

Two days later a letter from Miss Mary Smith was published: 'Sir, Mr Barry wrote, as did Jack Fingleton, in your columns criticising the length of Lillee's run-up. For those of us who do not merely write about cricket or, as Mr Barry, "idly" listen to commentators, but who actually pay, and support matches in person, the experience of watching Lillee thundering down from the pavilion end is one of the most exciting and thrilling experiences provided by the cricket world for many years . . .'

Less characteristically the Australians dropped catch after catch. In Arlott's words again, Edrich 'endured in his characteristically grim, unprepossessing fashion' until he was run out for 49. These were English conditions, and this was a very English sort of game: dour, slow, hard and grinding. Australia had more flair but were less consistent, and the bowler who could have best exploited the conditions, Bob Massie, was injured. England amassed 249 runs in 120.4 overs. Illingworth, wrote Arlott, 'plays his cricket tight and grudgingly until he senses an opening, when he then becomes a relentless attacker'. When Australia came to bat Geoff Arnold took four for 62, but had four catches dropped at slip. The selectors had the bowling and the batting worked out, but they had forgotten to give the team any close catchers. Keith Stackpole scored 53 of Australia's 142, cutting, pulling, gurning. Many of his teammates looked like members of the Partridge Family, or minor Osmonds, but Stackpole was a proper Australian – teeth gritted, jaw jutting, sleeves rolled up and anything a bit short thumped for four. With a first innings lead of 107, Boycott and Edrich started cautiously. With a first innings lead of 701, Boycott and Edrich would have started cautiously. Wickets fell, nonetheless, and at the end of the third day England were 136 for three. Smith had been hanging on 'by courage, experience and, perhaps, memory' (Arlott). It needed a bold 62 by Tony Greig on his England debut to bring the England total to the relative comfort of 234, leaving Australia 342 to win.

(A good example here of the Ur-team syndrome. I had no idea it was Greig's debut until this chapter was researched and nearly written and someone just happened to drop it into the conversation. He was only 23, but I assumed he had been playing for England for years. He dropped several catches at second slip. He fitted in like a native.)

The BBC video of this Test is an extraordinary document of a vanished age. Almost everyone in the Old Trafford crowd was wearing jacket and tie. Even the women. (A joke, of course. There were no women.) They all smoked and wore cloth caps. Then there were the astonishingly awful shots some of the batsmen played. Geoffrey Boycott, in Harry Hill shirt collars, played a horrible attempted sweep to a Gleeson half volley and was lbw. After their gruesome dismissals, they all walked. John Inverarity, Edrich, M. J. K. – none of them paused even a split-second to see what the umpire thought. Except Ian Chappell, who was in no hurry at all. Finger went up and he stomped off in a rage. Ah, that's more like it. That's what we recognise as Test cricket.

In their second innings Stackpole made 67, which, together with his 53, created the impression I retain to this day that it was effectively impossible to get him out. This was a strange Australian team, though, for as well as its stars, the Lillees and Marshs, Stackpoles and Chappells, there were several faces most of us would now struggle to put a name to. B. C. Francis, an opening batsman. G. D. Watson, middle-order batsman and change bowler. D. J. Colley, fast-medium bowler.* Francis and Colley made their debuts here too, but none of the three played beyond the end of the series. When Watson was out for 0 in the second innings, an attempted hook off Snow that looped gently back to the bowler, Jim Laker was commentating. 'Oh dear oh dear oh dear, what a bad shot,' he said, failing to mince his words. 'Really one couldn't describe anything as bad as that from a Test match player.' Soon Australia were 147 for eight. They clearly believed the conditions were against them. Heads drooped as they trudged back to the pavilion, although that might just have been an attempt to find some breathable air under the crowd's cigarette smoke. Then Rodney Marsh, pugnacious wicketkeeper and as yet *sans* moustache, started whacking Norman Gifford all around the place. Marsh and Gleeson put on 104 for the ninth wicket. They did lose in the end, by 89 runs, but my mother confirms that it is around this time that I started biting my nails. Victory, I learned, was never assured until after it had happened.

At Lord's, Bob Massie and Ross Edwards made their debuts, replacing Watson and Inverarity. Geoff Arnold was unfit, so John Price of Middlesex came into the team. You could understand the thinking. Price was 35 and looked like a geography teacher.

---

* Much loved by newspaper sub-editors. Every time he took a wicket it was because the batsman had 'suffered from the "Colley-Wobbles".

But he did have the longest run-up in county cricket, starting halfway up the steps to the Long Room and then curving in and out a couple of times before running the last seventy yards or so in a straight line. If he were playing today England would struggle to bowl ten overs an hour.

Tim C: He wasn't even very fast, was he? And he had a tiny head on a large body. Large bottom, like Angus Fraser.

As usual Illingworth won the toss; as usual England were 28 for three; as usual Greig and Knott led the fightback. A pattern was beginning to develop. The top order would be dismissed by good fast bowlers with a new ball, and the middle order would flourish against the second string ('not of Test quality', wrote Arlott). Massie was swinging the ball like a banana. You could see the surprise on his face every time he took a wicket. In the first innings he had eight for 84, several with late-swinging yorkers. Compared with Lillee he didn't look like anything very much, ambling to the wicket rather than sprinting, although some batsmen may have been distracted by his vast sideburns. In the second innings he took eight for 53, almost all of them caught in the slips. In between, Greg Chappell had contributed an elegant century, apparently without effort, and announced himself as the best batsman on either side. (Of this innings Richie Benaud would later write, 'It was as close to flawless as anything I have seen.') Australia had the best batsman and the best bowler – and it wasn't even the best bowler getting the wickets. Massie's match figures of 16 for 137 were the best by any bowler on debut, the best by an Australian bowler ever, and by some distance the best by a bowler sporting aerodynamically unsound sideburns that must have slowed him down by five mph. Everyone predicted a great future for him. What must have been greater for him? The thrill of this astonishing match-winning performance or the disappointment at never being able to follow it up? Massie played only five more Tests, and took 15 more wickets. Within 18 months he was out of

Western Australia's side and his career was over. This may be hindsight talking – well, hindsight screaming and shouting – but on the video footage you can see the modesty of his response, the surprise at his good fortune. Maybe he didn't have the steel and the singlemindedness of the fellow bowling at the other end.

Australia had won at Lord's again. I didn't know then that England had not beaten them there since 1934. (I know it now without having to look it up.) For Trent Bridge England dropped J. S. E. Price (another who had played his last Test) and brought in Peter Lever of Lancashire, who had 'a deposit of goodwill from his bowling in Australia and a record of honest effort', wrote Arlott. He was 31 years old and therefore represented a nod towards youth. Slightly more worryingly, Boycott was hit on the finger by Bob Willis in a Gillette Cup tie, and had to be replaced by Peter Parfitt of Middlesex. Where were all these players coming from? I was very confused. After just two Tests my Ur-team was in tatters.

Julian P: Parfitt? Who was he? Oh, the chap who used to be good when we were at primary school who'd played one Test in the last six years. I think this was the first time I thought the selectors were idiots and I was only 12.

To Trent Bridge, then a bowlers' paradise: no one had scored a century there all season. Illingworth put them in and Stackpole scored 114. Snow took five for 92, Parfitt took four catches at slip but several others were dropped. Marsh and David Colley cranked the score up to 315, and then the Lillee Show began. As David Frith wrote, 'He is one of the great fast bowlers of the twentieth century, possessing a full set of gear changes, a knowledge of aerodynamics equal to Lindwall's, an abundance of stamina and determination, and more courage than is given to most.' Off his first six overs, England managed two scoring shots, a two to Luckhurst, a single to Edrich. Luckhurst took most of the strike, and Lillee beat him for pace, again and again. In the

19th over Edrich hit Colley through square leg for four and England were 25 for no wicket. Another pattern was developing, one that would loom over the rest of our lives. Australia were playing like winners; England weren't. Edrich, with 37, was top scorer in an innings of 189 (Lillee four for 35). Australia led by 126, and ruthlessly extended their advantage. Of England's bowlers only Snow and, later in the innings, Illingworth seemed to pose any threat. Bruce Francis had a migraine, so Ross Edwards opened in his place and scored 170 not out. At 2.30 p.m. on the fourth day Ian Chappell declared, leaving England 451 to win. The pitch had slowed right down, and although England weren't terribly good at scoring runs, they were experts at escaping from apparently certain defeat with dour and relentless rearguard actions. Luckhurst had reached 96 when he tried to sweep the Australian captain's infrequent leg spin, and popped the ball up to wide second slip. England ground out 290 for four off 148 overs and the match was safe.

Three Tests down, two to go, and the strengths and weaknesses of both sides were becoming apparent. Of the touring party, Francis had scored 52 runs at 10.4, the legendary Doug Walters 47 runs at 9.4. Gleeson, the mystery spinner who had so confounded England in 1970/71, was a mystery no longer: three wickets at 52.33.* David Colley had six wickets at 52. Only Walters of these four kept his place for Headingley. Before the series he had had a Test average of 54, and would continue to score heavily everywhere in the world that wasn't the British Isles. No wonder we warmed to him.

Andy R: Dear old Dougie Walters, who was such a hero, my total

---

* At the Allan Border Medal dinner in 2008 – look it up on YouTube – the Australian comedians Roy and HG did a very funny routine about Gleeson's bowling. They claimed to have finally solved the mystery, which was that the ball didn't turn at all, in either direction.

Aussie cricket hero, and he never scored a run. Every time he came out to bat there was this Goweresque sense of anticipation, and he couldn't hit the ball off the square.

For Headingley England dropped M. J. K. Smith (who, like the three discarded Australians, had played his last Test), chubby-cheeked Gifford (whose only wicket in the series had cost 116 runs) and Peter Lever. Smith had concentrated throughout on survival, and as Arlott put it, 'There were already enough batsmen in the side who aspired little higher than to be survivors.' Keith Fletcher replaced him. Lever was said to have lost his 'nip', but happily Arnold was back from injury. And Gifford was replaced by Derek Underwood, whose name could not be prefaced by anything other than the word 'Deadly', by law. The Australians sensed conspiracy and dirty deeds, especially when they looked at the pitch.

There wasn't a lot of grass on it. And what there was had a curious grey-blueish tinge. Had the groundsman planted bluebells by mistake? The previous weekend, he explained, there had been a freak thunderstorm, during which the strip had apparently been infected with fusarium, a microscopic fungus whose spores must have been carried in the rain. Astonishingly none of the rest of the ground had been affected: just the bit that Underwood would be bowling on. The strip negated the skills of Lillee and Massie, but was perfect for grafting front-foot English batsmen of a certain age and temperament. The Australians were suspicious. They had only ever lost to England twice at Headingley, in 1956 and 1961. Each time they had thought the pitch unfit for Test cricket. But at least it had been the right colour. There was no point complaining publicly. They wouldn't give their hosts the satisfaction. Instead they grumbled and rumbled and collapsed from 79 for one to 146 all out, as Underwood bowled unchanged for 31 overs from the Experimental Microbiology End. England collapsed against Lillee as usual, but Illingworth and Snow put on 104 for the eighth wicket. Australia's two spinners, Ashley Mallett and

John Inverarity, both recalled for the match, were astonishingly
tidy – Inverarity took three for 26 off 33 overs – but less threatening than Deadly, who was waiting his turn. England led by 117
on first innings and Australia were all out for 136 in their second.
Paul Sheahan, one of those perennially underperforming batsmen
who was said to be 'picked for his fielding', top scored with 41
not out. Underwood took six for 45. I had forgotten, watching
him again after many years, just how swift he was. His 'faster' ball
was useful medium pace, turning just a little on this pitch rather
than a lot. England won by nine wickets and retained the Ashes.
'It was a very unusual Test match,' said Richie Benaud.

*Andy R: I was at the Cambridge Folk Festival during the fusarium
Test match. I was 15, 16, and getting into music, and wearing bell-bot-
toms and long hair, and cricket just didn't go with it. But I was
desperate to know what was going on in the Test match. If I heard a
radio, I'd start following people. And then I remember this guy running
across the grass – we were watching some band, can't remember who it
was – and he was shouting, 'We've beaten the bastards! We've beaten
the bastards!'*

It had also been a rare quiet Test for John Snow. He and Geoff
Arnold were the first England bowlers I can remember who
were visibly Good Enough. We could never have guessed that the
next 35 years would be dominated by bowling and bowlers that
were Not Quite Good Enough – and sometimes they weren't
even as good as that. Snow, though, was a strange one: a rebel, an
iconoclast, a published poet, picked less often for England than he
should have been because the blazers didn't trust him, but a
brooder and a seether rather than a shouter, exhibiting a very
English sort of rage. When Dennis Lillee took a wicket you
knew it. He would leap up in the air, his arms and legs flying in
all directions, like a vast hairy spider, or an out-of-control heli-
copter. When Snow took a wicket there'd be a brief smile, maybe
a thumb raised to whoever caught it, and then he would turn and
wander back to his mark. At Trent Bridge Doug Walters miscued

a wide long hop up in the air to Gifford at extra cover. The camera cut to Snow, standing watching, completely still, with his arms in what would come to be known as the Double Teapot formation. As the catch was taken, he just bowed his head. Maybe the uselessness of the ball that had taken the wicket weighed upon him; maybe it was the great randomness and pointlessness of all life; maybe it was the knowledge that there were still four balls left in the over.

England had the Ashes, but if Australia won the final Test at the Oval they would tie the series. Walters was finally dropped, for Graeme Watson. Luckhurst, who had scored runs at Headingley but was repeatedly being made to look daft by Lillee, also went, as did Fletcher (one innings of five runs at Headingley). In came John Hampshire, another perennially promising but underachieving middle-order batsman, for another of his occasional Tests, and Barry Wood of Lancashire for his debut. It was traditional for selectors to bring in a couple of likely lads for the final Test of the summer, give them the chance to fail, and then not pick them for the winter tour. England won the toss, stuttered to 284 (Knott 92, Lillee five for 58) and then the Chappell brothers did what they had been threatening to do all summer: score heaps of runs. As with the Waughs twenty years later, you always felt that an enormous unanswerable stand was just around the corner. Here they put on 201 for the third wicket, with Greg out just before the end of the second day for 113, and Ian out the following morning for 118. It was the first ever double-century stand in a Test by brothers. England should have been thinking about the draw and a series victory, but the authorities had scheduled an extra day, a sixth, in order to be sure of getting a result. How kind of them. Snow bowled with pace and fury, Underwood with guile, rattling through the lower middle order (Marsh, with scores of one, one and nought against him, was his new bunny), but Australia were acquiring an air of unstoppability. In the second innings Wood scored 90, 'one of the best innings of the whole series', according to Benaud. The following day, as Knott made 62, Jim Laker acknowledged 'a sparklin' display of battin' from the England players this mornin".* But Lillee took another five wickets, for a record 31 in the series, and Australia rolled home by five wickets on the afternoon of the sixth day. Are you sure you don't need a seventh? You can have one if you want one.

Julian P: I was rather crestfallen after the Oval Test. We should have won the Ashes, outright, not just clung on to them in a drawn series! History was not yet my strength.

John Arlott wrote that, 'No Test series of modern times between England and Australia has been so even, so entertaining and so constantly changing.' And none would be so for a while. Australia were a young team getting better, England were an ageing team showing signs of incipient decline. Soon they would be hanging on by their fingertips. Illingworth, Snow, Boycott and Edrich made themselves unavailable for the tour of India, Pakistan and Ceylon; Parfitt, D'Oliveira and Hampshire were not selected, and only Hampshire of these three played Test cricket again. Fletcher, having failed at Headingley and been dropped, was picked for the tour. Tony Lewis, future face of BBC cricket coverage and MCC President, was a very establishment choice as captain. Arlott thought 'it was sad that England could not find room for some of the younger players such as Owen-Thomas of Surrey, Randall of Notts, John Steele of Leicestershire, Turner of Hampshire or Hayes of Lancashire'.

Australia, though, were humming. As well as their established stars – all of them under 30 – there was the promise of

---

* When anyone hit the ball for four, he usually said, 'No need to chase that.' Richie's catchphrase, by contrast, was 'John Snow, no chance of cutting that orf.'

Bob Massie, Paul Sheahan and Ross Edwards. As it happens, none of these three managed to develop a long-term Test career, but we didn't know that then. I didn't know anything then, but I did have a feeling that the next Ashes series might be a bit tougher.

Two

1974/75

England were not happy with the aggressive way in which we approached the game, and not many of them stayed around for a drink after play.

Dennis Lillee

For spectators, away series have always been a little less stressful. Although England usually lose, we usually know they are going to lose, so there's none of the brutal raising of expectations that accompanies most home series. What's more, it's all taking place on the other side of the world in the middle of the night. In the 1970s we couldn't watch it live on television, and if we wanted to listen to it on radio, we had to forgo sleep. No one needs sleep more than a teenager. I was more likely to get my hair cut short and eat cabbage than stay up past one in the morning listening to *Test Match Special*. Not that I didn't have a go, but I soon realised that life became infinitely more bearable if you had your eight hours and then heard the bad news on the radio the following morning. Then you had the option of reading in the newspaper about the previous day's bad news and, that evening on television, watching the highlights package, with lots of clips of middle-aged England batsmen having fingers broken or prodding a rising short ball to Ashley Mallett in the gully. And if you didn't fancy that, you could just ignore it all and pretend it wasn't happening.

Actually, this latter is a learned skill: I can do it now, but I couldn't do it then. Besides, hadn't we drawn the previous series? Weren't the Ashes still ours? And hadn't Dennis Lillee been out of action for eighteen months with a career-threatening back injury?

David Frith called it 'one of sport's most impressive comebacks'. In 1973 Lillee had been diagnosed with four stress fractures in the lower vertebrae. He had endured six weeks in plaster and a long and punishing fight to regain fitness. Had England been defending the Ashes in 1973/74 they would have faced a new ball line-up of Max Walker and Geoff Dymock. A year later, Lillee was pronouncing himself fit and taking Ian Chappell's wicket twice in interstate matches. There was also talk of some young firebrand named Jeff Thomson. When England arrive in Australia, there's always talk of a new young bowler who is going to knock their blocks off. Only this time it was true.

Our primary text for this chapter is Christopher Martin-Jenkins's tour diary, *Assault on the Ashes*. CMJ was 30, and had just been confirmed as the BBC's cricket correspondent. It was his second book, following *Testing Times*, an account of the previous winter's tour of the West Indies. According to the flyleaf, 'He is well-known in Surrey club cricket circles as a skilful all-rounder (with some experience of playing for Surrey 2nd XI) and an entertaining after-dinner speaker.' The book is astonishingly authoritative for such a young writer, with many of his judgements borne out by subsequent events: 'Many cricket matches have been won by the lesser team; the game is all about making the most of one's abilities and playing according to one's limitations. The Australians in this series certainly did the former, whilst England conspicuously failed to do the latter. Australia played with skill, confidence, aggression, even ruthlessness. England, on the whole, played without method or discipline.'

Worse, they played without John Snow and Geoffrey Boycott. Snow hadn't been selected. Partly this was said to be a matter of form and age – he was now 33 – but as so often in the past, there was also the sense that his face didn't fit. Boycott had been picked, but had dropped out 'for personal reasons' a few weeks before the tour. No one understood this at the time – for many years people just thought he was a lily-livered coward, fearful of giant mad Australians – but we know now that he was offended by being passed over for the captaincy. Mike Denness of Kent had had the job since the West Indies tour, but was he a good enough batsman? Boycott clearly thought not, CMJ was unconvinced, and in the fourth form we just lived in hope. But England had a long history of this, of picking captains who weren't quite good enough players but were approved of by the blazers at Lord's. The distinction between amateurs and professionals had been abolished a dozen years before, but not in some people's minds, and particularly not in the minds of the people in charge.

Boycott had been replaced at short notice by old faithful Brian Luckhurst, who found out he was going while listening to Radio Luxembourg on holiday in Spain. Luckhurst was one of five changes to the squad that had toured the West Indies the previous year. Four of them were older than the men they replaced. Back in were John Edrich (37), Peter Lever (31), who had reinvented himself as an out-and-out fast bowler, and the ageless (i.e. very old) off-spinner Fred Titmus, now 41.* The only new young person was David Lloyd (27) of Lancashire, replacing John

---

* It's possible that Nigel Blackwell, future leader of the Birkenhead band Half Man Half Biscuit, was as surprised by this selection as anyone else. Twelve years later he would write and release his unforgettable paean to the Middlesex twirler, 'Fuckin' 'Ell, It's Fred Titmus'.

Jameson, whose 'generous girth [had] hindered him in the field' (CMJ). The selectors had finally realised that you needed at least one or two people in the team who could bend down to pick up the ball.

Australia, meanwhile, had lost Keith Stackpole and Paul Sheahan, who had both retired. In the early 1970s, all Australian cricketers played as amateurs and had proper day jobs, which occasionally they attended. Ian Chappell worked in public relations, Dennis Lillee was a director of an office-cleaning firm, Greg Chappell an insurance expert, Doug Walters a cigarette salesman (of course), Rodney Marsh a PE teacher and Max Walker an architect. Of the twelve regular players used by Australia in this series, only Jeff Thomson was unemployed. Sooner or later all of them would need to make proper money – the Australian board gave them a bonus on top of their match expenses for this series, but only with the gravest reluctance – which is why so many of them retired so young. (Sheahan had taken up a new post as a maths teacher.) Some did keep going. Replacing Stackpole was the jug-eared Ian Redpath, now 33 and the oldest man in the team. Youngest, at 24, were Thomson and Wally Edwards, who opened the batting for Western Australia. He was no relation to Ross Edwards, who had been out of favour for a while, but was now back in the side.

Against Victoria, Dennis Amiss and Brian Luckhurst put on 268 runs for the first wicket. Amiss had already scored more than a thousand Test runs that year; in his *Ashes '72* book, John Arlott had wondered whether he would be England's 'next great batsman'. Of Luckhurst, CMJ wrote that 'He plummeted swiftly from this high point and he ended the tour . . . as a virtual passenger.' The following week MCC played and beat New South Wales, with Lever, Arnold and Yorkshire's injury magnet Chris Old bowling lots of bouncers. Fight fire with fire, as someone would say years later, equally foolishly. David Lloyd acquired the first injury of the tour, chipping a finger during fielding practice.

Edrich pulled a back muscle, while Old 'needed only one serious bowl to claim his all-too familiar place at the top of the casualty list'. Arnold was struggling with his form, as so often abroad, so the seam attack for the first Test at Brisbane picked itself: Lever, Willis and Mike Hendrick of Derbyshire, who had made his debut during the summer. They did quite well. After Ian Chappell won the toss, Australia were 10 for two and 229 for eight, with both Chappells scoring fifties in between. But the last two wickets put on another 80. The fast bowlers' union was still active. The England quicks bowled not a single bouncer at the Australian quicks, until Greig lost patience and thumped one in to Lillee, who edged it high to Knott. As he walked off, Lillee said a few words to Greig: a statement of intent, maybe. When England came to bat on the afternoon of the second day, they faced what CMJ described as 'bowling so fearsome that even hardened campaigners of the press box were seen to blanch'.

There's something very special, cherishable even, about a truly fast bowler. Jeff Thomson had been a javelin thrower in his youth, and his delivery resembled Steve Backley's more than it did Ray Lindwall's. In 1972 Dennis Lillee had been the fastest bowler in the world. Now he was, at best, in second place. In his first spell Thomson took two for four in five overs. Amiss and Luckhurst were both caught off the glove, trying to get out of the way. Did they flinch? If they did, you couldn't blame them. As well as simple, stinging speed, Thomson got the ball to bounce from a good length 'with terrifying malignity'. Fortunately there was only one Thomson and he couldn't bowl all day. Edrich and Greig survived the final session in their differing styles: Edrich stoical, brave, introverted, Greig fired up, or maybe 'on fire' as he would later describe other cricketers on TV. At one point Lillee bowled a ridiculously short ball at him. Greig ambled up to the other end of the pitch and prodded a spot not far from Lillee's feet. Another time, he signalled his own four. Sometimes it helps to be six foot seven.

The following day Greig, slashing bouncers over the slips and playing and missing with remarkable frequency, became the first England player to score a Test century in Brisbane since Maurice Leyland in 1935, and brought England to within 44 of Australia's total. But when Australia came in to bat again, the disparity between the two bowling attacks was even more apparent. Willis had an injured thigh, while Greig's exciting new off-breaks, a revelation in the West Indies, didn't work so well here. Just before tea on the fourth day, Hendrick got two balls to rear up off a good length. If Hendrick, solidly and Britishly fast-medium, could do this, what might Thommo do? England needed to bat out the last day, something they had done many times before, but rarely against searing pace. Edrich, hit by Lillee in the first innings, had a puffed and heavily bruised right hand, later found to be broken. Amiss was hit by Thomson on the thumb, giving Walters a straightforward catch in the gully, and the thumb too proved to be broken. Chappell bowled Thomson in four-over spells: after each interval he seemed even faster than before. When he got Greig with a brutally swift yorker – sometimes it doesn't help being six foot seven – England were 94 for six. Thomson clearly wasn't a member of the fast bowlers' union: he bowled bouncers at everyone. Australia won by 165 runs. Perth's wicket would be even faster, and England had only five fit batsmen. Send for Cowdrey!

There is some great coverage of this series on YouTube. It may be a limitation of the source tape, but at times the ball seems faster than the eye can pick up.

Andy R: Again, it's those flickering TV images from Australia that I remember. And Ian Chappell's upturned collar. That won him more Test matches, frankly, than Lillee and Thomson. It was so sharp. You feared for his ears.

David T: My father had been an avid Test match watcher since before the Second World War. He always thought that, apart from one or two quiet, retiring, gentlemanly types, the Australians were a lot of yobs.

Street sweepings, Whitechapel convicts sent over, and these were their descendants. He loathed Ian Chappell, because he thought he was a complete git. He conceptualised it for me as a lot of English gentlemen playing cricket against a load of antipodean wastrels who just happened to be quite good at the game. It took me a while to see that these stereotypes didn't really apply. Except when they did.

Simon O'H: The BBC showed highlights between seven and seven-thirty in the evening, of the day's play that had finished about twelve hours before. It was like being allowed into an X-certificate film when you were far too young. I shouldn't have been watching it, it was so scary. And there was something about the light, the Australian light, that dazzled you, came burning out of the screen. Just the sight of Jeff Thomson running in . . . there's never been a more terrifying sight in the history of cricket.

Amiss, Willis and Edrich were unfit for the game against Western Australia, and Lever withdrew before start of play having injured his back sleeping on too soft a mattress. During the game David Lloyd ricked his neck, and in the nets Fletcher was hit above the elbow on an old Thomson wound and couldn't bat in either innings. Colin Cowdrey flew in, in a sky-blue suit. He had four days to acclimatise after a 37-hour flight and three months off. Hendrick went down with the flu, and for the Test match England left out Underwood for Titmus, who had bowled well in the state match. The Test began on Friday the thirteenth.

This time Chappell put England in. At 44 for one, out walked Cowdrey. His greeting to Jeff Thomson – 'How do you do, I'm Colin Cowdrey' – may be cricket's most famous introduction, our Stanley and Livingstone moment. Thomson replied 'G'day, I'm Jeff Thomson', and they shook hands. The 22 runs Cowdrey scored may not sound very many. Indeed, they weren't. But such was the cheerfulness and bravery he showed, at the age of 42, and looking it, and almost certainly feeling it, that these 22, and the 41 he scored in the second innings opening in place of the newly injured Luckhurst, have entered cricketing legend.

Alan D-J: My neighbour and I were in the notorious Bay 13, feeling slightly queasy from VB fumes. As Cowdrey took guard, a huge shout came from an extra-large Aussie standing behind us, with a tinnie in one hand and a pie in the other: 'Get back to Greyfriars, Billy Bunter!'

Despite these heroics, and a fearless 51 from Alan Knott, England could only reach 208 in their first innings. Australia scored 481 in theirs (Edwards 115, Walters 103) and won by nine wickets. They were assisted by more extraordinary close catching – of 18 chances, 17 were held, seven by Greg Chappell – and fallible English batting. Most fallible of all, it seemed, was the captain. As CMJ wrote, 'Denness could not work out a coherent technique to play Lillee or Thomson, and from this moment his days as captain were numbered.'

Most people fail at sport. Almost everyone reaches a level at which, they discover, they are simply not good enough. How appalling it must be only to discover this at the very highest level and, worse, during a four-month tour of Australia. Reading through all this decades afterwards, you get the strong sense that England didn't have a lot of luck. But then teams being walloped rarely do. An lbw decision not given here, a bat-and-pad catch not given there, and Ian Chappell disinclined to walk for anything under any circumstances: it's all you can expect. Maybe the worst stroke of luck, though, had come on 16 August 1950, with Jeff Thomson's birth.

Simon O'H: What sporting situations require the most physical courage? Standing there, in the heat of a Brisbane afternoon, when Jeff Thomson is running towards you: I can't think of anything more frightening in all sport. But the worst part of that series was Mike Denness stepping away towards the square leg umpire as Thomson released the ball. He did that thing you are always taught not to do. If the ball is rising and coming at you, you've got to move towards the off side and let it pass

*by you on the leg side. Otherwise the ball will chase you and chase you:
it will hunt you down and kill you. And Denness was committing that
cardinal schoolboy error. He was the England captain and he crumbled.*

England weren't always that bad. Many of them were old,
some of them were past it, and one or two weren't quite up to it
anyway, but they had more fight in them than one or two
England teams who would follow. Against all expectations, the
Melbourne Test was a thriller. Amiss and Edrich replaced
Luckhurst (walking wicket) and Fletcher (an automatic selection
for seven series, but averaging 10 in this one). Underwood and
Hendrick supplanted Arnold and Old, who wasn't even injured
this time. Chappell put England in again and wickets fell, usually
to short balls aimed at the body – bodyline in all but name,
really, except that the catches went to the off side rather than the
leg side – and a couple to questionable umpiring decisions. But
for once England didn't buckle. Alan Knott nurdled and whacked
another fifty and the score rose to 242. Then Hendrick, given
the chance to open the bowling at last, ripped a muscle in the
back of his left thigh. His tour was over and England had three
front-line bowlers, Willis, Titmus and Underwood, plus Tony
Greig. They bowled Australia out for 241. Willis took five for 61,
Titmus two for 43, Greig (finding control at last with his
medium-pacers) two for 63. In the second innings Dennis Amiss
(90) and David Lloyd (44) put on 115 for the first wicket. Then
came the collapse. Thomson took three for 13 in a devastating
spell and England lost eight wickets for 67. But Tony Greig and
Bob Willis added 50 for the ninth wicket, and Australia were left
with 246 to win and a day in which to do it. At last: a game of
cricket I wish I'd seen.

Wally Edwards and Ian Chappell went quickly. Redpath and
Greg Chappell put on a hundred for the third wicket. When he
was on 12 Redders survived a forceful South African appeal for
lbw; on 30, becalmed by Titmus, he mis-drove a simple catch to
Denness at mid-on, who dropped it. But at 106, Titmus got

one to shoot along the ground and Chappell was out lbw for 61. Seven wickets left, 140 runs needed. Half an hour later, after 205 minutes (by the end of the series he would have spent 32 hours at the crease), Redpath ran himself out coming back for a second. When Ross Edwards was out to Titmus a run later, England sniffed victory. But Walters and Marsh went on the attack, and at tea Australia were 145 for five, with an hour and fifteen 8-ball overs to go.

If anything could show how much cricket has changed over the past thirty years, it might be the final hour of this match. Walters holed out to Denness at cover, but with fifteen overs left Australia needed 55, with four wickets left and Marsh 30 not out. Titmus and Underwood bowled to three-six defensive fields, and Marsh and Lillee blocked. The crowd slow-handclapped. With eight overs left, Denness took the new ball. Scoring suddenly became easier; the field was changed with every ball; Marsh was out, caught behind off Greig; but a disastrous defeat still loomed for England. Off the last two overs – 16 balls – Lillee and Walker needed 14 runs. Underwood, the master of parsimony, bowled a maiden. Australia ended eight runs short, with two wickets left. It was the first competitive match of the series, and the first draw.

Maybe Marsh and Lillee were right to block: England, two-nil down, needed victory more than Australia did, and so to deny them that victory was more important than winning themselves. For Sydney Denness took the unusual decision to drop himself. He had captained England in 14 Tests over 11 months; he felt he had been relatively successful as a leader but a failure as a batsman. Would he have dropped himself if England had got those last two wickets? Surely not. Edrich replaced him as captain; Arnold and Fletcher were back in the team; and Rick McCosker, 28, the big batting find of the season, made his debut in place of Wally Edwards. Ian Chappell won his fourth toss of four and decided to bat.

We won't dwell too long on this Test, or the next one. Australia scored 405 in their first innings (G. S. Chappell 84, McCosker 80), England battled to reach 295 (Knott 82, Edrich 50), but the result was never in doubt. In their second innings Redpath (105) and G. S. (144) put on 220 for the second wicket. Then Greig hit another fifty and Edrich withstood unfeasible punishment and two cracked ribs for 33 not out in nearly four hours, but Ashley Mallett took four for 21, Australia won by 171 runs and the Ashes were lost. With his replacement captain *hors de combat*, Denness returned at Adelaide where, on a drying pitch, Underwood took 11 wickets and Knott scored an unbeaten 106 – only the second century in Ashes history by a wicket-keeper – but these only reduced Australia's winning margin to a more modest 163 runs. When England batted, wrote CMJ, 'the pattern of the day was set: controlled, hostile bowling; brilliant fielding; inadequate batting'. England seemed demoralised; the surprise was that it hadn't happened earlier. No one had an answer to Thomson. Greig and Knott went on the attack, which sometimes worked, sometimes didn't. Amiss, at Melbourne, had countered with aggressive, orthodox batsmanship, confirming the impression that he was now England's best batsman. But at Adelaide he made 0 and 0. At Sydney Edrich had endured through superhuman courage. Most of the other batsmen had been rendered strokeless. Sooner or later the unplayable ball would come along and get them out. Amiss called it the 'trap-door ball': it came out of nowhere.

As it happens, the most significant incident in the Adelaide Test took place on the rest day. Several cricketers on each side repaired to the Barossa Valley, South Australia's wine-growing district, for a day by the pool, guzzling wine and playing tennis on the grass court there. Jeff Thomson was playing the game for only the second time. Attempting a huge serve (that beat Doug Walters for pace), he ripped muscles in his right shoulder, and didn't bowl another ball in the series. It didn't affect the outcome

of the Test – Lillee and Walker cleaned up the following morning – but it had massive long-term repercussions. For Thomson
was never the same bowler again. He was fast, for sure: four
years later he would clock 99.7 mph in a televised time trial. But
he was never as fast. Some say that no one has ever been as fast as
Thomson was in those four and a half Tests.

With five matches done and one to go, Australia were 4–0 up.
Back at the MCG for a final money-spinning hurrah, they could
be forgiven for letting the intensity lapse a little. Or maybe
England saw their chance with Thommo out of action. Willis
too was injured, so Peter Lever came back, having become something of a Lucan since his mattress-related back injury. In
oppressive humidity, he took six for 38 and Australia made just
152. Lillee had time to dismiss Amiss for his third successive
duck, but then limped off on the second morning with a badly
bruised foot. Against Max Walker and Geoff Dymock, Denness
hit 188 (the highest score by an England captain in Australia),
Fletcher 146, Greig 89 and Edrich 70. Max Walker cleaned up
the tail to finish with eight for 143 and Australia had thirteen
hours to survive on a good pitch. Redders batted another six
hours and Greg Chappell made another century, but England
wore them down and won by an innings and four runs just after
lunch on the final day. It was their first innings victory against
Australia in nine years, and a slightly hollow one. Australia's tendency to lose Tests that didn't matter would become a feature of
the decades to come.

Three

1975

I enjoy hitting a batsman more than getting him out. I like to see blood on the pitch.

Jeff Thomson

The summer of 1975 provided a cricketing *embarras de richesse*, although, as usual, little of the *richesse* found its way to the players. The winners of the inaugural Prudential World Cup, contested by eight teams between 7 and 21 June, received £4000. The man of the match in a first round tie pocketed £50, and the best player in the final got £200. The first match suggested that one-day international cricket hadn't won everyone over just yet. At Lord's England scored 334 for four off their 60 overs. India managed 132 for three. Sunil Gavaskar opened the batting, stayed there to the end, and made 36 not out. In the last hour of play some Indian supporters ran on to the field to plead with the batsmen to speed it up a bit. Apparently Gavaskar believed that the total was ungettable, but it was a nice day and the bowling was reasonably challenging, so he thought he'd get in some batting practice. After the match the team manager, G. S. Ramchand, said, 'I do not personally agree with his tactics . . . It's a great disappointment to us, but he will not be disciplined.'

For our purposes, though, the crucial match was the semi-final at Headingley between England and Australia. Given what had passed in the winter, England would have preferred to play anyone else. And yet, in a group match, the West Indies had out-classed the Australians, passing their total of 192 with 14 overs to spare. Lillee had been hit for 66 off ten overs, mainly by Alvin Kallicharran, whose innings was described by Tony Lewis in his book *A Summer of Cricket* as 'genuinely rhapsodic, sometimes lissom, often brutal'. The Australian bowlers did not look so fearsome, it seemed, on slow English wickets. Nor was one-day cricket particularly to their taste. What's more, John Snow was back. England had a wonderful opportunity to reassert them-selves, maybe even put down a marker for the four-Test series to come.

Yet again, though, Australia had a secret weapon. In cloudy conditions, on a green pitch, the left-arm fast-medium Gary Gilmour opened the bowling, swung the ball prodigiously and took six for 14 in 12 overs (with six maidens). Only Denness (27) and Arnold (18 not out) managed double figures. England were all out for 93 in the 37th over. Alan Knott later said that the ball had been hard to pick up from the bowler's hand. The sightscreens were positioned perfectly for a right-arm over-the-wicket bowler, and weren't movable. An hour later, thanks primarily to Old and Snow, Australia were 39 for six, the crowd silent and unbelieving. But Walters and the dreaded Gilmour hung on for a four-wicket win and a place in the final.

So England had blown it again (a sentence I promise to use sparingly in this book, despite sometimes overwhelming tempta-tion). But we should probably be more generous. The psychological hold the Australian bowlers enjoyed over the English batsmen was absolute. Which might explain why Mike Denness, when he won the toss at Edgbaston a few weeks later, declined to make up his mind straight away and went back to his senior players to ask them what they would prefer to do.

What it doesn't explain is why Mike Denness was still captain in the first place.

Never previously known for their consistency, the selectors had stuck with most of the team who had been so humiliated in Australia. Alec Bedser, the chairman of selectors, felt that Denness had not done enough to earn the sack. Tony Lewis, newly retired from cricket and appointed cricket and rugby correspondent of the *Sunday Telegraph*, agreed. But he obviously knew and liked Denness, who had been brought into the side as captain despite not having proved himself as a captain (which may have rung a bell or two). Myself, I remember thinking of Denness as a weak man, much as any schoolboy would instantly diagnose a maths teacher who couldn't keep order. We could see that Ian Chappell could see this too. (He was the large hairy boy at the back of the class who was always making trouble.)

David T: My father had the most arbitrary likes and dislikes. He disliked Ian Chappell specifically for the way he fiddled with his box.

It wasn't that Denness hadn't done enough to be given the sack, it was that he hadn't done enough to be given the job in the first place. This appeared to be Geoffrey Boycott's view too, as he sulked in self-imposed exile in Yorkshire.

We have learned subsequently that if you don't remove a weak-link captain, it's difficult to make sweeping changes to the team surrounding him. Snow was back, and there was a first cap for a round-shouldered young Essex batsman called Graham Gooch. David Lloyd was the only notable casualty – a little unluckily, it seems now, as Amiss and Fletcher were still there. Australia were equally familiar: Lillee, Thomson and Walker kept their places ahead of Gilmour, and the only new batsman was Alan Turner, replacing jug-eared Redpath at the top of the order. Redders had opted out of the tour because he had an antique shop that required some attention. He should have come over anyway and stocked up on England batsmen.

So Denness went back to his senior players and they decided

to ask Australia to bat first. Sir Leonard Hutton had inspected the wicket earlier and told Alec Bedser, 'There are a packet of runs to be made on this strip – I'd be prepared to bet on that.' There was also an unfavourable weather forecast to consider. In 1975 all but the two ends of a Test strip would remain uncovered during the hours of play. If it rained, its nature would change markedly, and almost certainly for the worse. This is why captains rarely ever put other sides in to bat. Denness's decision was therefore what Sir Humphrey Appleby in *Yes, Minister* would have described, with a shudder, as 'courageous'. It was one of his last decisions as England captain. After two hours, Snow finally took the wicket of Alan Turner, caught at extra cover by Denness. Snow rather pointedly looked at his watch. Australia compiled 359, with McCosker, Ian Chappell, Ross Edwards and Marsh all scoring fifties and Jeff Thomson falling one short. It then rained and England were shot out for 101 and 173. Gooch made his legendary pair, only the third by an England batsman on debut. Denness scored three and eight, Lillee and Walker each took seven wickets and Thomson a further five. By mid-afternoon on the fourth day, Ladbroke's were quoting Tony Greig as 2–1 on for the England captaincy at the next Test.* Within 48 hours Denness had resigned – jumped before he was pushed, which was a disappointment to all of us who wanted to do the pushing.

Andy R: What I really remember about 1975 is one ball. Jeff Thomson bowled it to Mike Denness. Never seen a ball like it. It seemed to start going out, then came in and yorked him. But what was amazing was that Denness obviously never saw it. He just stood there. And then put his head back, as though he'd just thought, Ah yes, that's the end of my career, isn't it. It was one of those moments.

Thus began the era of Tony Greig. Cometh the hour, cometh

---

* Denness was 5–2, Richard Gilliat of Hampshire 6–1 and John Edrich 10–1. Richard Gilliat!

the immensely tall South African with mad, glittery eyes. Tony Lewis talked approvingly of Denness's 'gentle stoicism', and it's fair to say that Greig would offer different qualities. His England would be louder, more aggressive, more Australian. As Fred Trueman said, 'There's only one head bigger than Tony Greig's and that's Birkenhead.'*

So for Lord's England had a fresh new look, maybe not for the first time. Denness, Fletcher, Old and Arnold had gone (Denness and Arnold for good). Back came Barry Wood and Peter Lever, but the real headline-grabber was the dèbut of David Steele of Northants. Aged 34, bespectacled and prematurely grey, Steele was a solid county pro who had never been suggested by anyone, other than possibly his mother, as a potential England player. Greig, though, wanted gritty fighters, men of iron and steel(e) who wouldn't submit to the Australians' bullying. 'When I was appointed, the first thing I did was speak to county bowlers such as Bob Cottam,' he told *The Wisden Cricketer* many years later. 'I asked them who was the hardest batsman to get out. Two names continually popped up. One was Geoff Boycott. The other was David Steele.' England were 10 for one when Steele walked to the crease (having famously got lost on his way out of the pavilion) and 49 for four when his captain joined him. Dennis Amiss had been given another last chance at number four, and made 0.

Andrew N: In those days you could sit on the grass in front of the stands. I was sat there, in front of the Grand Stand, on the first morning of Lillee and Thomson. You knew then that you were in the presence of something special.

Simon O'H: It seemed to me that Thomson had found a whole new way to bowl fast. Lillee had the supreme classical fast bowler's action. Textbook, with a wonderful fluidity. Whereas Thomson was a slinger. It seemed to me purely about intimidating the batsman.

---

* But then he also said of Ian Botham, 'Can't bowl a hoop downhill.'

We all seem to remember that Steele scored an even 50, with his forward defensives and nudges through square leg. What we may forget is that Greig made 96 and Knott 69, and Bob Woolmer, also making his debut, batted at number eight and scored 33.

Chris D: I was in the Mound Stand that day, and I had an audition for a hospital series called Angels. *It was at three o'clock, and Greig and Steele were batting, and I stayed, and missed the audition, not to watch Greig get his hundred, but to watch Steele get his fifty.*

Tim C: I was sitting low in front of the Tavern. The wicketkeeper was further back to Lillee and Thomson than you could begin to comprehend. You were used to playing at school, where so-and-so guy is really quick, and you're terrified if you have to face him, and the wicketkeeper is about five yards back. But if you multiply that by seven, you think, how fucking fast is that?

Luckily for Steele, and unluckily for Thomson, the pitch was turgidly slow. First thing the following morning, England were all out for 315, and by lunch Australia were 81 for seven. Snow had taken the first three wickets, and after the third was actually seen to smile.

We have to cherish these moments, because moments are usually all they are. Every good team has its backs-to-the-wall expert, and Australia's was Ross Edwards. One of the last international cricketers known to smoke a pipe – although obviously not at the crease – Edwards adjusted to the pudding of a pitch and slowly batted his side out of the mire. Jeff Thomson hung around with him for an hour, and Lillee, if anything, looked even more comfortable. On 99, Edwards tried to clip Woolmer through the on side for his century, missed and was lbw. But the innings that sticks in my mind, because at the time I simply couldn't believe it, was Lillee's outrageous, barnstorming 73 not out. It made no sense, that he could get away with it, that he could be allowed to get away with it. I'm sure that Australians watching Botham's 149 not out at Headingley in 1981 would feel something similar. Although maybe we haven't been reminded of Lillee's innings quite so frequently.

For this was a match-saving rather than a match-winning innings. Lillee and Ashley Mallett put on 69 for the last wicket, and England had a first innings lead of just 47. Edrich hit 175 in the second innings, his seventh century against Australia (and his 93rd in first-class cricket). Then Australia batted out the final day for a draw. The pitch that had tamed Lillee, Thomson and Walker had also drawn the teeth of the England bowlers. Slightly smaller and blunter teeth, if we are to be frank.

Julian P: I went to the Friday and the Saturday with my friends Adrian W and Roy A: we were 15. We sat in what's now the Compton Stand. Edrich got 175 in a very, very long time. He really knew where his off-stump was. And in front of us a pair of Australians were drinking Swan lager. And behind us a pair were drinking VB. Their consumption was awesome. Roy went home, but Adrian and I stayed behind afterwards and counted the tins. The pair in front drank 87 cans between them, and the pair behind 112. So between them they drank more than one can for every run Edrich scored.

Simon O'H: I remember standing in the Tavern, and there being a group of two or three Aussies, and they'd come into the ground with a huge black bin-liner full of tinnies.

Ross C: The Lord's streaker was all over the news. I remember my mother and father having an argument in the kitchen, because the streaker had given his name to the police as 'Michael Angelow'. My mother was insistent that this was just a made-up name. And my father said, if his surname was Angelow, his parents might well have called him Michael. I still have no idea whether he was called Michael Angelow or not.

(It was the first appearance by a streaker in English Test matches. Angelow was a cook in the Merchant Navy, and hurdled nudely over each set of stumps at 3.20 on the fourth afternoon. A friend had dared him ten pounds to do so. 'We have got a freaker [*sic*] down the wicket now,' said John Arlott on *Test Match Special*. 'Not very shapely, as it's masculine.')

Would a more traditional, flighty spin bowler have made a difference at Lord's? Just in case it might have, England opted to give a debut to Philippe Edmonds at Headingley, and lose a batsman (R. A. Woolmer). The batting order was in a terrible flux anyway. Amiss and Gooch were put out of their misery, which couldn't be argued with, but back came John Hampshire and Keith Fletcher, which could. Old replaced Lever, who had sustained an injury midweek and, though he didn't know it, had played his last Test. Australia also opted for a fifth bowler: Gary Gilmour. In August 1977, during the next Ashes tour, an estimable punk group named The Adverts would release their best single, 'Looking Through Gary Gilmore's Eyes'. They claimed that it was about some American mass murderer with a vaguely similar name, but we knew who they were talking about.

Headingley was Headingley: grey of sky, slow of pitch, and full of Yorkshiremen. Spectators were furious that Fletcher had been picked again. Why hadn't Phil Sharpe been given a chance? Dennis Lillee wasn't complaining. The mere sight of Fletcher walking to the crease increased his speed by five mph. He quickly got his man, giving Mallett catching practice in the gully. This was after a good start for England: a useful toss won and fifties for Edrich and Steele, the two battlers. The following morning Greig was run out for 51, England were dismissed for 288 and Gilmour had taken six for 85. John Snow now bowled superbly – 16 overs, one maiden, one for 18 – but when Edmonds came on to bowl, Australia were 77 for two and Ian Chappell was prospering. Edmonds bowled a faster ball, a big soft juicy long-hop. Chappell's eyes lit up and steam came out of his ears. He missed it and was bowled. Ross Edwards padded up to his first ball. He hadn't scored a run here in 1972 either. He was destined never to get off the mark in a Test match at Headingley. Greg Chappell swept the third ball of the next over straight to Underwood at square leg. After tea Doug Walters was lbw and Max Walker caught by Old at slip. At close of play Australia were 107 for eight and Edmonds had taken five wickets for 17 runs. On the video footage he looks almost puppyish with delight. (Accentuating this impression is a very full head of blond hair, possibly modelled on Joanna Lumley's contemporaneous crop in *The New Avengers*.)

Could England win? We had a first innings lead of 153, which even impressed some Yorkshiremen, but sooner or later it was going to rain. England had to get on with it. Australia started working their way through the England line-up. (As Jim Laker put it, 'The familiar flash outside the off-stump from Fletcher again causin' his downfall.') David Steele, national hero, again stood firm, with a still head and a stout heart. It's strange to think that Steele played only eight Tests. Once the immediate danger of Lillee and Thomson had passed, he would soon be superseded. But that's fair enough: his talent was for playing fast bowling on slow wickets, and he made the most of that talent precisely when it was required. How many cricketers have been BBC Sports Personality of the Year? Not many. Racing drivers are more likely to win for coming second. In fact only four cricketers have won (as compared with 17 athletes and two members of the royal family): Jim Laker in 1956, Ian Botham in 1981, Andrew Flintoff in 2005, and David Steele in 1975. Such heroics, and all of them against Australians. Perhaps they are the only ones that really count.

Simon O'H: It was the apotheosis of the county pro. It was about England cricket rediscovering its core values.

Bill M: How many sports can you play wearing glasses?

Robin W: I've watched my brother become more and more like David Steele as the years have gone by. Including his batting. Measured, and studious. He used to look like Gooch: he had one of those Zapata moustaches. And then he evolved into David Steele. But without ever becoming Sports Personality of the Year.

Again, though, the crucial stand was between Steele and his

captain. What a contrast. The old pro, with his slightly Pooterish gait, not really looking like a sportsman at all. And Mr Belligerence, fuelled by who knows what demons, more Australian in some senses than many Australians. They made 92 and 49 out of England's 291, which left Australia needing 445 in five sessions. You wouldn't put it past them. By the end of the day they had reached 220 for three, with Rick McCosker 95 not out.

There's a famous photograph of the two captains the following morning both staring at the wrecked pitch. Tony Greig in check blazer, polished loafers, shirt and tie, neatly parted hair. Ian Chappell in open-necked shirt, casual jumper, slacks and stripy flip-flops. (By his own testimony he was hideously hungover.) Overnight, small holes had been dug in the pitch and engine oil poured all over it. On a nearby wall were painted the words 'G. DAVIS IS INNOCENT' and 'SORRY IT HAD TO BE DONE'. Not half as sorry as we were. George Davis, it emerged, was a convicted felon, serving a 20-year prison sentence for an armed raid on a branch of the London Electricity Board. His friends believed he had been stitched up and were campaigning to have him released. They had dug the holes with cutlery liberated from a motorway service station. I didn't want George Davis released. I wanted him tortured and killed. The leader of the protesters, by astonishing coincidence, was named Peter Chappell. He served 20 months for the outrage. George Davis was released early and caught two years later robbing a bank in north London. The third Test, though, was ruined. It had been England's best chance of victory; indeed, their only chance. As it happens, it started to rain at midday, and didn't stop until four o'clock. It would probably have been a draw anyway. Do we really think that? No, we don't, and neither does Tony Greig.

Ross C: It was a time of great economic strife, when inflation hit 29 per cent and the stock market collapsed by 70 per cent. But somehow I still feel the abandonment of the Headingley Test was the most significant event of the year.

One-nil up with one Test to play, Australia thus retained the Ashes. For the Oval England dropped Hampshire and Fletcher, brought Woolmer into the top five for the first time and recalled Surrey's Graham Roope, who had played eight Tests in 1973. To have any chance of squaring the series Tony Greig needed to win another toss. He didn't and on a slow but true surface Australia lost only one wicket on the first day. Rick McCosker, who had looked more impressive with every Test, finally got his century, and Ian Chappell batted for seven and three-quarter hours for 192. Australia 532 for nine declared; England 191 all out. David Steele made just 39, his lowest score of the summer. With their backs to the wall, rears firmly guarded, England's second innings, following on, was long, slow and resolute: Edrich 96, Steele 66, Roope 77, Woolmer 149, Knott 64. At six hours and 35 minutes, Woolmer's was the slowest hundred ever made against Australia. In all, England scored 538 over thirteen and a half hours. Even with the customary sixth day, Australia had nowhere near enough time to score the 198 runs they needed. As Tony Lewis wrote, 'A lot had happened in six days, and yet nothing had.' It's possible that the sage of Swansea had been watching too many episodes of *Kung Fu.*

So we lost one-nil, but the three draws after the single defeat lifted national spirits. Edrich, Steele, Greig and Knott had not just resisted the ferocious Australian quicks, they had scored runs against them as well. Snow's return made us all wonder again why he hadn't gone to Australia the previous winter. Edmonds and Woolmer demonstrated the fearlessness of youth. Greig's captaincy showed the benefits of almost unlimited aggression. He and Ian Chappell made a fine pair. Maybe feeling that he had done all he had set out to do, Chappell resigned as captain at the end of the series. Brother Greg would take over. Ross Edwards retired from Test cricket altogether, after just 20 Tests. You might begin to notice a preference in these pages for gritty, nuggety, hard-to-dismiss batsmen over fancy dans, and Ross Edwards was one of my favourites. The chin certainly helped. You could have shovelled sand with it.

Four

1977

The aim of English Test cricket is, in fact, mainly to beat Australia.

Jim Laker

In these times of plenty, when there's always a two-match Test series against Someone Or Other just around the corner, we are apt to get sated, if not bloated. But in the 1970s, Test series were longer and rarer and more of an event. Unless it was against Australia, whom we seemed to be playing all the time. The Packer revolution would soon change everything, but the cricket authorities' new enthusiasm for frequent Ashes series does suggest a growing awareness of the game's commercial possibilities. After the 1975 tussle, England sat at home during the winter and wallpapered the spare room. The following summer they were thrashed by the West Indies, and then flew to India for a five-Test series they would win 3–1. The unquestionable highlight of the 1976/77 schedule, though, was a one-off Centenary Test at Melbourne in March, to celebrate a hundred glorious years of sledging and sharp practice between the two nations. The Ashes would not be at stake, but they would be for the five Tests to be played in England the following summer. The Centenary Test therefore functioned as a tasty hors d'oeuvre, which both teams wished to gobble up, and also as an opportunity for these two grizzled, hard-bitten sides to take a good look at each other – as if they hadn't seen more than enough of each other recently anyway.

England, as usual, were a side in transition. Edrich, Steele and Snow had gone; Mike Brearley, Peter Willey and Geoff Miller had made debuts the previous summer; Derek Randall and John Lever had been capped in India. Dennis Amiss had made his great comeback, hitting 203 against Holding, Roberts, Daniel and Holder and then averaging 52 in India. Bob Woolmer and Keith Fletcher had fared less well but kept their places for the Centenary Test. How did Fletcher do it? Tactical nous, apparently. Greig didn't have much, but he knew a man who did. Australia, meanwhile, had lost Ian Chappell, Ian Redpath and Ashley Mallett, all retired. Ian Davis was opening the batting with his New South Wales teammate Rick McCosker; Gary Cosier was ensconced in the middle order; Kerry O'Keeffe was the main spinner; and David Hookes, 21, made his debut after five centuries in six Sheffield Shield innings (163, 9, 185, 101, 135 and 156).

But who cares who was in the teams? No one did at the time. The Centenary Test was an exercise in nostalgia, a celebration, a party. You probably needed to be a bit older than I was (16) to appreciate the wonder of it all. There were 214 former Test cricketers in attendance, 71 of them flown in from England, including Percy Fender, born in 1892. Every living Ashes captain was there bar one: Ray Illingworth, no doubt for stubborn Yorkshire reasons of his own. Old crocks were wheeled out before, during and after the game, often after a huge lunch, clad in blazers with shiny buttons, and noses to match. What struck me was how friendly all the old England and Australia players were, and keen to emphasise the good fellowship between them all. But that may just have been because Douglas Jardine wasn't there. He couldn't make it, sadly, on account of being dead.

Greg Chappell therefore tossed a specially minted commemorative gold coin, Tony Greig called correctly and put them in. A penknife belonging to assistant manager Ken Barrington had detected moisture under the surface, and a nervous England batting order may not have relished facing Lillee on it. As it is, Willis, Old, J. K. Lever and Underwood bowled superbly, sharing the wickets as Australia folded for 138. Greg Chappell blamed the pressure of the occasion rather than the pitch. In which case it worked both ways, because England made only 95. Lillee took six for 26, Walker four for 54. (Thomson wasn't playing, having dislocated his shoulder colliding with another fielder earlier in the season.*) The authorities began to get nervous. HM The Queen was due to drop by at three o'clock on the fifth afternoon. At this rate the game would be long over and the ground would be deserted. A few doddery old Test cricketers might still be wandering around, clutching throbbing heads, but no one else. Soon Australia were 53 for three, with McCosker unable to bat because a Willis bouncer had broken his jaw in the first innings. But the moisture in the pitch was gone: batting was becoming less fraught. Davis, Walters and Hookes all passed 50, and Marsh scored the first Test century by an Australian wicketkeeper against England. (Sad to say, it wasn't the last.) McCosker came in at number ten, his face swollen beyond recognition and his jaw held together with steel girders. He and Marsh put on 54 for the ninth wicket. When Greg Chappell declared, England's target was 463 runs in ten hours and fifty minutes.

* In *Wisden* 2008, Ian Chappell expressed the view that it was this injury that did for Thomson's fiercest pace, not the earlier tennis-related calamity. But what bad luck: two serious injuries, and both of them, to some extent, ridiculous.

There followed, of course, one of the great Test innings, which John Arlott would praise for 'its concentration, soundness, bravery and frequent handsome strokes'. After Woolmer's dismissal, Derek Randall skittered to the wicket to join Mike Brearley. Always a nervous starter – his fidgeting alone would have powered a set of floodlights on most modern grounds – he was helped on his way by some wayward bowling from Gary Gilmour. (No longer the menace of two years before, Gilmour was carrying an ankle injury, and playing his last Test.) When Lillee returned to the attack, Randall was the first batsman in the match to hook him. Later on he would doff his cap to the old monster, an act of genius in itself, in that it riled Lillee to even greater excesses of rage and violence. ('This is not a fucking tea party, Randall.') With Amiss in support, England reached 189 for two at the end of the fourth day. They needed 272 to win, with eight wickets left and Randall on 87 not out.

They didn't make it, of course, but they came magnificently close. Randall's 174 was the second highest score by a batsman playing his first England vs Australia Test, and Australia's winning margin of 45 runs was exactly the same as that of the first ever Test match between the two sides, a hundred years earlier. Best news of the day, from an Anglo-Saxon perspective, was that Dennis Lillee would not be on the tour to England. An X-ray revealed a reopening of one of the stress fractures in his back that had nearly ended his career in 1973. He also wanted to see more of the wife and kids. It must have been quite a day. HM The Queen turned up on time, Lillee asked for her autograph, and Tony Greig recruited a few more players for Kerry Packer's World Series Cricket.

Imagine an alternative universe in which Packer's Circus, as we all sneeringly called it, never happened. In this world Tony Greig played a hundred Test matches and is remembered as one of England's greatest players. Mike Brearley never became England captain. Ian Botham and David Gower didn't play for England for another two or three years. Derek Underwood took 400 Test wickets. The Australian Cricket Board continued to treat their players like serfs. One-day cricketers are still wearing white and playing with a red ball . . .

Kerry Packer, a huge, extravagantly ugly man thought by many of us to have been the original model for Jabba the Hutt, was a media mogul who wanted the TV rights to Australian international cricket. The ACB wouldn't have anything to do with him, so he set up his own rival cricketing event, seducing many of the world's best cricketers with substantial cheques. Nineteen of the leading Australian cricketers signed up, including a few, like Ian Chappell, Ian Redpath and Ross Edwards, who had recently retired. Tony Greig, enthusiastically embracing the Dark Side of the Force, secured the services of John Snow, Dennis Amiss and the two players of undisputed world class in the England side, Alan Knott and Derek Underwood. South Africans, West Indians, Indians, Pakistanis, they were all there and, with hindsight, who can blame them? Cricketers were paid atrociously and regarded with disdain by administrators. If Packer hadn't done it, someone else would have, sooner or later. At the time, though, he was the enemy, and having a face like an overfed lamprey probably didn't help. As it turned out, he probably contributed more than anyone to England's victory in the Ashes contest of 1977.

Well, he and Dennis Lillee. In the absence of the great one, the Australian bowling would be led by Jeff Thomson and Max Walker, with Geoff Dymock, Len Pascoe and Mick Malone in reserve (the last two uncapped). Kerry O'Keeffe and Ray Bright were the spinners; Richie Robinson was Rodney Marsh's understudy; and some new young batsmen supplemented Chappell, McCosker and Walters – Ian Davis, Gary Cosier and David Hookes had played a handful of Tests between them, while Craig Serjeant (25) and Kim Hughes (23) had played none. As ever, Australia favoured youth over experience for this long, exacting tour. As well as five Tests and three one-day internationals, they would play first-class matches against the MCC and every one of the 17 counties, and knockabouts against the Minor Counties, Combined Universities and Lavinia, Duchess of Norfolk's XI.*

Maybe the first hint that the balance of power was changing came in the second ODI, when Australia were bowled out for 70. Their batsmen struggled throughout the early games in some horrible weather, and with Cosier and Davis unable to score a run, Serjeant and Robinson were chosen for the first Test at Lord's, the latter playing as a specialist batsman. Thomson, fit again, returned and Len Pascoe also made his debut. Born Len Durtanovich, the son of Macedonian immigrants, this woolly mammoth of a bowler was said to be more Big-Hearted Trier than thoroughbred, although he looked pretty scary to me. Rick McCosker was also there, after a severely unpleasant few weeks, during which he had been fed on liquids and lost half a stone. The jawbone refused to knit at first, and had had to be rewired, and several splintered teeth repaired. It was an act of courage for him merely to put on his whites.

For many people, though, the series was tainted before it started. According to Christopher Martin-Jenkins, writing in *The Jubilee Tests*, 'The fact that ten of the Australians and four of the England team were prepared to risk their Test careers for forty pieces of silver, and the general uncertainty and nastiness in the air engendered by the Packer crisis, undoubtedly took away some of the spice from the traditional atmosphere for the Lord's Test.' Tony Greig had been sacked as captain and Mike Brearley installed in his place. But the Packer players

* Ask any group of cricket fans over the age of 35 who the Duchess of Norfolk is and they'll shout 'Lavinia!' as if they knew her personally. She died in 1995.

were still in the England side, at least for now. Good grief, the Ashes were at stake. The only casualty from the Centenary Test was Keith Fletcher, replaced by Graham Barlow.* I, for one, couldn't wait.

Richard B: It was the first series I saw in colour. My school holidays were so fucking boring that I just lived for the cricket.

Bill M: There was nothing else to do at that age. When a Test match was on, the whole day was built around it. The frustrating thing then was the time between getting up, at eight-thirty say, and the Test match starting at eleven-thirty. It was just the longest three hours of my life.

Richard B: Now I complain to my children that they're watching too much television. Of course I do. Entirely consistent behaviour.

England's record against Australia at Lord's was abject. Thomson had shown no form in the early matches. Now he roared in and dismissed Amiss and Brearley with consecutive balls. Randall and Woolmer put on 96, but after Randall slapped a wide half-volley to Greg Chappell at first slip, the innings fell apart. As CMJ put it, 'The contest between Chris Old and good fast bowling is rarely an even one', but Old wasn't the only batsman to fail against Thomson, Walker and Pascoe. After a diverting tenth-wicket partnership between Underwood and Bob Willis, England managed 216. On Friday it rained, and by the end of Saturday Australia were looking good on 278 for seven. CMJ was very keen on Craig Serjeant, who had scored 81: 'This tall, dark, personable Perth pharmacist played with astonishing maturity for a man in his first Test.' He had played only 15 first-class matches. Chappell made 66 and Doug Walters 53, nearly getting out around three hundred times. Willis and Old curtailed the

---

* The perfect example of a captain's influence on selection. Fletcher was Greig's tactical expert: Brearley didn't need him. And Barlow played for Middlesex, Brearley's county. Trebles all round.

fun with the second new ball, and Willis wrapped up the tail on Monday morning with seven for 78, his best figures (so far). Australia led by 80 on the first innings and had nearly two days to wrap up yet another Lord's victory. 'England were patently on the rack,' wrote David Frith in *The Ashes '77*. 'The ball was seaming. Aussie confidence was high – and it can reach peerless heights.' Survival was imperative. Thomson removed Amiss, bowling at somewhere approaching the speed of light, and nearly had Brearley caught at short leg when he was on 19. Next over, Woolmer was dropped in the gully by Serjeant, CMJ's new favourite. This appears to have been the turning point in the match – maybe even the series.

I remember this series primarily for Bob Woolmer's batting. We had long known he was a good player, someone who had made the most of his talents, brought into the side as a bowler who batted, and turning himself into a batsman who for some reason rarely bowled. Now he looked like England's next great batsman. Commentators and spectators drooled over his cover drives. His play had an authority that seemed to foretell great things. He and Randall would surely occupy the middle order for a generation.

Woolmer's 120 took five hours and 248 balls: it was an immense innings. Brearley made 49 and Tony Greig a belligerent 91 in England's 305. Australia needed 226 in an hour and three-quarters plus twenty overs. It was worth a try, but at 71 for five Marsh and Hookes opted for plan B and successfully blocked for the draw.

On, then, to Old Trafford. Worrying Australia was Rick McCosker's miserable form: maybe he had come back too soon after the jaw injury. England had a happier problem: a comfortable excess of opening batsmen. After delicate negotiations in service stations, Geoffrey Boycott had made himself available again. England didn't bring him back straight away: Geoff Miller for Graham Barlow was their only change for the second Test.

Australia gave a debut to Ray Bright, replacing Pascoe for a pitch expected to turn, and brought back Ian Davis, who was in the runs again, for Robinson.

So, an important toss, which Chappell won, and by lunch Australia were 80 for two. One of those wickets was the captain's. 'The big breakthrough . . . for such is Chappell's downfall always seen to be,' wrote David Frith. England's six bowlers – Willis, Lever, Old, Greig, Underwood and Miller – chipped away at Australia's inexperienced line-up, but at 140 for five Doug Walters suddenly perked up and unleashed a savage array of square cuts, off-drives and whippy clips through mid-wicket. On his fourth tour of England, this was only his fifth fifty, and the prospect of a century at last must have been running through his mind, especially given the remarkable numerical alignment noted by Mr Robert Lord in a letter to the Times the following week: 'The cricket Test between England and Australia commenced at Old Trafford on 7-7-77, which was the 77th day of the Australians' tour. In the 77th over, K. D. Walters took his score to 77, his partner at the wicket being R. W. Marsh, batting at number 7.'

But on 88, Walters hit a Miller full toss straight to Greig at extra cover. Australia were all out for 297.

Brearley and Amiss went quickly. 'England had once again got away to a miserable start,' wrote CMJ. 'Yet this was the prelude to as handsome an afternoon of batting from two English players as had been seen for years.' Randall and Woolmer played themselves in carefully against Thomson and Walker – and then let loose. Randall was the great instinctive batsman: it shouldn't work but it did. Woolmer had clearly been watching Cowdrey for years and thought, Yes, that's the way to do it. Just after he reached his fifty Randall played an O'Keeffe flipper, looked at the bowler, smiled and turned his wrist over, to let him know he had read him. 'Cheeky little bugger,' said Fred Trueman in the commentary box. Imagine Dennis Lillee, at home in Australia, watching this on TV with the wife and kids, steam pouring out of his ears.

On 43, Woolmer was dropped by McCosker at second slip. The Australians were becoming uncharacteristically buttery of finger, while England were catching everything. 'Thomson was a picture of dejection,' wrote David Frith. 'Brisbane 1974, with infallible catchers everywhere, Lillee at the other end, and a responsive pitch, were light-years away.' Woolmer batted a little under six and a half hours for his 137, adding 142 with Randall and 160 with Tony Greig. Lion-hearted bowling from Thomson and Walker and three wickets from Ray Bright restricted England's lead to 140. But in their second innings Australian wickets again fell regularly. McCosker mis-hooked Willis to mid-on for 0; Davis aimed his at long-leg; Serjeant glanced Underwood to forward short leg. At the other end Chappell calmly and elegantly scored his runs: 54 out of 92 for four by lunch. Years later Brian Lara would experience a similar quandary: how to lead and inspire a failing team when they simply aren't as good as you are. At tea Chappell was 92 not out, and two fours off Willis no-balls immediately afterwards took him to his 14th Test hundred, his sixth against England. It was like watching a high-performance vehicle ease past a lot of Morris Marinas and Austin Allegros. Derek Underwood snared him eventually, bowled off an inside edge for 112. In all, Underwood bowled 32.5 overs and took six for 66: my god, how we would miss him.*

Richard C: Derek Underwood is almost my favourite player in this era. One of the reasons, apart from his being a splendid bowler, is that he smoked the whole time. But the main reason is that he once said, I can't understand why all these people want to be captain. I don't. I just want to turn up and bowl.

---

* If you sold your soul to the devil in return for the ability to bowl world-class left-arm spin, chances are that you too would take 6-66.

Australia were all out for 218 and England took an hour and a half to score the 79 they needed. The winning runs, an extra cover drive for four, were hit by Dennis Amiss, in what turned out to be his last Test.* This was only the second England win against Australia in 14 Tests since 1972, only the eighth win at home against Australia since the war, and the first victory at home against anyone for three years. And for the next Test, Boycott would be back.

For Amiss, and us, the nightmare was over. In 50 Tests since 1966, he had scored 3612 runs at the impressive average of 46.30. In his first Test against Australia, in 1968, he had bagged a pair; in 1974/75, he had made 7, 25, 4, 90, 12, 37, 0, 0 and 0; in 1975, 4, 5, 0 and 10; in the Centenary Test, 4 and 64; and in this series, 4, 0, 11 and 28 not out. That's 305 runs at 15.25 against the ancient enemy, and 3307 runs at 57 against everyone else. In some ways he was our Doug Walters. The seeds of greatness were there, so you had to keep picking him, and he kept getting out.

Between the second and third Tests, an ICC meeting at Lord's confirmed the expected international bans on the Packer signees: this would be the last Test series for all of them. Australia brought back Len Pascoe for Bright and, slightly more controversially, Richie Robinson for Serjeant. Robinson had scored 207 runs in the game against Warwickshire without being dismissed; but Serjeant was the only man in the touring

---

* This seemed an interesting statistical point, so I contacted Steven Lynch at Wisden and asked him if he knew of any other England batsmen who had hit the winning runs in a Test and never played for England again. Nasser Hussain definitely did. Graham Roope might have done (he was certainly at the crease when the winning runs were hit). Justin Langer did it for Australia, and we thought Ian Chappell might have done it as well. What larks: an entire afternoon happily frittered away and only this footnote to show for it.

party known to have turned down Packer. The other non-Packers were Cosier, Hughes and Dymock, none of whom had yet played a Test match. Curiouser. The night before the match, Jeff Thomson announced that he had changed his mind and pulled out of his Packer contract. None of this can have been good for morale.

England made three changes for Trent Bridge. As well as Boycott for Amiss, Mike Hendrick came in for John Lever, who was said to be jaded after the long winter tour. Chris Old had a shoulder injury and was replaced by a young pup named Ian Botham, who at 21 was the youngest England debutant since Alan Knott. 'This move strengthened the batting but weakened the bowling,' wrote CMJ, lacking the precious gift of hindsight. With his second ball, Botham might have had McCosker caught at third slip, had there been one. Australia lost only Ian Davis before lunch, and McCosker just after, although he had reached 50 and started to look his old self again. Then Botham came back and bowled a long-hop at Chappell, who conveniently played it on to his stumps. Moments later Willis dismissed David Hookes to an amazing diving slip catch by Hendrick; Walters prodded to gully; Robinson slapped Greig to first slip; Marsh missed a straight ball and was lbw; Walker offered an outside edge to a ball that came back into him. Australia were 155 for eight and, at one point, Botham had taken three for one in 14 balls. O'Keeffe, Thomson and Pascoe added 88 for the last two wickets, demonstrating Australian grit and, maybe also, the innate soundness of the pitch. Botham ended with five for 74. He told waiting reporters that his wife Kath was eight months pregnant, and after his performance he was hoping she still was.

Tim C: Nobody in Somerset knew what he was. People used to say, is he a bowler or a batsman? And then come to the conclusion that he was a very good slip fielder. He'd get two or three wickets, and 25 or 35 runs, and every now and then he'd get a low fifty. After the cider had slipped down a bit, the big chant would be 'Denning for England! Denning for England!' It used to be sung the whole summer long. The mantra. 'Denning for England!'

Next day, 5000 spectators were locked out of Trent Bridge before a ball had been bowled. Brearley and Boycott made a cautious start against Walker and Thomson, who at one point bowled five maidens in succession. After the drinks break Boycott cut Walker dangerously close to O'Keeffe, diving in the gully, and in the next over Brearley was caught by Hookes. Woolmer lasted three balls before falling lbw, and out walked Randall, the first Notts man to play in a Test on his home ground since Reg Simpson in 1954.

What happened next, for some strange reason, is seared on the souls of all England cricket fans alive and functioning at the time. Randall, as well as being universally loved, was a slightly unlucky cricketer. His most prolific domestic season would be 1985, when England were crushing the Australians and he couldn't get into the side. Like Botham, he flourished under the imaginative and inclusive captaincy of Brearley, and would not fare as well during other, less supportive regimes. Today he had reached 13 with his usual *joie de vivre* when Boycott played Thomson straight down the pitch and set off on a run that wasn't there. Randall's first instinct was to turn round and make his ground, but Boycott wasn't stopping. Randall, decency personified, made a belated and obviously doomed attempt to reach the other end. Rodney Marsh smashed down the stumps with the glee of a pantomime villain, Randall wandered off in a daze and Boycott stood with his head in his hands. He had run out the local hero, and the crowd booed him.

Chris D: Boycott was interviewed afterwards on the BBC and he said, 'Oh, Jesus Christ!' And there was quite a bit of fuss about it, because he'd sworn in front of Peter West.

Boycott, of course, was notorious for both careless running and chronic self-absorption. But with England on 52 for three, the match was alive once again. Thomson now returned, bowling downwind at Greig. The West Indies had shown the previous year how to deal with Greig. Bowl wide at him and he will murder you, but bowl fast and straight and sooner or later he will miss one. Between 1972 and 1975 Greig had been superhuman. In 1976 and 1977 there came the worrying suspicion that he had been found out. This cut to the very core of our belief system. We needed to believe in Tony Greig. Otherwise, what was there? Geoff Miller? But if the great man's talents were waning, maybe Packer wasn't such a bad idea after all. Maybe he already knew that the game was up.

After two and a half hours at the crease, Boycott was 14 not out. Thomson bowled Greig, as planned, and Pascoe had Miller caught at short leg. At 82 for five, on 20, Boycott pushed forward to Pascoe and edged it to second slip, where McCosker dropped it. 'Catches win matches,' everyone says after someone has dropped one. What they mean is that 'dropped catches lose matches'. The Australians would drop six in this innings. Not long afterwards the sun came out, the ball swung less and Alan Knott embarked upon one of the most extraordinary and valuable innings of his career. Even Boycott seemed to relax a little, square-cutting O'Keeffe to bring up his fifty after 234 minutes. By tea he was 63 not out and Knott 34 not out; at close of play they were 88 not out and 87 not out respectively. Only the athleticism of Hookes in the covers stopped the wicketkeeper reaching his hundred that evening.

The following morning was a nail-biter. Boycott needed a century to atone for his sins. Knott deserved one for his audacity. Thomson was the threat, bowling at near to top speed, but spraying it about a bit. Both batsmen edged him through the slips, neither chance going to hand. Knott played and missed, then cut Thomson to third man to bring up his hundred in just under three and a half hours. Boycott reached his own six balls later: his 98th first-class hundred, his 13th in Tests, his fourth against Australia. England led by 121 on first innings, and by the close on Saturday Australia were 112 for two. Crucially Greg Chappell was already out, bowled by a ball from Hendrick that cut back and kept low.

How good were we? 'England were looking a most formidable side,' wrote CMJ, 'confident enough now to expect victory rather than merely hope for it.' I think that we, as England fans, have a dreadful tendency to write off any side we happen to beat. We look for reasons for them to lose rather than for us to win. The 1977 Australians were weakened by Lillee's absence and the retirements of several formidable talents. Their team was apparently divided between the Packerites and the non-Packerites, and led by their best player, a more aloof, introverted character than his flip-flop-wearing brother. But this doesn't mean they weren't any good. Chappell, Marsh and Walker were at their peaks; Thomson was only just over his (which was higher than everyone else's anyway); and McCosker might have been at his, had it not been for that terrible injury. Serjeant, Hughes and Hookes offered rich promise. Only in spin bowling and, arguably, back-up fast bowling were they weaker than usual. Whereas England were a really good side. Knott, Underwood and Boycott were world-class players; Willis, Old and Hendrick were coming into their own; Randall, Woolmer and Botham were great players to come; and all were lovingly nurtured by the massive cerebellum of J. M. Brearley. Crucially, this was an astoundingly good fielding side, one of the best England has ever had. In the 35 years covered by this book, I believe the 1977 England team were second only to the 2005 team. And, maybe controversially, better than any side we put out in the 1980s.

Rick McCosker, a tough old boot you couldn't help but admire, scored a valiant 107 in the second innings, but Marsh got a pair, Willis took five for 88 and England only needed 189 to win. Both Brearley and Boycott scored eighties, the latter not out (he had batted on all five days of the match). England hadn't been two up with two to play at home since 1905. We hadn't beaten Australia twice in a row at home since 1956, and before that 1890. Generations before us have suffered as we now suffer.

In between the third and fourth Tests, Boycott scored his 99th hundred. The fourth Test was at Headingley, his home ground. We all felt it: the sense of destiny, the inevitability of Boycott's century, the sheer irresistibility of his will. Also, crucially, Jeff Thomson had a bad case of piles. It's hard enough to bowl at 90 mph without haemorrhoids. Just imagine bowling 47 overs with them. Boycott reached his hundred with a clip through mid-on off Greg Chappell.

Ross C: I remember going out of the room and I missed it. I didn't think he was ever going to get there and I thought, I've had enough of this, so I cleared off and about three balls later he got it.

Julian P: Now why should I have been on a National Express bus going between Shrewsbury and Cheltenham, listening to Test Match Special? When he got his hundred, there was a riot on the coach – well, a riot of celebration – and the driver had to pull over to the side of the road for a few minutes while we all calmed down.

After that we hoped that Boycott would move up a gear and start to cut loose. As if. 'The progress after lunch was slow and miserable,' wrote CMJ with a sigh. Boycott eventually went for 191 and England had made 436; Australia were all out for 103. Hendrick took four for 41, Botham five for 21. In their second innings Rodney Marsh hit a furious 63 but Hendrick took four more wickets, Willis took three and England won by an innings and 85 runs just after tea on Monday. England had regained the Ashes. For five players in their dressing room – Greig, Knott, Underwood, Hendrick and Willis – it was the purest revenge for the horrors meted out in 1974/75.

Richard C: I don't have any live recollection of Boycott's hundredth hundred since I was in Penang at the time during the long school holiday.

However, I remember reading about it a week or so later in the airmail edition of The Times, *which we used to get once a week on very thin, brilliant white paper with a smell that I would instantly recognise now. In the same edition the death of Elvis Presley was reported. And at the same time, I got my A-Level results on a postcard from my school and had to explain to my parents why the A grade in my Maths mock A-Level had converted itself into an F grade in the real thing. Boycott, Elvis and A-Level results are inseparable in my mind.*

The final Test, at the Oval, was a rain-ruined draw that Australia were getting the better of, thanks to 85 from Hookes, 57 from Marsh and fine late-order biffing from Walker (78). Willis, with five more wickets in that innings, ended with a series aggregate of 27 – only Laker and Bedser had taken more against Australia in a home series. At least he wasn't going to Packer. The huge shock, after the series had ended, was the news that Bob Woolmer would be. How could he? We know now, from his remarkable coaching career, that Woolmer was a striver, an innovator, drawn instinctively to the new and the untried: he couldn't have resisted Packer even if he had wanted to. At the time his decision seemed ridiculous (for him) and disastrous (for us). You spend all those years waiting and waiting for a winning team, none too patiently, and when you finally have one, they fragment in front of you. Still, we were only losing half of our team. Australia were losing all of theirs. Writing in *The Ashes '77*, Greg Chappell refused to blame the spectre of Packer for their defeat. He thought the lousy hotels the team had been booked into had more of an effect. He said, 'Catching was the main difference between the sides. I said to Rod Marsh during Saturday's play, when we missed chances, that it seemed that we were being paid back for the previous five years, when everything that had gone in the air had been plucked safely out of it.' They have their vulnerabilities too. They just don't show them so often.

On 20 August 1977, *The Times* published this letter from Mr Paul Myers: 'Sir, Having recovered the Ashes in this country first in 1926, the year of the Queen's birth; then in 1953, her Coronation year; and now in 1977, Silver Jubilee year, will we have to wait until the next great event in the Queen's life for such an event to take place again? The year 2002, the Golden Jubilee, seems a long way away. Yours faithfully . . .'

Interlude

1977

Robin W: There was an incident with a dog. It was during the school holidays, and I was staying at my friend Mike's. They had a family dog called Pip, a very ancient boxer who had been a fantastic dog, a very colourful character. But as he got older – he was about ten at this stage – he started to have a sex change. He was a sight, really. His nipples were growing and he was a deeply confused dog. He also had a terrible wind problem, as old dogs often have.

There was one particular Saturday. Mike and his family had gone off somewhere, but there was a Test on and I just wanted to watch that. They had a really good TV snug, with very comfortable leather chairs. My idea of heaven was just to be there. So it was just me and Pip in this tiny snug. He was lying on the floor and I was really happy because Bob Willis was batting. Nothing I enjoyed more than Bob Willis's batting. But at this point the dog started to fart. And it was overwhelming: it was the worst fart you have ever smelt. And I didn't want to move him because he could be quite a dangerous dog when roused. Quite scary. But after a bit I couldn't bear it any more. The fug was unimaginable. And I got angry, because I was really enjoying the cricket. So I said, Pip! Out, Pip! Well, Pip wasn't having any of this. I don't blame him. It was his house, his snug. And he just leaped up. I've never seen an animal move so quickly. And he put both his huge great paws on my chest, and growled in my face. So I said, all right, Pip, all right. And eventually he got off. But I continued to watch the cricket, even though I couldn't breathe. He died chasing a postman. He was a traditional kind of dog.

Five

1978/79

A 1914 biplane tied up with elastic bands trying vainly to take off.
      Frank Keating on Bob Willis's bowling action

Fifteen months later, everything had changed. World Series Cricket, as Kerry Packer christened his escapade, had creamed off many of the world's best players, enriched several lawyers and come to dominate pub conversation (at least in the pubs I went to). White balls? Coloured clothing? Drop-in pitches? Floodlights? Disgraceful. It would never last. In the meantime England players had expressed a strong disinclination to play against Packerites in Test matches. Tony Greig blamed Geoffrey Boycott. Writing in the Sydney *Sun*, Greig said that Boycott was the last person in the world to complain about who he played against: 'His ability to be where the fast bowlers aren't has long been a talking point among cricketers. By some stroke of good fortune he has steered clear of the world's best fast bowlers for the past five years.' Sussex sacked Greig from the captaincy; he retired from first-class cricket and emigrated to Australia. As he was possibly the most hated person in Britain at the time, this wasn't such a bad idea.

Test match cricket went on, though, as it always must. During a dreary 0–0 series in Pakistan, a rare rising ball from Sikander Bakht broke Mike Brearley's left forearm. Boycott, his vice-captain, took charge for the New Zealand leg of the tour, which was drawn 1–1, but that defeat was the first England had ever suffered against New Zealand. Hard though it is to imagine such an eventuality, Boycott may not have had the full support of his team. During the second Test at Christchurch, they decided he was batting too slowly and selfishly, so Ian Botham ran him out. Brearley returned for the two summer series, against Pakistan and New Zealand again, both won. Of his 13 Tests as captain he had won eight and drawn five. Unfortunately he had also forgotten how to bat: his scores that summer were 38, 2, 0, 2 and 11 as an opening batsman, and 58, 33 and 8 not out when he dropped down to number five. Just as you were either for or against Boycott in his endless battles against the rest of humanity, so you were either for or against Brearley's captaincy. (Those for Boycott were often, by remarkable coincidence, against Brearley.) These were difficult times for Boycott. For the Ashes tour, the selectors gave the vice-captaincy to Bob Willis. A few days later Boycott's mother died after a long illness, and a day after that, Yorkshire sacked him as their captain after eight years. Paranoid he may have been, but it didn't mean they weren't all out to get him.

The sixteen chosen for the Ashes tour had a pleasingly solid look about them. The six batsmen were Brearley, Boycott, Randall, Gooch, Clive Radley of Middlesex and David Gower of Leicestershire. Gooch, now opening for Essex, had come back during the summer, and looked a different player. It was exhilarating to see an England opening batsman play so positively and fluently before teatime on the second day. Gower, aged 21, had pulled his first ball in Test cricket for four, scored a century in his fourth innings and sealed his place forever. Radley, 34, was the latest old sweat given an England chance when he had probably given up hope. In eight consecutive Tests he had hit two fifties and two centuries and averaged 48. Randall had lost his place the previous winter, but then scored 1525 runs in county cricket, more than anyone else in the touring team. The all-rounders were Botham and Miller. In eleven Tests Botham had scored three hundreds, was averaging 41 with the bat, had 64 wickets at 16, and had taken five wickets in an innings eight times. Hmm, shall we pick him, or not? Miller had a top score of 98 not out against Pakistan and best bowling of three for 99, and his moustache drooped as though it knew that things weren't going to get any better. He probably owed his place to Bob Taylor, universally acknowledged as the best wicketkeeper in the world, but not half the batsman Knott had been. An England off-spinner needed to be able to bat a bit these days, even if he only bowled a bit as well. The other spinners were Edmonds, who had stepped into Underwood's substantial shoes with his usual certainty, and John Emburey of Middlesex, capped once late in the summer. The faster bowlers were Willis, Old, Lever and Hendrick. Old was probably at his peak, although characteristically he had missed the last two Tests with injuries to his shoulder and neck. According to *The Wisden Cricketer*, there was 'barely a doctor in the land who didn't tinker with his knees at some point in the 1970s'. On one occasion, Old sneezed on the morning of a match and damaged a rib. Apparently, the first bowling machine installed at Lord's was nicknamed 'Chris Old' because it kept breaking down.

At the start of this tour, though, it was Ian Botham who was recovering from the freak injury. At a farewell party in a pub near his home in Lincolnshire, he had gone to the lavatory before leaving. The lavatory door had swung back on its spring, Botham had put out his left hand to stop it hitting him, the hand had gone straight through the glass partition and he needed ten stitches in his wrist. That was his story and he was sticking to it. But after an intense season, he probably needed some time off. The bigger worry was a tall mop-headed maniac who bowled very quickly indeed. 'It was an exaggeration to say that England's chances depended upon Willis remaining fit,' wrote the astonishingly prolific Christopher Martin-Jenkins in his latest tour diary, 'but he, more than any other player, Boycott possibly excluded, was the most feared man in the team in the eyes of the Australian cricketers.' The few who remained, that is.

For after Kerry Packer had nabbed most of their best players, Australia were having to rebuild, and fast. Bobby Simpson had come out of retirement the previous season to captain a painfully young and inexperienced side, even by Australian standards, in a home series against India (won 3–2) and five Tests in the West Indies (lost 3–1). This year the selectors told Simpson he could not be guaranteed a place in the side, so he retired again. The captaincy passed to 26-year-old Graham Yallop of Victoria, one of the few players left who had made his Test debut before the Great Schism.* Craig Serjeant had been and gone; Kim Hughes had had two undistinguished Tests and been dropped; Gary Cosier was still in the side but only just. Jeff Thomson had led the bowling, but he too had now signed for Packer and would not be available for the forth-coming series. England would be playing an almost entirely unfamiliar team.

Before that, though, came the many warm-ups, up-country knockabouts alternating with tougher games against the states. Against South Australia they faced the new Great White Hope, Rodney Hogg, a 27-year-old former milkman only marginally less fast than Thomson. He had Gooch caught behind and, two balls later, hit Radley above the left eye with a brutal lifter. Radley staggered back, inadvertently dislodged the bails and went straight to hospital for seven stitches. Later on Hogg

* The previous year he had become the first batsmen ever to wear a helmet in a Test match. Now everyone was wearing one.

removed Boycott and Miller, and went into tea with four for 38, and the knowledge that a first Test cap would soon be his. South Australia won by 32 runs, the first time they had beaten England (or MCC) since 1925. Subsequent state matches passed off more satisfactorily for the tourists. Reading the scorecards now, you spot the names of players who will come to represent Australia with some distinction in years to come. John Dyson, Andrew Hilditch, Allan Border and Geoff Lawson for New South Wales; Trevor Hohns for Queensland; Geoff Marsh and Terry Alderman for Western Australia; Peter Sleep for South Australia; John Hampshire and Jack Simmons for Tasmania . . . sorry, what?

Clive Radley, though, was struggling. Discombobulated by the pace of the pitches, he scored 4, 3, 22 and 13 before the first Test and lost his place to Randall. Thus a near automatic selection was transformed into a Lucan within a few weeks, and never played a Test for England again.

At Brisbane Graham Yallop won the toss and batted. Australia were soon 26 for six. Gary Cosier was run out, Graeme Wood caught behind off Old, Peter Toohey bowled Willis, Yallop caught first slip . . . it was a sorry display. The two new caps, Hogg and wicketkeeper John Maclean, put on 60 for the eighth wicket. CMJ described the innings as 'an unequal struggle between very good bowlers using suitable conditions to the full and a determined but inexperienced batting side who were given very little chance to settle'. Conditions were little easier when England came to bat: the ball was swinging and Hogg was swift. Gooch went for two, Boycott for 13 but Randall's 75 and forties from Gower and Botham dragged England up to 286 (Hogg six for 76).

The pitch was easing, and in Australia's second innings Yallop and Hughes added 170 for the fourth wicket. During this tense and, by all accounts, absorbing struggle, a young man climbed on to a rostrum wearing a T-shirt marked 'Boycott: King Pom'.

Australian supporters hailed him with cans (presumably empty), wrestled him down, ripped off his T-shirt and publicly burned it. Yallop was out, c & b Willis, just after reaching his century, his second in nine Tests and his first as captain. Kim Hughes's century, in 369 minutes, was the slowest for Australia in all Tests. He was last out for 129; England needed 170 to win.

Are there any easy victories in Test cricket? Maybe, but very rarely do England seem to win them. Australia, written off, mildly patronised, had fought their way back into the game. England hadn't bowled badly; Australia had batted well. Now there was a tricky smallish target to achieve. Bobby Simpson gave his verdict: 'They are easily the best-drilled and most enthusiastic England side in the field I have ever seen, but their batting looks brittle, and because, unlike many England sides, they have so many strokeplayers, they are vulnerable.' In the second innings Gooch and Boycott failed again, as did Brearley at number five; Randall (74 not out) and Gower (48 not out) brought England home.

Off to Perth, and an eventful match against Western Australia. John Inverarity's side had won the Sheffield Shield in five of the previous seven seasons, and Inverarity, a giant-brained leader in the Brearley mode (he would later become a headmaster), had been unlucky not to be given the Australian captaincy during the current crisis. Brearley was keen to give his batsmen practice, so chose to bat despite a fierce breeze, grey skies and a lush, green pitch. In the fourteenth over England were 31 for six. Spectators overheard a certain Yorkshire opening batsman saying that no one would criticise Brearley 'because he had been to Cambridge'. In the event, England rallied to make 144, dismissed Western Australian for 52 and eventually won by 140 runs. For the Test England left out Phil Edmonds and Chris Old (who had complained of a sore back, and been taken at his word) and brought back John Lever and the in-form Mike Hendrick. Australia recalled Geoff Dymock and South Australia's opening batsman

Warrick 'Rick' Darling. Gary Cosier, in last-chance saloon, would bat at six.

In cloudy and muggy conditions, Brearley called heads and Yallop invited England to bat. Hogg saw off Gooch and Randall, which brought Boycott and Brearley together, the two grafters. At lunch England were 30 for two. If you hadn't been watching World Series Cricket before, you would be now. After Brearley fell, Gower made batting look several hundred times easier. Boycott had had two and a half hours' start, but Gower drew level with the Yorkshireman when he reached 25. Boycott scored not a single boundary all day. In the morning he made 17 runs, in the afternoon 19 and in the final session a heart-stopping 27, unfurling yet more of those flowing clips off the legs down to long leg for a single. At the other end, after some torrid treatment from Hogg with the second new ball, Gower glided to a second Test hundred before close of play. Both were out the following morning, Gower for 102, Boycott after seven and a half hours for 77. Poor man, he was in no sort of touch, and the external pressures on him appeared to be overwhelming. But 309 was a more than decent total in the conditions. Hogg, the fastest (former) milkman in the west, had taken five for 65 off 30.5 eight-ball overs.

Even the best fast bowler needs support from his batsmen. Australia could muster just 190, with diminutive Doug Walters lookalike Peter Toohey toughing it out for 81 not out. Hogg took another five in England's second innings of 208, and Australia needed 328 to win. Graeme Wood and Gary Cosier put on 83 for the fifth wicket, but it wasn't really in the nature of either of these players to grind out the long, slow, attritional innings the situation demanded. No, they went for everything. After Cosier tried to sweep Miller one time too many, the lower order folded, and England won by 166 runs to go 2–0 up.

Were these victories devalued by the weakness of the opposition?

Australians certainly decided so at the time, and history has tended to agree with them. It scarcely seems to matter that, in Willis, Old, Hendrick, Botham, Lever, Miller, Emburey and Edmonds, England had their strongest bowling line-up of the 1970s. Willis barely wasted a ball. His control and concentration were absolute. Eighteen months before, England had beaten a full-strength Australia 3–0. Who is to say that we wouldn't have beaten that same team this time around?

After another match against South Australia, this one drawn, England celebrated Christmas with what may have been the first of their legendary fancy dress parties. David Gower went as a cowboy, Derek Randall as HM The Queen, Bob Taylor as an executioner, tour manager Doug Insole as Inspector Clouseau, and Bob Willis as a faceless blind umpire with a white stick. Insole won first prize, a toy duck.

For Melbourne Australia dropped Cosier – that was it for him – and gave a first cap to a young left-hander named Allan Border. England played a second spinner, John Emburey, instead of Lever. Yallop won the toss and chose to bat first on a dry and patchy pitch. The Australians rode their luck a little to score 243 for four on the first day, with Graeme Wood reaching a maiden Test hundred just before the close. The following morning the England bowlers woke up and took the other six wickets for 15 runs. But the outfield was slow, the pitch was getting worse, and Rodney Hogg was steaming in, no doubt enraged by all the 'one extra pinta' jokes. England were shot out for 143. Bobby Simpson may have been right about the brittleness of the batting. Hogg took five wickets, steady old Geoff Dymock another three. Curiously the wicket seemed to behave a little better when Australia batted again: they were able to set a target of 283. Boycott survived more than three hours for 38, but England were all out for 179. Hogg took five for 36. The pitch gave him neither pace nor bounce, but he bowled straight and fast and now had 27 wickets in three Tests. It was Brearley's first defeat as captain in his 16th Test.

We were two-one up with three to play, against a team we were expected to beat easily. For Sydney both sides named unchanged XIs, although the Aussie keeper John Maclean was passed fit only an hour before play, having been hit by a ball in the nets just above the left eye. Brearley finally won a toss, and walked out with Boycott into intense heat, only some of it generated by Rodney Hogg. Oddly enough, the heat got to Hogg first: after three overs he had to leave the field. It was left to the worthy Alan Hurst to take Boycott's wicket, caught by Border at second slip. Randall hooked his second ball straight to Graeme Wood at backward short leg; Hogg came back and bowled Brearley; and the last ball before lunch Gower gloved a ball from Hurst to Maclean. England were 51 for four. After lunch leg-spinner Jim Higgs bowled a great fat cafeteria long-hop, and Gooch pulled it straight to Toohey at deep mid-wicket. A few balls later Maclean walked off the field. The drugs he had been taking to reduce the swelling around his eye had taken away all feeling in his hands. Yallop took over behind the stumps. Why not? It was a nice day, and England would soon be 98 for eight. When Willis came in, Botham decided it was time to give it a bit of humpity. The ninth-wicket pair added 43, Botham made 59, Hurst took five for 28, and England were all out for 152. Australia ended the day at 56 for one and Brearley called a team meeting. Standards had slipped. Riot acts were read. Bob Taylor suggested that they should see every new day as the first day of the tour. Starting tomorrow.

Next day England bowled with greater purpose, but Darling and Yallop passed England's feeble total in mid-afternoon. When he had made 91, Darling glanced Miller straight to Botham at leg-slip. Out walked Allan Border at number six. England teams would have to get used to this sight. His unbeaten 60 –

all cuts and pulls and bristling determination – helped raise Australia's total to 291. For the next dozen years, Border's would be the wicket everyone prized above all others.

Until recently that had been Boycott's. Now he was out first ball, lbw to a gentle loosener from Hogg. It was his first duck in 67 innings. At tea on the third day, England were 74 for one. Brearley reached his fifty soon after, but on 111 missed one from Border that turned a fraction and was bowled. At stumps England were just nine runs behind, with eight wickets left and Randall on 65.

On Monday, both the game and the ground hotted up. Gooch was nearly caught by Wood at short leg and dropped by Higgs at slip, while an ABC cameraman fainted in the heat, fell twenty feet and fractured his skull. Maybe he should have been wearing a helmet as well. Randall and Gooch added 58 in two and a quarter hours, before Gooch was caught at bat-and-pad off Higgs. After lunch Yallop took the new ball, and Randall hooked Hogg for four to reach 99. Next ball, another short ball, another four, just in front of square. His century had taken six hours and 51 minutes in savage heat. He was eventually out for 150, padding up to Hogg. Taylor and Miller hung on for the last twenty minutes and England were 162 ahead, four wickets to the good.

And so, the final day, Tuesday 11 January 1979. Both sides felt they could win. Australian supporters were less confident: only 8755 of them bothered to turn up. Higgs ran through England's tail, for five for 148, and Australia needed 205 in four and a half hours. At tea they were 76 for six. Again, Border (45 not out) looked in a different class. Australia were all out for 111, England were 3–1 ahead with two to play, and the Ashes had been retained.

Gloom enshrouded Australian cricket. As if to mock, World Series Cricket unveiled its latest innovation, 'co-ordinated colour clothing'. The Australian rebels were elegant in wattle-yellow from head to toe, the West Indies positively fetching in Barbie pink.* The WSC theme tune, 'C'mon Aussie C'mon', was climbing the charts. 'Lillee's pounding down like a machine, Pascoe's making divots in the green, Marsh is taking wickets, Hooksie's clearing pickets, and the Chappells' eyes have got that killer gleam.' For the fifth Test at Adelaide, Australia dropped Dymock, Toohey and John Maclean, brought back the off-spinner Bruce Yardley, and gave debuts to the Queensland all-rounder Phil Carlson and Western Australia's wicketkeeper Kevin Wright. No, I've never heard of them either. You can always spot a losing team by their revolving-door selection policy. England were unchanged.

Brearley lost the toss yet again. The pitch was so green you could serve it as salad. Hogg, on his home pitch, was fast and hostile; Hurst pitched it up more and swung it late. After eleven overs, England were 27 for five. Could no side in this series get to tea without a precipitous batting collapse? It was humpity time again. Botham's 74 included six fours and two sixes, Willis slogged 24 in 20 balls, and England were all done for 169. Hogg took only four wickets this time, but the last of them was his 37th of the series, beating Arthur Mailey's Australian record of 36 in a series against England set in 1920/21.

All of which was instantly forgotten when the fifth ball of Bob Willis's first over lifted and cut back and hit Rick Darling just under the heart. He collapsed in a heap. The ground went silent. 'He's not breathing,' said umpire Max O'Connell. John Emburey, fresh from first-aid classes at Middlesex, gave Darling the precordial thump, a blow above the heart, which brought him around with a cry and a gasp. A passing physiotherapist pulled Darling's tongue back to the front of his mouth and removed

---

* Many years later, when I had been bought a pink shirt and was trying to pluck up the courage to wear it in public, I saw Michael Holding wearing one in the commentary box, and thought, If he can . . .

some unhelpful chewing gum. Darling went off to hospital, but
the only injury they could find was a large bruise on his chest
where Emburey had thumped him. Whether this incident
unnerved his teammates, or whether they would all have got
out anyway, we cannot know, but Australia were 24 for four
before anyone blinked, 69 for four by close of play, and 164 all
out the following day. England had a first innings lead of five.
And were quickly 132 for six. This wasn't a series for the front-
line batsmen. Bob Taylor and Geoff Miller joined forces, two
Derbyshire men who had scored precisely no first-class centuries
between them. They brought up their fifty partnership in 70
minutes, and by tea the lead had passed 200, with Taylor on 46
and Miller 31. Their stand had reached 135 when, ten minutes
before the close, Miller tickled one going down leg from Hurst
and was caught by Wright. Next day, Bob Taylor moved steadily
towards a maiden century. No one would have begrudged it –
even Ian Chappell, the old villain. Possibly only Steve Waugh,
then aged 13, would have wholeheartedly approved of what now
happened. It was the last ball before lunch. Taylor was on 97.
Hogg angled the ball across him, and he flicked it down leg,
straight into Kevin Wright's gloves. The eight-year-old Glenn
McGrath might have issued a mighty cheer, too. Or was he
watching WSC?

Australia would have been expecting to chase 200. A target of
366 was beyond them. Only Hughes (48) and Yallop (36) played
innings of consequence. They were all out for 160 in 67 overs. As
David Frith wrote in his great pictorial history, *England versus
Australia*, 'England's all-round superiority in all departments was
boldly underlined.'

The sixth Test, back at Sydney, demonstrated just how quickly
the balance between two sides can change. (It also suggested
that six Tests was one too many.) Australia's selectors dropped
Rick Darling, a marginal decision, and Allan Border, a lunatic
decision. (It was the only time he would ever be dropped from

the Test team.) Toohey came back and the NSW opening batsman Andrew Hilditch made his debut. Yallop won the toss as usual and Australia batted, and England rolled them over for 198, of which Yallop himself made 121 – pure frustration and maybe rage bringing out the best in those strangely sloping shoulders. (He also had an unusually small head. No Test batsman more resembled a bottle of champagne with the cork still in.) Botham took another four wickets, but everyone contributed. England had the usual early scares, but Brearley made 46, Gower 65 and, most significantly, Gooch 74, as this might otherwise have been his last chance for a while. CMJ compared Gooch's struggles against the high pace and accuracy of Hogg with Dennis Amiss's waking nightmare in 1974/75, which is intriguing, given Gooch's later excellence against the fastest bowlers. Bob Taylor, full of confidence, added 36 not out, and the first innings lead was 120. In Australia's second innings the spinners got to work. Emburey took four for 52 and Miller five for 44, as Australia were all out for 143. 'England are often chided for fragility facing leg-spin,' wrote Alex Bannister in *Wisden*. 'But it seldom gets them into the type of trouble Australia have in coping with off-spin.' It was probably only appropriate that Brearley hit the winning runs.

It is, in effect, the forgotten series. It was probably a career high point for Geoff Miller (23 wickets at 15), John Emburey (16 at 19) and Mike Hendrick (19 at 15.7). For Australia, Hogg had been a revelation, with 41 wickets at 12.85. Hurst hadn't done badly, either, with 25 at 23. But bowling figures can never reflect the number of dropped catches. Aussie dropped loads.

Doesn't matter: no one was watching. When you see the video coverage of this series, you can see why: low-scoring matches, on dodgy pitches, with lots of faces under baggy green caps you had never seen before and would never see again. Nonetheless, this was a Test series between England and Australia, and therefore it is part of something much bigger. It still has resonance, thirty years on. Whereas World Series Cricket, which was only ever a means to an end, had no resonance, only consequences. The actual cricket in WSC has faded out of memory completely, and might as well never have been played.

Six

1979/80

*He is arguably second only to Bradman amongst Australia's
batsmen.*

John Arlott on Greg Chappell

In May 1979 the Australian Cricket Board and Kerry Packer
signed a peace deal. Packer could have the TV rights to everything he wanted, and in return he would dismantle World Series
Cricket. In the two years of WSC, the Board had lost $810,000,
partly because they were having to pay players much more than
before, and partly because gates were well down on the boom
years of the mid-1970s. WSC was losing money as well, but
Packer's pockets were deeper (his trousers being absolutely enormous). The long-term consequences of the whole kerfuffle were
that television would control international cricket as never
before, cricketers would be paid properly and administrators
would do as they were told. And England would come back to
Australia in November for their seventh series against the ancient
enemy in ten years.

Back at Lord's, the Test and County Cricket Board felt let
down. They had supported the ACB to the hilt, if not quite
beyond. The only way they could have supported them more was

to send a substandard England team to Australia in 1978/79, who would have been beaten, and official Australian cricket might then have seemed stronger and more marketable than it turned out to be. Unfortunately, as we have seen, Mike Brearley's team were just too good. Now the TCCB were being asked to send another team, only a year later, for a much shorter tour and one geared wholly to Packer's requirements. India had been booked in as well, but they were summarily sacked and replaced by the West Indies, who were better box office. Both England and the West Indies would play three Test matches against Australia, and the three countries would engage in a triangular tournament of one-day internationals with coloured clothing, white balls, floodlights and Tony Greig in the commentary box. On television this would be the first series in which anyone out for nought would be accompanied off the field by a cartoon duck quacking hilariously. Maybe I was an unusually conservative and hidebound teenager, but the first few times I saw this, I wanted someone harmed.

On one issue, though, the TCCB refused to budge. This series wouldn't be for the Ashes. If England had been playing five or six Tests, with several first-class games in between, that would have been fine. But a three-Test series, with pyjama cricket in between? We're doing you a favour by coming, matey, and don't you forget it.

In fact English cricket would have been better off if we hadn't gone at all. By going we effectively allowed the Australians to say that the previous year's series didn't count. Now we have our Packer players back, we are at full strength, so these games have a legitimacy that the 1978/79 games didn't. If you say it's not for the Ashes, that's up to you, but we know better. The TCCB may have thought they were doing the ACB a favour, as one board of administrators to another, with the health of the beloved game at heart, but in reality they had been outmanoeuvred. I suspect that Mike Brearley knew this even before he started growing his Ayatollah Khomeini beard.

In the summer just past, his side had beaten India 1–0 in four Tests, although India had nearly pulled off one of the great upsets in cricket history at the Oval when, asked to score 438 to win, they finished on 429 for 8. Sunil Gavaskar and Chetan Chauhan put on 213 for the first wicket. Gavaskar scored 221 and, off the last over, India needed 15 runs to win, and could score only six. A close call, but England had still only lost one of the 23 Tests under Brearley's captaincy. Maybe suspecting that his luck could not hold for ever, he announced that this would be his last tour. The following summer, when West Indies were touring, England would need a new captain.

For the moment, they were an unusually settled side. All but five of the previous year's tourists were on the plane again this time. Clive Radley and Roger Tolchard, last year's reserve wicketkeeper, had drifted out of view. Chris Old had had a busy benefit year and his usual crop of injuries, and his extensive team of medical advisers had recommended a winter at home, straining crucial muscles doing the washing-up. More controversial, perhaps, was the omission of Phil Edmonds and John Emburey. Edmonds had been replaced by the only Packerite to be selected, Derek Underwood. Emburey had been superseded by Peter Willey, his superior as a batsman, if a lesser bowler. The other new picks were Wayne Larkins, the bish-bash-bosh Northants opener, Yorkshire's wicketkeeper David Bairstow and Kent's 20-year-old fast bowler Graham Dilley.

The established players, meanwhile, had enjoyed wildly varying seasons. Geoffrey Boycott, all but written off a year earlier, averaged 102.53 in 1979, and scored two centuries in four Tests. Bob Willis, 'the player the Australians feared the most', had looked weary and off the pace against India. Mike Hendrick took 12 Indian wickets at 18 but, on the final day of the series, aggravated a shoulder injury he had incurred earlier in the season. He rested it and suffered no pain in early training, but in the first tour match against Queensland it flared up again, and a specialist told him it might continue to do so whenever he placed the shoulder under physical stress. (Which is as good a definition of bowling as you can get.) England's most incisive bowler of the past year faced a career-threatening injury. The balance of the side was subtly altering, and not for the better.

In order to stay sane, we shall disregard the one-day matches, which were played in apparently random batches before and in-between the Tests. But England did quite well. They won all four of their group matches against Australia, and in the third, Boycott scored a century ('It is doubtful whether he has ever played better,' said Peter Smith in *Wisden*). They lost 2–1 to the West Indies, with one match abandoned. Australia were eliminated – the worst possible result for both the ACB and Packer, and there-fore the most satisfying for everyone else – and England lost 2–0 in the finals to the West Indies.

We won't quite disregard the Australia vs West Indies Test matches, however, if only because they alternated with Australia vs England Test matches. This was a new arrangement which, unsurprisingly, did not catch on. It was almost as though one Test series at a time wasn't good enough. Australia's first Test against the West Indies was the first since the Great Schism to feature the Packer players. Kim Hughes had succeeded Graeme Yallop as captain for a six-Test tour of India (which India had won 2–0); Greg Chappell now took over. Hughes, Allan Border and Rodney Hogg were the only survivors of the previous regime; back came McCosker, Hookes, Marsh, Bright, Lillee and Thomson, and Western Australia's opening batsman Bruce Laird, a success in WSC, was given his first official cap. The West Indies, too, were at full strength, with points to prove. Their record in Australia was abject: they had never won a series in six attempts, and the last one, in 1975/76, they had lost 5–1. This first Test at the Gabba was also notable for a couple of significant changes in playing conditions: the six-ball over had been restored to first-class cricket in Australia after more than forty years; and it was the first Test without a rest day for more than twenty years. In addition, Lillee was beginning to go bald. Truly, a bright new dawn for Australian cricket.

Australia, then, scored 268 against Roberts, Holding, Croft and Garner. Laird made 92 and Chappell 74. West Indies surged to 441, thanks to a masterly 140 from Vivian Richards. But Chappell (124) and Laird (75) had been facing these bowlers for two years on pitches far worse than this, Hughes hit an unbeaten 130, and the draw was secured. For the first Test match against England at Perth the following week, the selectors dropped McCosker in favour of Julian Wiener, a 24-year-old Victorian of Austrian origins. Hookes and Hogg, both injured, were replaced by Peter Toohey and Geoff Dymock. England had already waved goodbye to Mike Hendrick, who had flown home because his shoulder wasn't healing. They gave a first cap to Graham Dilley, their youngest debutant since Brian Close in 1949. Brearley was no longer scoring enough runs to open the batting, so Derek Randall was pushed up to the top of the order. Peter Willey had been playing well in the one-dayers, and was preferred to Gooch. But with Brearley at six, England would be fielding three players batting higher than their normal positions for their counties: Randall at one, Willey at three, Miller (who was carrying a back injury) at five. Depending on your point of view, this was either adventurous, risky or completely bonkers.

Brearley, with his terrifying new macho beard, won the toss and put Australia in on the world's fastest wicket. Within an hour Botham had two lbws, Wiener had been run out and Australia were 20 for three. Chappell went after lunch, caught by Boycott in the gully, but Kim Hughes was batting with 'gymnastic flamboyance,' according to Christopher Martin-Jenkins in his latest tour diary, the amazingly boringly titled *Cricket Contest 1979–80*. On 99, Hughes pulled Underwood and was caught by the captain at square leg. He had batted a little under four hours and hit ten fours.

Australia resumed the following morning on 232 for eight, and Lillee walked out to the crease holding an aluminium bat. He and a friend were marketing this item to feckless Australian youths as a cheap alternative to the wooden bat: an enterprising idea, although the glorious sound of leather on aluminium may not have had the same resonance. More of a clang, in fact. Greg Chappell did not approve, and Mike Brearley was aghast. After two balls, he said the ball 'looked as though it had twice been hit against a concrete wall'. Chappell sent out Hogg with two wooden bats, but Lillee sent him back. The umpires conferred, and told Lillee to change his bat because, in their view, it amounted to unfair play under Law 46. Lillee stomped back to the pavilion. A few minutes later he walked out again, still holding the aluminium bat. The umpires again told him to change it. Greg Chappell himself came out with a wooden bat and told Lillee he had to use it. In his rage, Lillee threw the aluminium bat twenty yards towards the pavilion.* In the commentary box Tony Greig predicted that the bat would outsell all others within a year. Four months later, the MCC amended the laws of the game to read that all bats 'shall be made of wood'.

If it achieved nothing else, though, the incident did serve to fire up Australia's premier strike bowler. After his side were all out for 244, Lillee dismissed the makeshift new opening pair, Randall and Boycott, for ducks. England were 14 for three, 41 for four, 74 for five, 90 for six. Brearley wrote that Botham 'played with reckless fury . . . enraged at what he saw as the faintheartedness of our early batsmen . . . He was right to be cross . . . but wrong to let it affect his game.' After he went, the Ayatollah and Bob Taylor, 37 and 38 years old respectively, inched their team to

---

* 'I now hold the record for throwing an aluminium bat the furthest in a Test match, and I know it will stand for ever,' Lillee later told *The Wisden Cricketer*. 'At the end of the game, I got each side to sign the bat, and Mike Brearley wrote, "Good luck with the sales".'

respectability. The following morning, on 64, Brearley edged behind to become Lillee's 100th England victim. Graham Dilley hit a brisk 38 not out as England conceded a first innings lead of just 16. It was about the last moment in the series when anything went right for them.

Cricket matches, as we all know, turn on isolated moments, close calls, marginal decisions, strokes of luck. Who is to say that Julian Wiener wasn't lbw to Botham on 14 or to Willis on 20? And what if Laird hadn't been dropped by Willey on eight, or edged the ball at catchable height between Taylor and Brearley two balls later? As it is, Australia's openers put on 91. After they went, Allan Border was dropped by Miller in the gully and then held the innings together with 115. Dennis Lillee stayed with him for two hours, before bequeathing to future generations possibly the most satisfying scorebook entry in cricket history: Lillee c Willey b Dilley 19.* Graham Dilley had taken three wickets in his first Test; Botham followed his six for 78 in the first innings with five for 98 in the second – his 11th and 12th five-wicket analyses in 22 Tests. It was a heroic effort that hadn't been enough: England needed 354 runs to win, or had seven hours to survive for a draw. In the ensuing misery, the aggression of Lillee and Thomson were overshadowed by the more solid fast-medium virtues of Geoff Dymock, who took six for 34 in 17.2 overs. 'In this, his finest hour, he was the master of both wind and wicket,' wrote Robin Marlar. The wickets, however, were only falling at one end. At the other stood Boycott. '[His] judgement was flawless,' wrote CMJ. 'His technique has seldom looked more perfect.' When on 97, with last man Willis at the other end, Boycott clipped a ball from Lillee off his legs for what should have been an easy three. But after two runs Willis held up his hand and sent him

---

* Has there ever been another three-way rhyming dismissal in first-class cricket? Answers on a postcard to the usual address.

back, because the plan was that Willis would not have to face Lillee. In Dymock's next over Willis was out for 0, England were all out for 215 and Boycott was left stranded on 99. ('Geoffrey wasn't terribly pleased,' Willis told *The Wisden Cricketer*. 'It took him a little longer to leave the pitch than it took me.') He was the fourth England batsman to carry his bat through a completed innings (and the first since Len Hutton) and the first person from any country to score 99 not out in a Test match. By contrast, Randall, Willey, Gower and Botham had all played poor shots, and both Miller's dismissals suggested problems against high-class fast bowling. The usual problems, in other words.

Still, it was only one defeat, and the pitches at Sydney and Melbourne were more likely to suit the England bowlers, if they had any left. Geoff Miller was now flying home: his back problem had not responded to treatment. His replacement was John Emburey. Surely they wouldn't make him bat at number five as well.

After Christmas, several ODIs and at least one fancy-dress party (won by England physio Bernard Thomas, as Rasputin), West Indies quietly overwhelmed Australia in their second Test. The crowds stayed away. They much preferred to go to the one-dayers and boo Brearley. He was said to be the most hated England captain since Jardine: he was too posh and too clever and kept winning, at least in the shorter version of the game.* This was why he had grown the beard. It was a psychological ploy, an aggressive act in itself.

---

* Brearley had also complained about some of the dafter innovations proposed by Packer's people for the one-day games, like playing with a white ball when all the players were wearing white. For this he was damned as a 'whinger'. In his book *Phoenix from the Ashes* there's a wonderful photo of a banner someone in the crowd displayed at Melbourne: 'Gold Medallion Award For Greatest Winger [sic] would have to be won by J M Brearley, Classical Music Lover'.

Ken R: There were an awful lot of moustaches on the Australian team. And I think Brearley sussed that out and decided, we've got to counter that with some beards. A suitably masculine riposte. The battle of the facial hair.

In Sydney, meanwhile, England were dismayed not to see the usual dry, spinning wicket, but something muddy and under-prepared that had accidentally been left uncovered during a heavy downpour a few days earlier. (I have a mental image of Dennis Lillee, out there in the storm at the dead of night, physically removing the covers himself.) Graham Gooch replaced Geoff Miller, but there was still no place for J. K. Lever, who might have enjoyed this pitch. Boycott had a stiff neck and played only because he was told to. For Australia, Rick McCosker came in for the injured Laird, while Ian Chappell played his first Test for four years, replacing Peter Toohey, who had just played his last. Hogg and Thomson were both still injured, so Len Pascoe, next cab on the rank, was given his chance. 'Winning the toss almost guaranteed victory,' said *Wisden*. Brearley lost it, Greg Chappell inserted, and England were bundled out for 123 (Lillee four for 40, Dymock four for 42). When Australia batted, Botham (four for 29) was all but unplayable, but five catches were dropped in the slips, and Australia scrapped their way to 145. At the end of the second day England were 38 for three. Brearley survived for an hour the following morning, and night-watchman Underwood was out just after lunch for a staunch 43. Gradually, though, the pitch was flattening out. Gower played streakily before reaching his fifty, and sublimely thereafter. He was 82 not out when the last man, Bob Willis, loped out. Gower hooked and square-cut Lillee for successive fours, but on 98 not out, he could only watch as Willis was caught low in the slips. Big Bob had done it again. Batting conditions were now the best of the match, and Australia quickly knocked off the 216 runs they needed. With one to win, Greg Chappell was on 94 and facing Botham, who, with a grin, bowled a kindly slow long-hop. Chappell hit it first bounce for four, so that he too ended on 98 not out. In the first innings he had made three. So had Gower.

Two–nil down with one to play, Brearley thought the opposition 'might be better than us, though I doubt it'. In the first Test (Boycott excepted) England had batted feebly on the final day. In the second Test they had lost a vital toss. How would they cock things up in the third Test at Melbourne? For Australia, Bruce Laird was fit again and replaced Wiener. Thomson was also fit but had bowled like a drain in the one-day matches, and Pascoe kept his place. And, at the age of 34, Ashley Mallett was back. For England Wayne Larkins was given a first cap, in place of Randall, and John Lever replaced Graham Dilley, who had a strained side. CMJ thought that Lever might have played anyway, instead of the out-of-form Willis: 'It was to be, in all probability, Willis's final Test match.' For any other bowler, it might have been.

England won the toss and batted first on a good-natured pitch. Gooch and Boycott put on 116 for the first wicket, and many observers would have been placing their lager money on Boycott scoring his 118th first-class century. But on 44 he drove hard at Dymock, and Mallett took a typically brilliant diving one-handed catch in the gully, reminding everyone of his astonishing exploits there in 1974/75. Larkins, the first Wayne to play for England,* staggering under the weight of his proto-mullet, scored 25 but the crucial moment in the match occurred just after his dismissal. Gooch, on 99, played a ball from Pascoe down the pitch, past the bowler, and called David Gower for a run. Kim Hughes sprinted round from mid-off, had three stumps to aim at, and Gooch was out by a foot. He became the third man in the series to miss a century by one run. England's 170 for one, just before Larkins

---

* The first Darren would not play for England until 1994. The first Dean had to wait until 1997 (unless you count Harry Dean, who played three Tests in 1912). No Clint or Gary has yet played for England, unless you count Gary Pratt.

was out, quickly became 177 for five and then 192 for six. We had blown it again. Brearley was booed to the crease, and booed even louder at the end of the innings when he walked off with 60 not out. But 306 wasn't enough on this placid surface. Lillee had taken six for 60, with what Willis called 'some of the best bowling I've seen'. Australia then batted England out of the game. Laird scored 74, Ian Chappell 75, Border 63 and Greg Chappell, batting at number six because of a dodgy knee and a sore throat, limped and coughed his way to 114. Lever, Botham and Underwood took four, three and three wickets respectively, but Willis was again off the pace. Australia led by 171 on first innings.

And this is where things get interesting. Batting again, England seemed to be worrying about missing the flight home. Boycott, Larkins, Gower, Willey and Brearley all fell cheaply to Lillee and Pascoe. Gooch made 51 but could not go on. England were 92 for six, still 79 behind, with Ian Botham and Bob Taylor at the crease. What could possibly happen next? 'Botham at his best makes the game look wonderfully simple,' wrote CMJ. True, but few players could have set about the Australian quick bowlers as he now did. With England on 178, Taylor tried to hook Lillee and gave a catch to short leg, but at least Australia would have to bat again. Lever and Botham put on another 89 for the ninth wicket, and England were all out for 273. Botham had scored 119 not out, Lillee had taken five for 78, Pascoe four for 80. Australia needed 103 to win.

Surely not? They couldn't, could they?

No, you're right, they couldn't. Greg Chappell led the way with an unbeaten 40, and Australia won the Test by eight wickets. It's a double act: you need Botham to score the century, but you also need Willis to take the eight for 43. (And don't forget Lillee. Brearley would later describe his bowling in this match as 'the most masterly bowling performance I have ever seen . . . Bowling medium-fast leg-cutters and off-cutters, interspersed with faster deliveries, and a modicum of swing with the new ball, [he] took 11 wickets for 138 runs on a pitch that was unhelpful to fast bowlers.')

Were England so bad? Were Australia so much better? As previously suggested, this was the tour that should never have happened. Its only purpose, in the wider Ashes scheme of things, was to invalidate the previous year's tour. It succeeded completely. No one now remembers that Australia failed to get to the final of the one-day triangular tournament, but we all have 3–0 carved on our memories. There's no doubt that England were less strong than a year earlier. Willis, Randall and Gower had lost form; Willey's highest score was 12; Underwood was less potent than he had been; but the loss of Old and Hendrick may have been most significant, not just for their bowling but for their wonderful close fielding. And I can't help wondering whether this had been a tour too far for Brearley. As we have seen several times since, most England captains simply wear out, like washers on taps. Brearley was almost certainly the best captain we have ever had, but even he was tested on this tour as he never had been before. CMJ said that his batting improved, but his captaincy suffered. And let's face it, he wasn't there for his batting.

Seven

1981

What does this man have? A mystique has settled over him. He no longer wears whites and carries a bat; he plays in a cloak and waves a wand.

Tony Lewis on Mike Brearley

It was the greatest one-off sustained effort I ever saw from a fast bowler in the entire time I played cricket.

Dennis Lillee on Bob Willis's eight for 43 at Headingley

This series will be remembered in a hundred years. Unfortunately.

Kim Hughes

In February 1981 Mike Brearley wrote an article for *Punch* magazine about success. 'The urge for success may get out of hand,' he wrote.

Jardine went too far in his strategy for containing Bradman. Ian Chappell, going beyond an admirable identification with his own players, turned cricket matches into gang warfare. But the opposite is more common: when an often unacknowledged uneasiness about our own aggression may make us both less successful than we should be and less capable of enjoying whatever success we do achieve.

I have seen England players, overwhelmed by the aggression of the opposition, lose touch with their own combative powers and surrender to the legend of Lillee and the Perth pitch. There's a fear, too, that showing one's aggression will invite even fiercer retaliation. But one may also be afraid of one's own destructiveness. Some individuals (and teams) let their opponents off the hook when they have them at their mercy ... Respecting an opponent includes being prepared to finish him off.

And there you have, in a nutshell, the essence of Mike Brearley's captaincy: a sort of super-awareness of your own team's and the opposition's skills and strengths and flaws and vulnerabilities − as human beings, not just as sportsmen. The paragraphs above may have gained something from the eighteen months he had already spent training to become a psychoanalyst, and later that year (I think it's fair to say) we would gain something from them too. But, as he wrote, England had just arrived in the West Indies for a five-Test series under the captaincy of Ian Botham. We had lost a five-Test series at home to them already, 1–0: not a bad result, in the light of what was to come. The second Centenary Test against Australia, at Lord's in September 1980, had then been drawn. Graeme Wood, Kim Hughes and Geoffrey Boycott scored centuries, Len Pascoe took five for 59, and ten hours of play were lost to rain. But Botham's own form was suffering. He had injured his back at Oxford in April 1980: X-rays showed that the vertebrae were out of alignment. By August his bowling was innocuous, he had put on weight, catches were being dropped, runs were no longer being scored. And as Brearley noted in *Phoenix from the Ashes*, captaincy was weighing him down: 'In the Centenary Test I felt that he lost his nerve a little: the earlier, optimistic Botham would have leapt at the chance of having a go at Chappell's target on the last afternoon.' Allen Synge put it more brutally in *Sins of Omission*: 'Like Dexter before him, the natural adventurousness of his play was not matched by similar qualities of leadership.'

Brearley's impression was that Botham 'found it hard to take advice and even harder to take criticism'. One England player told him that he was physically afraid to pursue a suggestion if Botham disagreed with it. That said, the tour of the West Indies had been unusually demanding. The home team were the best in the world, close to their peak. Political posturing had caused the cancellation of the Guyana Test and, for a while, threatened the whole tour. Worst of all had been the sudden death of Ken Barrington, their beloved assistant manager and mentor. Amid this chaos, said Brearley, Botham kept the team together. They hadn't fallen out with each other or anyone else, and had never been overawed by the opposition: 'He maintained within the side the feeling that the West Indies could be held, even beaten.'

A home series would be different. The attentions of the media would be unrelenting. And they would only reflect what the rest of us were thinking anyway. I remember the sense we all had that Botham wasn't up to it, that he had been promoted to the one job on a cricket pitch he couldn't do, and that it was preventing him from doing the other ones he could do better than anyone else. We had been let down. We were angry. This is how lynch mobs come about. For a brief period it is probably fair to say that, as a cricketing culture, we were not quite sane.

Nonetheless, the Australians were again lacking some famous names. Ian Chappell had retired for the last time, while Greg Chappell, who had long complained of the frequency and length of overseas tours, chose to sit this one out. Len Pascoe needed an operation on his knee, while Jeff Thomson wasn't picked. The famed ruthlessness of Australian selectors also saw off Dymock,

Laird and McCosker, as well as Doug Walters, who had played
throughout the three-Test 1980/81 series against New Zealand
and India. New Zealand had been brushed aside 2–0, but the
Indian series came to a more surprising conclusion. One–nil up
going into the third Test at the MCG, Australia needed 143 to
win on the final day. They were all out for 83, their lowest total
against India and worst against anyone since 1968. Kapil Dev
took five for 28. It was the first series India had ever played in
Australia that they hadn't lost.

So changes had been made, old faces brought back, fresh faces
introduced. Graeme Wood and John Dyson were the established
opening partnership, Graeme Yallop was back, Ray Bright was
the only spinner, and uncapped players included bowlers Geoff
Lawson and Terry Alderman, and batsmen Martin Kent and Dirk
Wellham. Trevor Chappell, younger brother of Ian and Greg, was
in the party, on the assumption that any Chappell was better
than none. Kim Hughes skippered. Only Marsh and Lillee survived of the players who had established themselves before
Packer, just four years earlier.

The first Test was a low-scoring thriller at seam-friendly
Trent Bridge. England, put in on a cold and cloudy morning,
managed 187, and Australia 179. Middlesex's Mike Gatting,
adding ballast to the England middle order, and Allan Border
both hit half-centuries. Neither side had bothered with a front-
line spinner, and England had recalled Bob Woolmer for the
troubled number-three position, where everyone scored 0.
Woolmer scored 0. There was variation in bounce, and one or
two balls an over deviated unplayably off the seam. Lillee,
Alderman (in his first Test) and Hogg took wickets, as did
Dilley, Willis, Hendrick and Botham. Brearley felt that none of
the batsmen had let themselves down, and yet in their second
innings England could make only 125, with Lillee and
Alderman each taking five. Woolmer made 0. But it wasn't
their batting that lost them the match: it was a flurry of

dropped catches. The most personally costly was that by Middlesex's 24-year-old wicketkeeper Paul Downton, who had come into the side in the West Indies. He dropped a sitter from Border early in the first innings, and was himself dropped from the team. Whereas Yallop took a screamer in the gully to dismiss Gooch in the second innings, and sub fielder Martin Kent another at fourth slip to see off Gower. Australia squeezed home by four wickets. Lillee, with match figures of eight for 80, was man of the match. In May he had contracted viral pneumonia, and was still far from full fitness. Brearley reckoned he did not bowl at full pelt until the sixth Test, at the end of August.

Before the second Test the Australians played Middlesex, and who should they come up against but Jeff Thomson, signed up for the season by Brearley. On the evidence of this match, he thought Thomson was faster than any of their bowlers and as accurate; also that Australia were a stronger bowling than batting side. All their batsmen looked vulnerable against Thomson and Wayne Daniel, although 'it was unlikely that England's attack would be as penetrating as ours'. For the Lord's Test England brought in Emburey for Hendrick and recalled Bob Taylor, now 39 and as fit as ever.* Australia brought in Ray Bright for Rodney Hogg, whose back was troubling him. Hughes put England in for the second Test in a row. In between showers England made 311, with fifties for Gatting and Willey, and Geoff Lawson took seven for 81. Botham made 0. Australia batted with their customary *joie de vivre* at Lord's to reach 345, Border top-scoring with 64. England were then 55 for two, but Boycott, playing his 100th Test, made 60 and Gower caressed 89 in

---

* I am now 48 and still consider myself a relatively young man, especially if I don't look in the mirror before mid-morning. But I remember that in 1981 no one in the world seemed older than Bob Taylor. It seemed a miracle that he could walk unaided.

increasingly awkward circumstances, with Bright turning it out
of the rough. Botham was again out for 0, this time first ball. The
members in the pavilion did not stir.

*John S: I was there on a school trip. That silence when he walked off:
it was just extraordinary. Absolute silence. People just reading their
papers. No sympathy. Just this class contempt for Botham.*

Andy R: Typical MCC response.

What we tend to forget is that we drew the match, and given
more time and/or better weather might even have won it.

Botham resigned the captaincy on television, and Alec Bedser
admitted they were going to sack him anyway. Bedser then rang
Brearley from a call box in a pub. He couldn't get the coins in the
slot: he kept being cut off. Finally the operator rang Brearley,
asking him whether he would take a reverse-charge call. 'OK,'
said Brearley. The chairman of the selectors came on the line.
'We'd like you to captain the side for the rest of the series,' he
said.

Two days before the Headingley Test, I celebrated my 21st
birthday. I had recently left university, with what would turn
out to be a third-class degree and no job. I had scurried back to
the parental home in north London, and started preparing for my
birthday party on the Saturday of the Test. Most friends were
coming down from one university or another: some were en
route elsewhere; a few would stay several days in sleeping bags on
the floor. The most adhesive, it would transpire, was my good
friend Richard C, who had left the same university under a small
cloud earlier in the year. With nothing much better to do he
arrived in time for the first day's play, found the seat nearest to the
television, lit a cigarette, poured a glass of whisky and sat down to
watch. During the preparations for the party, the party itself and
its prolonged aftermath, he was a beacon of stillness and concentration. As far as I remember, he did not miss a single ball.

Australia were unchanged. For England, Brearley displaced
Woolmer (whose Test career was now at an end) and, in deciding

to play four seamers, brought in Chris Old for Emburey. Had they played only three seamers, Willis would have been the one left out. He had only just sneaked into the XII in the first place. At Lords he had been suffering from a chest infection and bowled 32 no-balls. But the Headingley pitch promised awkward bounce and, if the cloud remained, seam and swing. 'It was mid-July, but felt like mid-April,' wrote Brearley. At the end of the first day he said to umpire David Evans that if all went well, you could bowl out a side for 90 on this pitch. Unfortunately, by this stage, Australia were 210 for three.

It was the old story: inconsistent bowling (Old aside) and dropped catches. John Dyson, yorked by Dilley just before the close, had scored 102. The following day England bowled better, but Hughes still hit 89 and Yallop 58. Declaring on 401 for nine, Hughes said it was 'worth about a thousand on this pitch', and Brearley agreed. Botham, provoked by his new captain to bowl more quickly, had taken six for 95. Lillee and Alderman, though, made the ball talk. It usually said, 'You're out.' Lawson bowled Boycott with one that cut back and kept brutally low. Gower was out to a good length ball that leaped viciously and touched his glove. Marsh took the catch above his head. When Botham came in the score was 87 for five. He had clearly decided that there was no point hanging around. His 50 came off 54 balls. England were all out for 174 at tea on Saturday. Brearley thought this was about par for the pitch, and that England would have made less if Lillee had been bowling at his best. (He still took four for 49, in a shocking orange headband.) As we were laying out food and drink and moving furniture in preparation for my party, England followed on, Gooch was out for 0 and the batsmen were offered the light.

Sunday was a rest day, both for the Test players and for us. In my house, much bacon was consumed.

On Monday four or five guests remained, I was wondering what to do with the rest of my life and Richard C was still on the sofa, five feet from the television, smoking, drinking, watching. At 41 for four Willey joined Boycott and they both played rather well, but after three and a half hours' gritty resistance Boycott was lbw to Alderman for 46. ('A very reluctant leaver of the crease,' said CMJ on TV.) England were 135 for seven, still 92 runs behind. Ian Botham was one of several players who had already booked out of the team hotel.

David T: When they quoted odds of 500 to 1 against England winning, I can remember walking down the drive with a five-pound note in my hand, to go to the betting shop a mile up the road. And I remember turning round, thinking, No, this is just a waste of time, there's no way they can win.

Botham played quite carefully before tea, scoring 39 in 87 minutes. It was Graham Dilley who began the onslaught. After tea Botham joined him, driving Alderman to all parts, and memorably leaping down the pitch and thumping him for an astonishing straight six. Wrote Brearley: 'Gradually, our hopes became more ambitious. If Dilley could stay with Botham until the close . . .' At a quarter to five, he played on to Alderman for 58. I knew that without looking it up, and that Chris Old made 29, and that Ian Botham made 149 not out. Of the other significant thing that happened that year – my degree – I remember the subject (maths) and the class (third) and really not a lot else. None of it can compete with the visual memory of Ian Botham winding up to club something over mid-wicket and edging it high over the slips for four. Indeed, I suspect that these memories have actually supplanted the earlier ones of applied analysis and non-Boolean groups. Maybe the mind is like videotape: some memories simply get taped over and are lost for ever. If so, it's more reliable than real videotape. My VHS copy of *Botham's Ashes* wore out years ago.*

---

* The poet Gavin Ewart wrote: 'One particular six, a tremendous one, parabola-tall, / Made one feel pretty sorry for the ball.'

Dilley and Botham put on 117 runs in 80 minutes. When Dilley was out England were 25 runs ahead with only two wickets left.

Robin W: I hit my head in a car park. I was listening on headphones and trying to get into a car, and Dilley hit a four and I banged my head on some concrete. It was so exciting! My dad said, it's brave and wonderful, but futile.

Even so, the momentum was now with England. Botham and Old clubbed another 67 runs; Botham reached his century, off 87 balls; Australia started to look desperate. Even after Old was out, Botham protected Willis so effectively that another 31 runs were added. At the close we were 351 for 9, leading by 124.

How did any of us sleep that night?

Bob Willis was soon out on Tuesday, and Australia needed 130. Amazing to think, now, that Brearley opened the bowling with Botham and Dilley. Botham swiftly dismissed Graeme Wood, caught behind off a half-volley, but Dilley was struggling, conceding eleven runs off two overs. On came Willis for the sixth over, bowling uphill and into the wind. Nothing was happening. Brearley persevered with Botham and Old at the other end, hoping for swing, which didn't come. Dyson and Chappell played and missed occasionally, but survived. Willis changed ends. Brearley had told him to bowl faster and straighter and hold nothing back. He bowled the perfect bouncer, fast and straight, at Trevor Chappell's head. Chappell lobbed it up to Bob Taylor. Last over before lunch, Kim Hughes edged a short ball to Botham at third slip. He could catch again! The Australian captain was gone for 0, and Brearley really started to think that it could be done. England hadn't won a Test match in over a year. Three balls later Yallop fended another short, fast, lifting ball to Gatting at short leg. Australia were 58 for four at lunch.

Did we eat? Could we breathe yet? Could we still get 500 to 1 at William Hill?

Thirteen minutes after lunch Old bowled Allan Border: 65 for five. He had been bowling uphill with tireless accuracy, and conceded only 11 runs off his first eight overs. Next over Dyson tried to hook Willis and gloved the ball behind: 68 for six. And then the one I remember most vividly: Rodney Marsh, also trying to hook, getting a top edge and Dilley taking the catch at long leg, just inside the boundary. Marsh, it was said, wasn't the player he had been, but in 1981 getting him out cheaply seemed as crucial as getting Adam Gilchrist out cheaply would be in 2005. This was when I thought it could be done: 74 for seven.

Richard B: I'd had an ex-girlfriend for lunch, which is always a bit tricky. Quite why I thought it was a good idea to invite her, and listen to the Test match, combine the two, I really don't know. Cricket of course being the priority, which may be why she was an ex.

Anyway, I was doing the washing-up and listening to the radio, and Marsh hooked Willis to long leg. Ball in the air, great tension, Dilley took the catch and I punched the air. We had a small kitchen and we had one of those thick white opaque bowls over the lightbulb. It shattered on impact. I only heard the result of the Test match when I was in hospital being stitched up. I needed 30 stitches and I was cut quite deeply in three fingers. It seemed like a sacrifice that absolutely had to be made.

Next over Willis had Lawson caught behind: 75 for eight. He had taken six wickets in six overs. In 58 minutes seven wickets had gone down for 19 runs.

And yet Australia still needed only 55 to win. In the next four overs Lillee and Bright scored 35 of them. Oh god oh god oh god. You always felt that Willis would get them out sooner or later, but we were rapidly running out of later. Finally Lillee spooned a ball up to mid-on, where Gatting ran in, dived and caught it inches off the ground: 110 for nine. 'Oh what a good catch,' said Richie Benaud, but it was better than that. Twice in Botham's next over, Old dropped Alderman at third slip. 'Just as well it's not Keith Fletcher,' said Richie. Then Willis to Bright, the perfect ball for a tail-ender, a fast yorker on middle stump: 111 all out. England had won by 18 runs. Only once before in

Test history had a side won after following on. But you know all this. Of course you do. It's like a small child wanting to hear the same story at bedtime every night for years. 'Daddy, can you tell me the one about the big bowler with the hair and the glassy eyes who took eight for 43?'

Julian P: The thing that does live in the mind is the maniacal determination on Bob Willis's face.

Ken R: It's a pity it's called Botham's Test, isn't it? Because Willis . . . well, 'bowling like a man possessed' summed it up perfectly. It was awesome to watch, the destruction. You could feel it, it was a palpable thing, his anger, his aggression. And afterwards he looked like a zombie. He'd given his all.

Twenty years on, in 2001, two cricket writers constructed an entire book about this match.* BBC Sport Online invited people to email in their memories of the last day. 'I was working in an operating theatre and the surgeons kept sending me out every ten minutes to the back corridor to check the score on the radio,' wrote Andrew Ponsford from Wales. 'I was 12 years old and had skipped school pretending to have stomach pains,' wrote Mark Proffitt from England. 'I spent all day gripped with excitement, watching my two heroes Ian Botham and Bob Willis. The only downside was when my father came home . . . I was in trouble but it was so worth it.' 'It's a little sad when you need a talking point topic on something that happened twenty years ago. Haven't England won anything since?' wrote Mark Schuller from Australia. 'I have no memories of this Test at all, ' wrote Daryl, also of Australia. 'However, I do remember the last seven Ashes series quite well. I'd be happy to let you know where I was on each of the occasions these series were won if you'd only ask.'

As it happens this series wasn't won: far from it. With three Tests to go, the score was 1–1. The series was alive, and so was I, luckily, to see it.

* *500–1: The Miracle of Headingley '81* by Rob Steen and Alastair McLellan.

Edgbaston would provide a flatter, drier pitch. The selectors left out Dilley, and told him he would be back before long; Emburey returned in his place. Graham Gooch had privately declared a preference for number four, so Brearley opened with Boycott and Gower went in at three. Australia left out the token Chappell and gave a first cap to the Queensland batsman Martin Kent, while Hogg came back for the injured Lawson. England won the toss. At lunch they were 68 for three, which became 145 for six, and 189 all out. Terry Alderman took five for 43, and now had 25 victims from three and a half Tests. In his first spell, said Brearley, almost every ball landed in the same place, on a perfect length just outside off stump. But England had batted poorly on a flat pitch. Australia had eleven overs to survive, and lost Dyson and Border, both to Old, who was bowling so well that an injury had to be just around the corner.

On day two the clouds arrived but the ball swung less. At lunch Australia were 111 for three. After Graeme Wood ran himself out, Hughes and Yallop put on 50 before Hughes was lbw to Old, not playing a shot. Martin Kent should have been caught at short leg first ball, but Brearley and Old had just decided they didn't need one. Kent went on to score 46 out of 258. Australia led by 69. England ended the day on 49 for one. If only we could set them a decent target, we might even have a chance.

On day three it was 'cricket for the connoisseur', i.e. far too slow and dull for the riff-raff. By mid-afternoon England were 115 for six – 47 ahead. Some batsmen had been beaten by the pitch, others had played daft shots. Gatting was still there, and Brearley sent in Old to attack the spinner. The pair added 39 in half an hour. Hughes brought back Alderman, whose first ball Old edged behind. Gatting was then bowled behind his legs attempting to sweep Bright: 167 for eight. Emburey and Taylor heroically added 50 for the ninth wicket. England were all out for 219 and Australia needed 151 to win. Chris Old swung one in to trap Graeme Wood lbw for two: at close they were nine for one.

You have to wonder how much the events of Headingley weighed on the Australians' minds overnight. Lucky old Graeme Wood. He was probably in the bar by himself. There was no rest day for this Test: indeed, this was the first ever Sunday on which Test cricket had been played in England. As a sop to the religious lobby, play did not begin until noon. All around the country, cricket fans prayed for an England victory. Bob Willis, in the zone once again, dismissed Dyson, lbw to another that kept low, and Hughes, timing a hook so well it flew directly to Emburey on the boundary: 29 for three. Yallop and Border struggled to survive. Finally Border attempted to drive Willis, and edged the ball to Brearley, who dropped it.

Oh shit, I thought, that's it.

At lunch Australia were 63 for three. Border, labouring with a stomach upset, had scored 13 in two and a half hours. After lunch Willis began to look tired: he had bowled twelve overs without a break in the morning. Emburey was now getting last-day turn and bounce. On 87, he tempted Yallop to on-drive him; the batsman edged the ball into his pad; Botham caught him at silly mid-off. Australia needed 64 to win. Emburey starved Kent of his favourite off-side shots, but it took a sharp lifter to remove Border, caught off his glove for 40. Five wickets down, 105 runs on the board, 46 runs to win.

Legend has it that Botham was reluctant to bowl. Someone had to bowl at the other end from Emburey, but the ball wasn't swinging or seaming or bouncing for the quicker bowlers. Botham suggested giving Willey a go. Brearley disagreed. In the subsequent 40 minutes Botham would bowl 28 balls, concede one run and take the last five wickets. Marsh was bowled middle stump: 114 for six. Bright went first ball, lbw, beaten for pace: 114 for seven. Lillee played and missed the hat-trick ball, stuck around for a few overs, edged behind where Taylor caught him at the second attempt: 120 for eight. Kent tried to play Botham through the leg-side and missed: 121 for nine. Alderman bowled for 0: 121 all out. England had won by 29 runs. Among other things it was the first Test match played anywhere in the world since January 1935 in which no batsman had scored a fifty.

Robin W: I remember Kim Hughes saying about Botham, 'You gotta wrap this guy in cotton wool, really take care of him.' And I remember thinking that wrapping Ian Botham in cotton wool, what a horrible thing that would be. Especially after he'd bowled fifteen overs.

England were 2–1 up with two Tests still to play. And here comes the perfect illustration of another characteristic of Mike Brearley's captaincy: his ruthlessness. 'Respecting an opponent includes being prepared to finish him off.' But what about your teammates? Just as you would have thought Dilley was safe after Headingley, so you might have imagined that Bob Taylor, who had kept without blemish, would at least have seen out the series. But Brearley was keen to get Derek Underwood into the side, and if he played five bowlers, Taylor or Emburey would be batting at number seven: too high. So he brought in Knott for Taylor, and Chris Tavare for Peter Willey. As it was, Underwood was left out of the twelve, which must have irked Bob Taylor no end. Then Chris Old pulled up on the Monday with an injured knee. (He had played his 46th and last Test.) Paul Allott of Lancashire was given a first cap. Australia were also a fast bowler short. Lawson and Hogg were still injured, so Mike Whitney, a 22-year-old left-armer playing for Gloucestershire, was called up, and brought his John Snow hair with him.

England won the toss, and when he reached seven, Boycott passed Colin Cowdrey's aggregate of 7624 runs in Test cricket (in eleven fewer matches). Only Gary Sobers (8032) lay ahead of him now. But too far ahead, obviously, for three runs later he was out. When Gooch was lbw to Lillee, England were 25 for two. Tavare came to the crease. He started as he meant to go on: forward defensive prod, no run, little walk to short leg, twitch of moustache. It was like David Steele all over again, except without the runs. Well, occasionally he'd score one, but we could see that it wasn't his main priority. With his first innings 69, scored almost inadvertently while at the other end wickets fell steadily, Tavare divided the cricketing public into two. On one side were the appreciative, the amused, the truly thankful. On the other were the horrified, the bemused, the downright hostile. Already he had been the subject of barracking from some sections – possibly the drunker ones – of the Old Trafford crowd. But when John Emburey was out an hour after tea we were 137 for eight. Now Tavare perked up and with the other new boy, Allott, put on 38 in an hour before edging Alderman to first slip. The following morning Allott and Willis added another 56 in twelve overs for the last wicket. Allott's 52 was his maiden first-class half-century. And Willis was Lillee's 150th wicket against England alone.

Once again, though, England were up against it. The sun was coming out, the pitch was easing, birds were tweeting in the trees and 231 wasn't enough. In Willis's first over Wood was beaten twice and hooked the last two balls for four and six. In his second, Wood again pulled him for four. On *Test Match Special*, Fred Trueman was furious. 'I should be ashamed to draw my pay if I bowled like this in a Test,' he raged. 'The worst bowling with a new ball I have ever seen.' In his third over Willis took three wickets. Dyson was caught low down at third slip, not quite over a lifting ball; Hughes hit his second ball for four and then was lbw; Yallop edged his second ball to Botham at second slip. The first ball of the next over, Allott had Wood lbw to an inswinger. Four wickets had fallen in seven balls in excellent batting conditions.

Australia had obviously had a team talk and decided to go for it. If it had worked for Botham, and latterly Allott and Willis, it could work for them too. Border, though, was injured: he had cracked a bone in his left hand taking a catch the previous day. (You or I might crack a bone *dropping* a catch, but Border was Border.) When he sliced a Botham half volley to Gower at fourth slip, Australia were 58 for five off just 11.4 overs. Marsh followed soon after lunch, but Kent and Bright continued to bash the ball around, with Kent's fifty coming off just 42 deliveries. Willis took four for 63 and Botham three for 28 as Australia were all out for 130 in 30.2 overs. It was their shortest innings in a Test since 1902. At tea on the second day England were seven for one. Boycott and Tavare took this to 70 for one at the end of play with some magnificently unexciting batting.

So, 171 ahead with nine wickets left? Time for the Australians to give up completely, as England would, many times in later years. But cloud cover was helping the bowlers, and Lillee and Alderman were immaculate. In two hours and twenty minutes before lunch on Saturday, England scored 34 runs and lost four wickets. Tavare clung on, scoring just nine in the session.

Tom R: My first guinea pig was called Tavare.

At 104 for five, we were 205 ahead. Fortunately, next man in was Botham.

Consensus has it that this was an even better innings than the one at Headingley. Botham had the advantage here of an easier pitch: his savagery could be altogether more orthodox. He started slowly, scoring three singles off his first 30 balls. When he was on 28, the Australians took the new ball. This turned out to be a mistake. Botham hooked Lillee for three sixes in two overs. He wasn't wearing a helmet; the bouncers were coming straight for his head; at the very last split-second, he ducked and went through with the stroke. Two long legs, stationed for the purpose, saw the balls fly over their heads. Off one Lillee over Botham scored 22. Alderman and Whitney scarcely suffered any less. At the other end Tavare stood impassively. I remember wondering what he was thinking. Botham reached his century off 86 balls. His six sixes were a new record for any Test innings in England and the most in any innings against Australia. Tavare, by wondrous contrast, reached his fifty in 306 minutes, the slowest in the history of English first-class cricket. He sped up a little after that: his 78 took 423 minutes. At one end, non-stop action. At the other, all action had stopped. Botham's 118 made the front page of *The Times*: no one could remember a mere cricket match having done that before. The paper's sagacious (and fun-sized) cricket correspondent John Woodcock said that Botham had showed himself 'able to scale heights beyond the reach of ordinary men'.

David T: It was a very odd summer to be alive. It was the summer of the riots, but also the summer of great sporting glory. I remember saying to my dad, what about Ian Botham, Dad? And he'd say, he's a yob, but you'd love to have him batting at number six for your team. He's a yob, but he's our yob.

Andy R: I was working in a kids' home in Peckham, and that was rough. It was also the year of the Brixton riots. Working in Peckham, living in Vauxhall . . . and I had mates who lived in Atlantic Road [in Brixton]. They were literally on the frontline. And then in the midst of all this, these amazing Test matches. It's a cliché to say that Botham cheered the nation up, but it's still true.

Later both Knott and Emburey scored fifties, and England were all out for 404. With ten hours left, Australia were set 506 to win. Kim Hughes had said they would feel happier chasing 500 than 150. He may even have believed it himself.

Still, Australia quickly lost both openers. Wood ran out Dyson, then edged Allott behind. Yallop and Hughes set about the bowling, particularly Allott, and the hundred came up in the nineteenth over. Only 400 to go. Botham returned, had Hughes lbw. When he was 89 Yallop edged Allott just wide of Tavare at first slip; soon after he hooked Botham for four to reach his century. Yallop's batting tended to resemble the little girl who had a little curl: when it was good, it was very very good; when it was bad, it was awful. Today had been a good day. Emburey came on and bowled Yallop for 116 with a low full toss: awful. Kent gave a bat-and-pad catch to silly mid-off and 198 for three had declined to 210 for five at the close.

The last day was Border's: he batted for as long as he could for 123 not out. Marsh got 47 and Lillee 28: only when Lillee was out, says Brearley, did England feel certain that they would not lose. (Myself, I can never quite believe England will win any match until they have actually done so and are standing on the balcony pouring champagne over each other's heads.) There were 25 minutes plus 20 overs left when Willis had Whitney caught at short leg by Gatting. Australia were all out for 402 and had lost by 103 runs. England had won three Ashes Tests in a row. Happy days.

Brearley had been appointed captain for the third, fourth and fifth Tests only, at his own request: if the series went wrong, he felt that he and the selectors should both have a get-out clause. Now he was confirmed as captain for the sixth Test at the Oval, his last and final Test before his last and final retirement. As ever at the Oval, the selectors could not resist a little random experimentation: this year's fall guys were Paul Parker of Sussex whose only England appearance this would be and Wayne 'Pop' Larkins. Amazingly, in retrospect, Gower and Gooch were the batsmen dropped, but both were told they would go to India in the winter. Mike Hendrick came back, as much for his slip fielding as for his bowling, while Paul Allott was gone after one Test in which he had taken four wickets at 22 and scored a half-century. Australia dropped Dyson, who had top-scored in both innings at Headingley and been run out by his batting partner at Old Trafford. Martin Kent moved up to open and Dirk Wellham, a 22-year-old schoolteacher from Sydney, came in at number six. He had been scoring heavily in the county matches, and would be Test cricket's first recorded Dirk.

It was, unavoidably, a bit of an anti-climax. Australia scored 352 in their first innings, with Border unbeaten on 106. All three England seam bowlers had managed to crock themselves. but Botham disregarded the trapped nerve in his back to take six for 125.

Mark McC: Border had to shield the tail. It was fantastic to watch Brearley's endless machinations in the field, basically giving him singles when he didn't want them, and Border's ability to work the ball around and keep the strike, which he did really well. It was an absorbing after-noon's cricket, watching these two top professionals, each in their respective way at the top of their game.

In response England scored 314. Boycott's 137 was his seventh century against Australia; Gatting got 53; poor Paul Parker made 0; and Lillee took seven for 89. England had Australia at 105 for four on Monday morning, but the pitch was easing, the English bowlers were toast and Dirk Wellham moved confidently to 99, where he stopped. Boycott dropped him at mid-off. Ray Bright got out. Grey clouds started to loom. I went and made a cup of tea, took a phone call, ate a bag of Maltesers. And still Dirk Wellham was on 99. After 25 minutes he drove Botham through extra cover for four, and was out lbw soon after for 103. Hughes declared overnight, giving England six hours to score 383 and go 4–1 up. With two and a half hours left, they were 144 for six, and Alderman had just taken his 42nd wicket of the series, breaking Rodney Hogg's 1978/79 record. Brearley was joined by Knott, who yet again justified his recall in place of Bob Taylor. The second new ball was Hughes's last chance. Lillee had Brearley caught behind for 51, but Emburey and Knott hung on for the last twelve overs. Knott ended on 70 not out, in several senses, for this was his last Test innings as well.

An extraordinary series. When England lose, we lose big. When we win, it's often by the narrowest squeak. Australia should have won at Headingley, but losing that game not only lost them the series, it doomed their countrymen to 25 years of boredom. Was it Steve Waugh who said that England are good losers but unbearable winners? What the 1981 series did show, though, is that if you're English, you recognise no time limit on celebration. We are still exhilarated by the victory, over a quarter of a century later. Misty-eyed old men will be sitting in bars droning on about it in another quarter of a century's time. I intend to be one of them.

Interlude

1981

Tom H: I was 13, and I wasn't only not interested in cricket, I was vehemently hostile to it. I was like Saul before the vision on the road to Damascus. I was an active persecutor. But my mother was in hospital, so my father had to look after us. My brother was away, so it was just him and me, and he said, let me try and convince you that a Test match can be interesting. And I said, fine, OK, let's do the next one. Botham had just lost the captaincy, and I felt sorry for him, so I thought, I'll try and root for him. Because that's what my father said: pick one player and follow his fortunes. So I was quite interested because he got six wickets in the first innings at Headingley, and then he got 50. It's like backing a horse: it raises your interest. And then there was the calamity of the follow-on. My father said, there's no way they'll win this, I can't bear to watch it, let's go and see a film. So we went to the cinema and saw Excalibur, which I enjoyed.

Now, he didn't have a radio in the car or anything, so when we came back home he said, we might as well see if they've lost yet, so we switched on the TV, and Dilley was coming out to bat. I was really pleased that Botham was still there, and I thought, I'll watch it till the end till they all get out. And we sat there, and we sat there, and we sat there, and by the end of the day England still weren't all out . . .

It was an utter revelation. I had no idea that sport, let alone cricket, could be as exciting as that. I was completely hooked. And the moment it was over I started looking forward to the next one.

And of course my father sagely advised me that lightning doesn't strike twice. You've been lucky with this first one but you have to know that not all matches will be as exhilarating as that. He was right, because Edgbaston wasn't as exhilarating as Headingley. But only just. And again it was Botham who did it.

Then it came to the Old Trafford Test, and we were out and we had a radio on and Botham came out to bat, and he was out first ball. And that was the sudden realisation that this isn't a fairy story, that there are going to be times when you get disappointed. I was so anxious about him getting a pair that I couldn't bear to watch it when he came out in the second innings. I kept the radio on at low volume, not so that I could hear what was being said, but so that if he was out I would know from the voice intonation. And I could hear the commentator getting more and more worked up, so I turned the volume up and Botham was on about 50. So I went in and watched it on TV. That was the best innings of all in a way.

From that moment on I was so gripped that I didn't actually need cricket to be exciting. Which was just as well, because then there was the Oval, and Boycott got a hundred, and then there was the India series, the most boring series of all time. It didn't matter. I was hooked.

Chris P: On the fifth day of Headingley I was in a town called Girvan in Ayrshire, loading up a tanker with pure alcohol to bring it down to London. Test Match Special was on medium wave in those days, on the Radio 3 wavelength. You were fine coming up the coast from Girvan to Ayr, but then you would turn inland and lose the signal. So I left the distillery just as play was starting. Not a lot happened in the first hour, and then I lost the signal. But I knew exactly where I would get a signal again, and when I got there I turned it on just as The World at One was ending. And Robin Day was saying, at lunch England have got Australia three or four down. So, straight into a lay-by. You see, I had a telly. Nine-inch screen, black-and-white portable. So I'm sitting in this huge lay-by just outside Dumfries watching the cricket, and I'm going nowhere until it's finished.

And this old man drove a caravan in, with what I assumed to be his wife and, maybe, granddaughter. You know how, sometimes, you're conscious of being watched? The wife and granddaughter had gone back into the caravan to make a cup of tea, but he just sat in the car, looking at me. Eventually he could resist it no more. So he came wandering over and, in a broad Yorkshire accent, said, you're not watching the cricket, are you? I said, well, yes. And he said, can I? And I said, by all means. And he said, I'll be back. Two minutes later he came back with a four-pack of John Smiths bitter. And we sat and watched it till the death, with his wife and granddaughter sitting there, arms folded, very very annoyed. But there was no way this man was going to leave until the game was over.

Andy J: I was about 15, and there was this girl I really fancied. She used to go to the church I went to, and I remember the first time I saw her: it was a baptism and I was an acolyte in the choir, and I looked to my right and there was this absolutely stunning girl guide. The light was shining on her, it was like something out of a film. I had to get to know her. They'd have little church dos, and her friend would come up and say, she wants to dance with you. And we'd dance but I wouldn't say anything because I was too shy. This was before alcohol, you see. Didn't talk to any women before alcohol.

But every now and then our vicar would have get-togethers round at his house. There were only about seven or eight of us there. He was a cricket fan so he had the cricket on the telly. He'd made us all some lunch, and the idea was that we'd go in his really big garden and play some games. But the cricket was on, and it was the last day at Headingley, and it was just getting to the exciting bit. Thinking, they can't turn this round, can they? And everyone was saying, we're going out into the garden, and she's there, saying, Andy, we're all going out into the garden. I said, all right, I'll be out in a minute.

So they're out there, playing rounders and whatnot, and I'm thinking, I've got to get out there, this has got to be one of the best opportunities I'll ever get. I'll go in a minute. And then I'd watch a bit more. Every so often I'd go to the window. They were down in the garden, playing, laughing. But the cricket got so exciting that I watched it to the end. And then I ran downstairs, and her mum had just turned up to take her home. And I went from elation to depression in an instant – because I wouldn't get to see her again for the rest of the summer. My plan had been, hook up with her then, arrange a date at the pictures, see her through the holidays, who knows what would happen? And the cricket ruined it. She was stunning. We never did hook up. Every now and then I get a little pang about what might have been. But then I really wouldn't want to have missed that final day.

Eight

1982/83

I think that was the start of AB being a great player under pressure . . . it started with that innings.
Geoff Lawson on the Melbourne Test

When I went out to bat there was no pressure on me. Everyone expected me to play a stupid shot and get out. I went up to AB and said, 'Let's beat these fruits.'
Jeff Thomson

In 1981, as has been mentioned, there were riots in Brixton and Toxteth. 'Green Door' by Shakin' Stevens was number one for four long weeks. *Brideshead Revisited* was on TV for even longer. It all feels like ancient history, whereas I can remember the appointment of Keith Fletcher as England captain for the 1981/82 tour of India with pinpoint clarity. Had they gone mad? Wasn't there anyone else? I would have done it if they had asked.

It all comes down to the English preference for appointing a captain first and then building the team around him. This can sometimes work if the captain is a genius (J. M. Brearley), but if the captain isn't already an automatic selection (M. H. Denness, A. R. Lewis), it can end in tears. Fletcher had missed 47 Tests, and there were sound cricketing reasons for this. In the event, the Gnome would preside over one of the dreariest series in modern times. England lost the first Test on a poor pitch at Bombay, after which the Indians, under the single-minded leadership of Sunil Gavaskar, protected their lead with five high-scoring and agonisingly boring draws. When the tourists returned, Peter May, the new chairman of selectors, appointed Bob Willis captain without having first told Fletcher he had been sacked. By then, though, our attention was elsewhere.

For it was during the Indian series that the famed South African Breweries XI had come into being. Inspired by the Packer shambles, the South Africans recruited a squad of England players to go and play a 'rebel' tour there. Geoffrey Boycott was chief recruiting officer, which may account for the relatively large number of Yorkshiremen in the party. Large cheques were involved: a cricketer's professional life can be short and, in those days, was not well remunerated. Even so, a few of them can't have been thinking straight. Of the fifteen who took part, five had just been in India with England: Boycott, Gooch, Emburey, Lever and Underwood. Others may have been near the end of their international careers or beyond it: Amiss, Knott, Woolmer, Old, Hendrick. Yet others were still on the margins: Willey, Larkins, Arnie Sidebottom of Yorkshire, Les Taylor of Leicestershire, and Warwickshire's batsman-wicketkeeper Geoff Humpage. The furore the tour caused seemed to come as a shock to them, for the team didn't play well. Graham Gooch, appointed captain by the rest of the side, became by default the tour's front man and the primary target for people's contempt and bitterness. Cricket tends to be deeply conservative in its politics, but I wasn't and none of my friends were, and we felt badly let down. It seemed only appropriate to us that the players were banned from Test cricket for three years.

Yet again, the England team would be weakened by circumstances beyond their control. Boycott, Underwood and several others would not have been playing Test cricket in three years' time, but Gooch? Emburey? I was sad to see Lever and Old go as well. What was left of the England team, though, pulled together under Willis's captaincy. Although he still tended to switch off when bowling, he had been a highly effective vice-captain for several series under Brearley, and the summer of 1982 was a small triumph for him. India were beaten 1–0 in three Tests, and a strong Pakistan side (Javed, Zaheer, Mudassar Nazar and Mohsin Khan opening, Abdul Qadir with his twirlers, and Imran Khan in charge for the first time) were dispatched 2–1. Willis missed one game, and that was the one England lost, under David Gower. There were no other candidates for captain on the 1982/83 Ashes tour. Now all we had to worry about was the rest of the team.

According to Robin Marlar, in his typically trenchant book of the series, *Decision Against England*, six players picked themselves for the tour and could expect to play every Test: Willis, Gower, Botham, Bob Taylor, Chris Tavare and Allan Lamb. Taylor's longevity was extraordinary: his standards never seemed to slip. Tavare had replaced Boycott in the affections of all those who like their batsmen sound in defence and liable to stick around for a while; Allan Lamb, South African in origins but qualified for England earlier in the season, was an infusion of class we could scarcely afford to ignore, given the loss of Gooch. Two other batsmen had had good summers: Derek Randall, mercurial as ever, and Lancashire's opener, Graeme 'Foxy' Fowler, who brought the number of stylish left-handed batsmen who kept the slips interested up to two. The last batting place went to the stolid Northants opener Geoff Cook, who had been in and out of the Test side during the summer. This meant no tour for Mike Gatting, who had become England's latest enigma: immense talent, prolific against the counties, not enough runs in Tests. Nor, again, was there room for Phil Edmonds: the selectors chose three off-spinners. Eddie Hemmings was the obvious

replacement for Emburey after two productive seasons; Geoff
Miller, chosen once again to bolster the batting; and Vic Marks
of Somerset, possibly earmarked as a one-day specialist. The
other quick bowlers were Robin Jackman (gnarled old pro),
Norman Cowans of Middlesex (speedy tyro) and Derek Pringle,
who had scored tons of runs for Cambridge University, been
rushed into the Test side and found a role as the third-string
bowler who could bat a bit. With Old, Hendrick and Lever
gone and Willis in the last phase of his long career, the cupboard
looked a little bare. Dilley had faded in India and was rebuilding
his action from scratch; Allott, beset by injuries, had lost his
place during the summer; and Jackman, at 37, was hardly an
investment for the future.

Australia, of course, had their own problems. Yet again Greg
Chappell was back as captain for a home series, after Kim
Hughes's side had been walloped 3–0 in Pakistan. Only the best
players could pick and choose tours, and so they did: Lillee had
made himself unavailable for Pakistan as well. It's worth noting
that Rodney Marsh, the third of Australia's old stagers, went on
every tour as a matter of course. Why was he never given the
captaincy? I always wondered, and we can be sure that he did too.
Hughes was in danger of being remembered more as an unsuccessful captain than as the superb batsman we knew him to be.
But at least he kept his place in the side. Since 1981 Martin Kent
(for good), Dirk Wellham, Graeme Yallop and Ray Bright had all
gone. David Hookes, Australia's Gatting, was back for another go,
while Bruce Yardley was the incumbent spinner. Lillee,
Alderman and Lawson were all fit and eating raw meat for breakfast.

England lost their first four-day match, as was now traditional,
against Queensland, for whom Greg Chappell and Kepler Wessels
scored centuries. Wessels – left-handed, South African, a crab-
stanced run machine – was newly qualified for Australia, and they
would be fools not to have him. Fortunately for England, the

Australian selectors remained loyal to their opening pair, Graeme Wood and John Dyson, for the first Test. Whichever one of them Wood ran out would surely lose his place. For England, Gower, Lamb and Tavare scored good runs in the early matches, while Hemmings, Cowans, Willis and Botham all took good wickets. Miller made 83 against South Australia, the 51st time he had passed fifty without making a hundred. The only real problem was that the first Test was at Perth, Australia's fastest wicket, and scene of so many English humiliations, past and future.

Willis called incorrectly, and Chappell put England in. As Tavare and Cook walked to the crease, Robin Marlar found it 'impossible not to cast a thought in the direction of absent friends'. England without Gooch was 'like tonic without the gin', while England without Boycott was 'like gin and tonic without a glass'. Every side needs a Boycott, a batsman who has to be prised out with pliers. Maybe Tavare could do the job. Marlar was less impressed with his opening partner, who he felt lacked speed of reaction against the fastest bowlers. After 35 minutes Lillee undid Cook with a shortish rising ball that he lobbed up to short leg: 14 for one. Listening at home late at night, tens of thousands of Britons sighed, took another sip and feared the worst.

But this was a blander Perth pitch than in 1978/79, with little pace or seam movement, and at lunch England were 66 for one. Not long afterwards Lillee had a huge hairy shout for lbw against Gower. The umpire said no. In his fury, Lillee kicked the ball towards the slips. Two balls later Gower went to his fifty with an all-run four. No doubt he raised a nonchalant Roger Moore eyebrow at the same time. One can only imagine the extent of Lillee's rage. On 72, however, Gower flicked Alderman in the air to Dyson just in front of square leg. Bruce Yardley said he 'had looked as if he would get 300'. (Gower confirmed, years later, that he had never felt better at the crease.) At tea England were 140 for two. Tavare had been given one life, dropped by

Alderman in the slips off Lawson, but nothing else had pierced that cocoon of concentration. If a plane had crashed into the pavilion it might have been several minutes before he noticed. (Why is no one bowling at me?)

In the final session Yardley and Lawson picked up a wicket each. Lamb was caught by Marsh off inside edge and thigh, and given a rousing reception by the Australian fielders (who thought he had been caught behind off Lillee some time before). Botham smacked three fours off Lawson and then was given out caught behind off the last ball of the over. Marsh hadn't even appealed. Marlar said it was 'a disgracefully incompetent piece of umpiring'. With England on 204 for four and the second new ball available, Tavare went into his shell. Not that he had been seen to leave it very often since 1981, but even by his standards, staying on 66 for an hour and nine minutes was some feat. The big question the following morning was, could 'Rowdy' (so named because he never said a word) break the record? Mohsin Khan had once remained on the same score for an hour and 33 minutes, for Punjab against England in 1977/78. Tragically Tavare fell three minutes short. When he was out, mishitting a sweep off Yardley to short leg, he had batted five and three quarter hours for 89. Randall made 78, Miller 30, Taylor 29 not out and the skipper 26 in a total of 411, with Yardley taking five for 107.

But that wasn't the half of it. The day's most memorable incident came when England reached 400. Some drunken England supporters decided that this would be a good moment to invade the pitch. One of them, possibly drunker and stupider than the others, danced around Alderman, fielding at long leg, and jeered at him. Alderman gave him a shove. Another of the invaders approached and gave Alderman a glancing whack on the side of the head. Alderman pursued the perp and brought him down with a magnificent flying tackle (he played Australian Rules football in his spare time). Lillee and Border sprinted over to lend assistance and, in the ensuing melee, Alderman dislocated his bowling shoulder. 'He was the first man to do the chasing and he came off second best,' said the TV commentator. Endless action replays of the incident were shown. 'And here's looking at this again from another angle. And that looked to be a punch going in there.' The thuggish English fans were escorted from the ground. Many of them are doubtless now respectable estate agents and minor criminals.

On the third day the Australians came back as strongly as we expected, scoring 333 for six. Willis's opening spell was, said Marlar, 'the toughest examination opening batsmen had to face in this match'. Unfortunately, they passed it. Dyson, Hughes and Hookes made fifties and Chappell scored 117, his 21st Test century. He had survived a testing spell by Botham and, as all great players seem to, cashed in thereafter. Geoff Miller bowled all afternoon and deserved his two wickets, but the initiative had slipped away. In *The Captain's Diary*, Bob Willis admits he gave his team a severe bollocking: 'If we had kept it tighter we might even now be in a winning position, but the inexperience of Pringle and Cowans was crucial. With hindsight, Eddie Hemmings should have played after all. But we were not to know quite how easy a batting pitch this would turn out.'

On the rest day, six of the England side took a boat trip, which, after a return journey in heavy seas, Willis described as 'probably a mistake'.

On the fourth morning Australia were able to declare with a lead of 13, but with Alderman gone they had only three frontline bowlers. Lillee and Lawson alternated, with Bruce Yardley closing up the other end, and England batsmen got themselves out. Cook hung his bat out to dry for seven. Gower reached 28 before falling lbw to Lillee. At the other end Tavare was, in Robin Marlar's words, 'as becalmed as a yacht in the Sargasso Sea'. At tea England were 71 for two and Tavare had made nine of them, with six scoring shots, in two hours. There is no problem in this if, like Boycott, you then go on to score a distinguished century that either saves or wins the match. But if you then get out for nine, as Tavare did, caught at first slip off Yardley, you just look daft.

Bren S: At our school in Hobart, that became the biggest sledge you could throw at somebody when they were batting. You'd just say, 'Come on, Tavare.'

Botham then missed a straight ball and England were 80 for four. Australia were now rueing Alderman's flying tackle. Lillee had twisted his right knee in a foothold and his pace had dropped. Lamb and Randall added 71 for the fifth wicket, before the annoyingly nicknamed 'Legga' edged to Marsh for 56.* On the last day, though, Derek Randall came into his own again with 115, his fifth century in Tests and third in Australia. ('A monumental effort,' said Willis.) Again the tail wagged: nightwatchman Taylor hung around until after lunch for 31, and later, Pringle and Cowans put on 66 for the last wicket. England were all out for 358 (Lawson five for 108), and there was only really time left for Wood to edge Willis behind for 0 and therefore lose his place for the second Test. Chappell blamed poor catching for his team's failure to go 1–0 up, not his shortage of fit bowlers.

A dislocated shoulder, though, is a horrible injury for a bowler. Terry Alderman was out for the season and beyond. Lillee's knee continued to inconvenience him, and he broke down completely in a Sheffield Shield match the week after. Jeff Thomson, now 32 and 'a fading comet' according to Marlar, was recalled, and Carl Rackemann summoned for the first time. Aged 22 and of the brick shithouse school of fast bowlers, Rackemann had taken 25 wickets for Queensland at just under 15. The terrifying Kepler Wessels took Graeme Wood's place. England's only planned change for Brisbane was Hemmings for Pringle. Geoff Cook had scored 99 against New South Wales, while Graeme Fowler remained dismally out of touch. But then Cook

---

* Apparently 'Larry' and 'Chop' had been rejected by Lamb himself. But surely 'Bestendnecka' would have satisfied all imaginable criteria.

took a blow in the ribs from Botham in the nets, so Fowler played anyway.

Willis would have put them in if he had won the toss, despite finding out the previous day that England had only ever beaten Australia once after putting them in. It was irrelevant, anyway: he called wrongly, Chappell inserted, and England were all out for 219, roughly 150 short of a competitive total. The highlight was a 50 partnership between Lamb and Botham, of which Botham scored 40. First he slapped Rackemann back over his head, his customary greeting to a new fast bowler. Then he decided to hit Jeff Thomson out of Test cricket. He had clumped six fours and a six, scoring at a run a ball, when he sliced a wide ball from Yardley straight to Rackemann at third man. Willis reckoned that every top order batsman other than Tavare had contributed to his own dismissal. 'The truth is we were miserably bad.' Lawson, new leader of the attack, had taken six for 47.

England's only hope, on an easy-paced pitch, was the new ball, which accounted for both Dyson and Border. But this only brought Chappell in to join Wessels. Robin Marlar wrote that Chappell had 'grown increasingly vulnerable to his first few deliveries', but not today. As Wessels concentrated on survival, his captain breezed to yet another fifty. It took a run out to remove him, as Chappell called for a non-run and Wessels hesitated too long before sending him back. Hughes was out for 0, Hookes got a dodgy caught behind and just after tea Marsh nicked one more audibly. Australia were 171 for six. Wessels was still there, and just before the close reached his century. It hadn't been pretty: it never would be with Wessels, whose bizarre crustacean stance didn't lend itself to elegant Chappell-like off-drives. But it had been the innings his team needed, the one we were always willing Tavare to play. The following day Yardley cut and carved his way to 53, and Wessels was last out for 162. Willis (five for 66) had bowled magnificently, Cowans hadn't (six overs for 36) and the spinners, though steady, had taken one wicket between them.

Australia led by 122 on first innings and, barring an astounding rearguard action from England, the match was probably lost.

Now it was the home side's turn to falter. Dyson dropped Tavare. Hughes dropped Fowler, who was then caught off a no-ball. Marsh caught Tavare down the leg side for 13. But then Yardley dropped Gower in the gully. After tea, in fading light, Thomson bowled a silly bouncer, and the umpires offered the batsmen the light. Greg Chappell was enraged. It wasn't dark. You could easily play on in that. The Brisbane *Courier-Mail's* headline the following morning read 'England Make Their Escape Into The Night'. Wrote Willis in his *Captain's Diary*: 'I'm afraid I am going to be without both big toenails in a matter of days . . . Went to bed early, after a barbecued steak.'

Next day, the sun shone and escape still looked possible. Gower and Fowler, each dropped off Thomson, put on 90 for the second wicket and wiped out the deficit. Rackemann tore a groin muscle, and off he went. But this time England could not make the most of their good fortune, as Thomson, apparently whacked out of international cricket in the first innings, took three for eight in 37 balls. Gower mishooked and edged to Marsh, Lamb clipped a ball to Wessels at short leg and Randall went to a snorting catch by Yardley in the gully. Both Fowler, for 83, and Botham, suffering a migraine, were out c Marsh b Thomson. Lawson took the other five wickets, for 87, but Yardley did his bit as well. 'It is impossible to praise these three Australian bowlers too highly,' said Marlar. 'It strikes me that the Perth pitch invasion did us no favours,' said Willis. 'That injury to Terry Alderman merely opened the way for Jeff Thomson's comeback.' England's total of 309 gave Australia a target of 188 and five hours in which to score them. Wessels, dropped in the gully in Willis's first over, made 46. Norman Cowans finally took his first Test wicket, when Chappell hooked him to Lamb at long leg. But then Hughes (39 not out) and Hookes (66 not out) made it look easy. Australia won by seven wickets, and were one-nil up.

For Adelaide Cowans was replaced by Pringle and Australia, whose cupboard wasn't bare, could bring back Rodney Hogg in place of the injured Rackemann. Mike Brearley always thought that, because they had faced him in his pomp in 1978/79, England had a higher opinion of Hogg than some of his current teammates did. Everyone presumed that it was the thought of sending his openers out to face Lawson, Hogg and Thomson that influenced Willis, who finally won a toss and chose to bowl. 'Mistake,' wrote Robin Marlar in his notebook, in large red letters. In fact Willis had been outvoted by his committee and teammates: 'Now I am faced with trying publicly to justify a decision I thought absurd.' Within the first half-hour Wessels had hooked Botham in front of square, which suggested that Botham's pace wasn't what it had been, and that the wicket was a peach. At the end of the first day Australia were 265 for three. Willis reckoned that three balls had passed the bat all day. Greg Chappell was out just before the close to the second new ball for 115. England bowled with more purpose on the second day, Kim Hughes ran himself out for 88, and Australia were all out for 438. If we had a decent start the match could even be saved. Tavare scored one run off Lawson's first over and faced Hogg for the first time. The third ball was fast – 90 mph or more – and straight, and Tavare could only edge it to Marsh. The crucial difference between him and Boycott, we could now see, was self-confidence. 'By nature he is slightly insecure,' wrote his captain, 'and certainly worries a good deal.' Test cricket he found 'a great mental strain'. The team's social committee, whose job was to raise funds for the Christmas party, had fined Tavare for being 'too brainy', and Allan Lamb 'for not being brainy enough'.

Even so, by lunchtime on the third day, England were 140 for two and tiptoeing to safety. Gower and Lamb had put on 119 in just over three hours, 'defiant, determined and not unsuccessful in the vital matter of scoring runs,' wrote Marlar. Just after lunch, a shortish ball from Lawson bounced sharply and Gower, trying to withdraw his bat, gloved a catch. He had made 60. On 181 for three, Lamb was out hooking for 82, and seventy minutes later England were all out for 216. The details are too painful to recount here. Let's just be thankful that we were asleep at the time. Lawson had four for 56, Thomson three for 51, Hogg two for 41. Before anyone could get their breath back Tavare was out for 0, bat and pad off Thommo.

Nick N: That was the one, I'm sure, where I went to sleep and England were batting, and I woke up and England were batting, again. They had followed on. Gower was on about 10, and I woke up and he was on three.

Willis called his chapter on this match 'The Fateful Adelaide Toss'. England could have prayed for rain, but they would have been wasting their time: there hadn't been more than a shower in Adelaide for four years. The following day Gower made 114 in six hours with great care, while Botham batted three hours for 58, a long time for him. But again the innings fell away: the last seven wickets were lost for 68 runs, with another five wickets for Geoff Lawson. He had taken 25 in three Tests. England were all out for 304 and Australia won by eight wickets. The Ashes weren't yet lost, but we would need to win the last two Tests in order to keep them.

What had gone wrong? The opening partnership wasn't working. Nor was the back-up seam bowling. Ian Botham wasn't taking his usual hatful of wickets. For the first time people were suggesting that he might be carrying a little extra weight. (In my local pub the phrase 'fat bastard' had been used.) But like so many England captains, Bob Willis was having to use him as a stock bowler. The big question was, which first-change bowler would you rather face? The Australians had Jeff Thomson. We had Derek Pringle.

Mark McC: No one in Australia could figure that one out. They were mystified. He couldn't bat, he couldn't bowl. I've never seen a big man hit the ball so weakly.

And the Tasmanians had Michael Holding. In a 50-over match, Whispering Death bowled a brute of a ball at Derek Randall. 'It simply could not have been avoided,' wrote Marlar. Randall was wearing a helmet but not a visor. He was hit on the top lip, just under the nose. Several teeth were shattered, the bone attached to the upper jaw that supports the gristle of the nose was broken and the upper jaw itself cracked close to the sinus passage, which filled with blood . . . and Randall was out of the next Test. In the Christmas fancy dress party, Bob Willis went as Napoleon, Derek Pringle as a Hell's Angel, and manager Doug Insole as showjumper Harvey Smith, with two fingers permanently aloft. Chris Tavare impersonated Hilda Ogden, and was photographed brandishing a fluffer.

And so to Melbourne for the Fourth Test. The MCG had become a bogey ground for the Australians. They had lost all five ODIs there the previous season; they felt the wickets didn't suit them. Indeed it was his profound suspicion of the pitch, more than anything, that made Greg Chappell put England in to bat when he won the toss. But Willis would have done the same thing: Hemmings had been left out, and both Cowans and Pringle were playing. Geoff Cook replaced the injured Randall, allowing Tavare to drop down to number three, his preferred position. Lawson's sixth ball leaped far over Fowler's head. At the other end Cook got into position to defend, and several days later the ball arrived. Before lunch both openers had perished to slip catches, and England's new number three was greeted by a banner saying 'Hey Tavare What's The Rush?' Gower went soon after and England were 56 for three. At tea they were 183 for three. Lamb and Tavare had hit the leather off the ball. In one over from Yardley, Tavare smashed three fours, two over square leg and one through the covers. How wonderful it must have been to see this. All the disappointments of the previous two Tests had been wiped out with a single twitch of that funny little moustache. The Australians were certain they had Lamb caught behind down the leg side off Thomson when he was 20, but Lamb wasn't going anywhere. What, me guv? At 219 Tavare was out, slashing to gully, for 89. Lamb went shortly afterwards for 82 and the now familiar batting collapse saw England dismissed for 284. Hogg and Yardley picked up four wickets each.

Maybe it was sheer excitement, but Willis and Botham were unusually profligate with the new ball, and it took Cowans to remove Dyson lbw. Dyson wasn't happy. If it wasn't the pitch, it was the umpires. Next ball, Cowans pitched one short on leg stump, Chappell hooked, and Lamb took the catch inside the square leg boundary. Wessels, with years of experience on unreliable English pitches, looked as comfortable as anyone, but Willis probed a perceived weakness on leg stump and eventually bowled him for 47. When Border was bowled by Botham for two, Australia were 89 for four. But then Hughes, Hookes and Marsh each made fifties, all three aided by some remarkably generous umpiring decisions. The tail squeaked a first innings lead of three. It could hardly have been closer.

If England had an advantage, though, it was their familiarity with this sort of pitch – slow, unreliable, more likely now to keep low than smack you in the throat. The umpires had quite a day of it as well. Gower missed the ball by a foot and was given out caught behind. At 129 for five, despite 65 from Fowler, Australia were favourites once again. But Botham (46), Pringle (42) and Taylor (37) pulled things back. Taylor was given out lbw by a ball from Thomson that hit him high on the thigh: even Australians were astonished by that one. The quickies shared the wickets and the home side needed 292 to win.

Unfortunately Willis had one of his stomach upsets. ('I was like a wet paper bag,' he wrote.) On the fourth day he would be able to bowl only nine overs. Step forward N. G. Cowans, wild and raw fast bowler and genuine number-eleven batsman, whose finest cricketing hour this would be. In the second innings he took six for 77, including the wicket, for the third time in the series, of Greg Chappell, caught at cover for two. Hookes made 68 and Hughes 48 but when Jeff Thomson, the last man, came out to join Allan Border, Australia were 218 for nine. In his first innings Thommo had taken a giant mow at Miller and missed. Patience was not his watchword. My strongest memory of this partnership (the highlights taped on our new VHS recorder and watched many times until mysteriously 'lost' in a house move) was the way England didn't really try and get Border out. They gave him singles, which often turned into twos, threes and fours, and waited to get at Thomson. In the process they helped play Border back into form. On the fourth evening the pair scored exactly half of the 74 runs needed to win. On day five they would seek to score another 37, and England would seek to get one of them out. I'm sure I wasn't the only person who took a radio to bed with me that evening. How could you sleep, not knowing?

Ben D: It's a very personal thing, following cricket. Lying in bed listening to Test Match Special *into the early hours: it's like a vigil, a semi-devotional sort of thing. And feeling the searing heat . . . and here it's cold, and you're tucked up in bed.*

Ken R: You could almost feel the heat from those broadcasts. There was some sort of bizarre quality to the sound. You just got the impression that the grounds were huge and everyone was baking hot.

Border and Thomson edged closer and closer to the target. How had we let them get so close? It seemed ridiculous. The more you know of cricket, the more ridiculous it becomes. Fourteen wanted, nine wanted, six wanted. As Botham started his fourth over of the morning, Thomson was facing and they needed four to win. One shot. Botham bowled his stock delivery, the outswinger, well pitched up, slightly too wide if anything. Thomson got a thick edge. The ball flew to Tavare at second slip. He put his hands up to catch it, and said later that it had grown big on him. It hit the ball of his right thumb and flew up in the air behind him. Miller, fielding some way behind Tavare at first slip, moved to his right, stooped and took the ball in both hands. He threw it straight up in the air and ran all the way to the pavilion. And thousands of miles away, an awful lot of people lying in bed with a transistor radio for company whooped with joy.

Julian P: It was very late at night, and we were trying to work out what we could do. You're completely powerless, it's going on on the other side of the world, and you maintain this ludicrous fiction that if you sit with your feet off the ground or your fingers in your ears or you don't have another cigarette, then you'll change the luck of the team. In this case one of us must have done the right thing, because it was entirely down to us that we won.

No one remembers the resounding victories. (Not that there are many.) But the nail-biters stick in your memory for the rest of your life.*

Bill M: Your emotions go into a whirl. You think he's dropped it, then it rebounds. But I was so delighted to have been listening to it live, because it wouldn't have been the same to have woken up the next day and it's – oh, we've won by three runs.

England still needed to win the final Test at Sydney, starting only a couple of days later. Graeme Fowler had had his toe cracked during his second-innings 65 at Melbourne, but Derek Randall, though dentally challenged, declared himself fit and ready. The ball was expected to turn as always at Sydney, so Hemmings came in for Pringle. It was vital that Bob Willis won the toss, so of course he didn't. For the first time in the series, the winner of the toss decided to bat. In Willis's first over Wessels called John Dyson for a quick single. Not renowned for his light-ning fast ground fielding, Willis picked up and threw down the

---

* As do some of the daft statistics. To protect Thomson, Border turned down 29 obvious singles during their stand. And the match was the first in Test history in which all four innings totals were within ten runs of each other (Eng 284 and 294; Aus 287 and 288).

batsman's wicket. Dyson was 18 inches short. The umpire said, 'Not out'. Later he told the press, 'You can only decide it as you see it. It was either six inches in or six inches out. That was close enough not to give him out.' The following afternoon Dyson was out for 79. We can't just blame the coin and the umpires, though. With heavy cloud cover and rain in the air, these should have been perfect conditions for Botham. 'This was a day on which he might have run half-way through the Australians,' wrote Marlar, 'had he been bowling in what we must sadly look back on as his heyday.' Australia made 314, with Border, back in good touch, scoring 89. England were soon 24 for three – two to Lawson, one to Hogg. Gower and Randall put on 122 for the fourth wicket, and each scored 70, but Thomson took five for 50 and England were all out for 237. In Australia's second innings, Hughes swept a ball from Miller on to his toe, and the ball bounced up to Geoff Cook at bat and pad. The umpire said, 'Not out'. The following afternoon Hughes was out for 137. On a pitch now offering generous if slow turn, Hemmings and Miller each took three expensive wickets. Border made 83 and Australia were all out for 382. 'It is days such as this which have brought home to me the problems of a captain with a mediocre attack,' wrote Bob Willis. 'Whatever he may do, he cannot create the gunpowder to blast out the opposition, and consistently through this series we have been unable to dismiss a rather ordinary Australian batting side.' In his last innings for England, Cook was lbw to Lawson for two. He had scored 54 runs in six innings. Hemmings came in as night-watchman, and on the last afternoon was out for 95, having outscored and outplayed the recognised batsmen. England were playing for the draw now, and the two Derbyshire men, Geoff Miller and Bob Taylor, blocked out the final overs to secure it. Kim Hughes was named man of the match, and to regain some of the world's attention, Greg Chappell resigned as captain for the 458th time. Australia's next Test, in Sri Lanka in April 1983, would be captained by Greg Chappell.

In the one-day series that followed, and lasted longer than anyone could have thought possible, England narrowly failed to reach the finals, which were contested by Australia and New Zealand. Maybe the most pertinent comment on England's tour came from a fat little pig that was unleashed on to the field during an Australia vs England match at Brisbane. On one side of the pig, someone had written 'EDDIE' in marker pen. On the other side was written 'BOTHAM'. Happily grazing in the outfield, the pig was disturbed by a passing policeman, who managed to overpower the porker with his bare hands. No arrests were made.

Nine

1985

They dropped me and picked Richard Ellison. So in a way I won the Ashes for England.

Paul Allott

In his book of the 1982/83 series, Bob Willis singled out three players for praise: 'David Gower has grown in confidence as a player and person, Derek Randall surpassed even our expectations, and Bob Taylor showed that the years have not impaired his brilliance behind the stumps.' Two and a half years later, only Gower was still in the team, and he was captain. Willis had led England in the World Cup and to a 3–1 home victory over New Zealand, but the two three-match series in 1983/84, away to New Zealand and Pakistan, had each been lost 1–0. Willis had been injured in Pakistan, and Gower took over as official captain for the 1984 home series against the West Indies: the notorious 'blackwash', an ignominious 5–0 defeat. What a relief it is not to have to write about this series, which destroyed careers and broke hearts. Taylor had already retired, and Willis called it a day after 90 Tests and 325 wickets, but Randall never played another Test after 1984, and nor did Geoff Miller. In 1984/85 England went to India and Botham took the winter off. Gower's party lost the first Test but recovered brilliantly to win 2–1. Gatting, raised to the vice-captaincy, at last scored his first Test century, and followed it up with a double two Tests later. Tim Robinson of Notts averaged 63 in his first series, Neil Foster of Essex took 11 for 163 to win the third Test, and the Middlesex pair, Paul Downton and Phil Edmonds, re-established themselves as first-choice wicketkeeper and spinner respectively. Maybe the strangest case of all was that of Graeme Fowler, whose last two innings on the sub-continent were 201 and 69, but then lost form so utterly at the beginning of 1985 that he never played Test cricket again. A great shame, as his uppish slashes through gully stick in my memory to this day.

Australia had also had an interesting time. After helping to beat Pakistan 1–0 at home in 1983/84, Lillee, Chappell and Marsh announced their retirements. Kim Hughes, the poor bugger, had to take a weakened side to the West Indies. They lost 3–0. Not once, in any of the five Tests, did the West Indies lose a second-innings wicket. Border averaged 74; Wayne Phillips, the new wicketkeeper, was next best on 25. In 1984/85, the West Indies made the return journey, and won 3–1. After the second Test (and second crushing defeat), Kim Hughes resigned in tears, which now is all he is remembered for. Australia used 19 players in the series. Kepler Wessels scored 505 runs at 56, and Geoff Lawson took 23 wickets at 25, but other reputations were ruined. According to *Wisden*, 'It is not often the case that a touring team can be said to have had no single individual failure, but it was so with this West Indian team.'

South Africa were waiting. Weren't they always? It amazes me now to recall that, in England, a sizeable rump of Con-servative MPs were sympathetic to the South African regime, and saw no reason why they shouldn't be brought back into the sporting fold. I hated the South Africans because they had taken away Gooch, Emburey and the others for three years, but at the beginning of the 1985 season the ban on these players lapsed, and they could be selected for England again. So South Africa looked elsewhere. Australia had a lot of disaffected cricketers who had been made to look daft by the West Indies. A 'rebel' squad was recruited, including Rodney Hogg, Terry Alderman, John Dyson and Carl Rackemann. Then, when they weren't selected for the tour to England, Kim Hughes and Graeme Yallop signed up as well. All were immediately banned for three years. In *Wisden*, John Woodcock suggested that the 'rebel' side might have been stronger than the official side sent to England under the leadership of Allan Border. It was certainly more experienced; and if Alderman had taken his usual 40 wickets in the English season, I doubt we would have enjoyed ourselves half as much.

Border's squad had several familiar faces: Kepler Wessels, Graeme Wood, Geoff Lawson and Jeff Thomson were all there, the latter with a disturbing new bleached blond mullet. As his captain told the press, 'He can bowl a brisk medium pace now and move the ball around, which is going to be very useful.' (This was pure kidology. He still ran in and tried to bowl it as fast as he could.) Of the batsmen, Dirk Wellham and Andrew Hilditch had been recalled, while there were first tours for Greg Ritchie and David Boon. Wayne Phillips was the incumbent keeper, Simon O'Donnell the promising all-rounder. New bowlers included baby-faced tearaway Craig McDermott, punk off-spinner Greg Matthews, and 38-year-old leg-spinner Bob 'Dutchy' Holland, who would have to get used to being called 'ageless' if he so much as took a single wicket.

John S: That was the peak of my cricket nerdery. I can recall – and I've probably still got it – drawing up a sheet with all the names of the Australian tour party, and I got all their autographs. Murray Bennett. Bob Holland. Even Dirk Wellham.

England were unusually confident. The horrors of the black-wash had been forgotten, or at least airbrushed from memory; the triumph in India was fresh and famous. Graham Gooch and

Peter Willey came straight back into the squad for the three ODIs, as did a refreshed Ian Botham, who had lost some weight.

Tom H: It was Botham's mullet year. The blond highlights in his mullet radiate in my memory like beams of sunlight.

England duly lost the first ODI. Botham was out for 72 playing a reverse sweep and, the following day, Peter May banned England players from attempting the stroke. He said he had thumbed through the MCC coaching book and been unable to find it. Australia won the second match as well, mainly because of Border's 85 not out. It was his seventh innings on the tour, and his seventh score of 50 or more. Gower, by contrast, couldn't score a run. The rumbles were beginning. Was the captaincy affecting his form? Was his form affecting his captaincy? When was Gatting going to get the job? In the final ODI at Lord's, Gower scored 102, Gooch got 117 not out (after 115 at Edgbaston), England won by eight wickets and the rumbles ceased.

For the first Test at Headingley, Phil Edmonds was dropped in favour of two 'rebel' off-spinners, Willey and John Emburey. Willey was 35, had dodgy knees and was amazed to have lasted this long. In his book *Ashes '85*, Matthew Engel diagnosed 'a classic committee botch', a compromise between Peter May's desire to have the country's best off-spinner in the team and Gower's worries over the batting. Which was odd, as to most of us it looked like the strongest England batting line-up in years. Derek Randall, for instance, would score 2151 first-class runs this summer and not get within a sniff of the Test side. Boycott, with 1657 runs at 77, was ready for the call that never came. Even so, England went into the match with only four front-line bowlers, Allott, Botham, Cowans and Emburey. When Gooch came on for a trundle, someone in the crowd shouted, 'Get a proper bowler!'

Andrew Hilditch batted well, nevertheless, to score 119 out of Australia's first innings 331, which looked a decent score on

another slightly iffy Headingley wicket, with occasional low
bounce, uninterrupted cloud cover, occasional stoppages for rain
and spectators in mufflers. At the end of day two, England were
134 for two, with Tim Robinson on 66 not out. He had started
with an edged four and Greg Ritchie dropped him at third slip
when he was on 22. But on Saturday the sun came out and
England roared on to 484 for nine. 'It would be churlish to be
critical of the pitch at this stage,' said Gower at the press conference. Border said Australia's bowling performance had been the
worst in years. Lawson had been ill before the Test and hadn't
recovered; Thomson was off the boil. Craig McDermott had
carried the attack, such as it was. Robinson's 175 was the highest on an Ashes debut since 1904, just pipping Randall's 174 in
the Centenary Test at Melbourne. The innings we'd remember,
though, was Botham's 51-ball 60, with ten fours and two sixes.
The following morning Downton (54) and the bowlers took
the score up to 533, England's highest total against Australia in a
decade.

But having selected their side for a draw, how were they going
to force a win? After Wood hooked Botham to long leg's waiting
hands, Hilditch and Wessels settled in and put on 139 at four an
over. 'The pattern of the match was holding,' wrote Engel, 'with
the batsmen in control to a bewildering extent.' Then Emburey
changed ends to bowl uphill, got one to keep low and Wessels
was bowled off his pads for 64. Hilditch went soon after for 80,
but Phillips hit a handsome 91, and England were set 123 to win.
In 1981, Australia had had to chase 130, and failed. England
supporters grew nervous. Good grief, I had feigned illness to take
the day off from the job I wasn't doing very well to watch this.
Fortunately Australia had no specialist spinner: they had gone for
the four bowlers option too. England lost four wickets for 83,
and five in all, but Lamb and Willey brought us home. Willey, the
extra batsman. So what do I know?

Less than the selectors, obviously, who dropped him for the

Lord's Test in favour of Phil Edmonds. Norman Cowans went too, replaced by Neil Foster. 'Cowans has no divine right to play for England,' wrote Engel. 'But [he] is capable of deliveries, overs, and even spells of world-class speed and hostility . . . One up in the series, Australia in disarray, England's best stroke-making line-up in years in prime form, and one of the reasons for dropping the main strike bowler is to strengthen the batting. You want to weep sometimes, you really do.' The selectors had demonstrated their traditional preference for fast-medium reliability (and, let's be frank, uniformity) over potentially match-winning speed. Four years later Allen Synge would write that 'somewhere along the chain of command, there was a failure to capitalise on the promise of Cowans. Like other fast bowlers during the [Peter] May era, he gradually faded from the England scene.' Aged 24, he had just played his last Test.

And here's another selectorial oddity: England had picked Emburey and Edmonds, 32 and 34 respectively, together for only the second time. Australia brought in Bob 'Dutchy' Holland for Jeff Thomson, thus increasing the average age of the side by four months. The match was similar to the first one, except it was the other way round. England made a slightly under-par 290 in the first innings. Gower scored 86 – 'no one in cricket habitually makes better 80s,' said Engel – and McDermott took six for 70, having been rather more carefully nurtured than our Norman. Australia responded with 425, thanks mainly to Border's 196 and Greg Ritchie's 94. The pair put on 216 for the fifth wicket, Border with his usual bristly commitment, and Ritchie occasionally loose but an imposing presence at the crease. Indeed, a certain fondness for pies had been detected. 'Strong man, powerfully built,' said Tony Lewis on the BBC. 'Elegant, though rounded of profile,' wrote David Frith in *Wisden*. When Border had made 87, the Australian bogey number, he ran down the pitch and clumped Edmonds straight to Gatting at short leg, who made the mistake of throwing the ball up in celebration before he had caught it. Border was already on his way to the pavilion, but the ball was on the ground and Dickie Bird ruled that Gatting hadn't been in control of it for long enough for the catch to count. Border was more than happy to carry on.

Botham, though, was bowling genuinely quickly at times, despite a sore ankle, and his five-for was his 25th for England. Batting again on Saturday evening, England lost Gooch and Robinson in swift succession and sent in two nightwatchmen, Emburey and Allott. When a team sends in two nightwatchmen, you know they are going to lose. By the time Botham joined Gatting the following morning, England were 98 for six, still 37 behind. Of the 131 they put on, Botham made 85. It was another savage onslaught. Border dared not bowl Simon O'Donnell, who had been given the treatment at Headingley. So 'Dutchy' soldiered on, greyer at the end of the innings than at the start, and finally got his man, caught at cover point while trying to hit it over long on. Gatting was the not-out batsman on 75, 'Dutchy' had five wickets, England had 261 and Australia needed 127 to win. Maybe foolishly, Border had expressed the opinion that anything over 150 would be tough on this wicket. What he meant, of course, was anything under 150. Australia were 22 for three when Allott bowled Ritchie, and 65 for five when Edmonds bowled Boon. The crowd roared every ball. 'Still a lot of cricket to be played in this match,' said Jim Laker. Needless to say, it was Border who played it. He was 41 not out at the end, and Australia won by four wickets. With uncanny timing, the selectors announced that David Gower would remain England captain for the rest of the summer. If he had lost the first Test too, maybe they would have confirmed him for the rest of his life.

For the third Test at Trent Bridge, Neil Foster (back injury) was replaced by Arnie Sidebottom, who had been twelfth man at Lord's. England won the toss and batted on a flat-looking pitch. Gooch (70) and Robinson (38) made a sound start, and then Gower and Gatting put on 187 for the third wicket. Gower's tenth Test century took three and a quarter hours. At work I watched some of it on the TV in the conference room: a sacking offence, but it would have been worth it. 'How good it is to see David Gower moving that front foot to the ball,' said Tom Graveney. 'Majestic stroke.' 'Majestic' was but one adjective that would be overused by BBC commentators describing Gower's batting this summer, the others being 'nonchalant', 'casual' and 'elegant'. Richie Benaud went one better, and called him 'casually elegant'.

At 358 for two, though, Gower mis-pulled a short ball straight past Holland, who got a touch on it as it went by. The ball hit the stumps at the bowler's end, and Gatting, on 74, was out of his ground. He looked very cross indeed. England collapsed to 456 all out. Gower's 166 had taken six hours and Lawson, without bowling particularly well, had taken five for 103. Australia needed 257 to save the follow-on, but England's latest attack was less than incisive. Graeme Wood, having made only 77 runs in eight innings on tour, scored 172 and Greg Ritchie 146 in a match-killing total of 539. Allott went down with a stomach bug, and Arnie split his left big toe painfully and messily. To cheer us all up England used 41-year-old Basharat Hassan as a substitute fielder, under the lid at short leg, his speciality. Only that day he had announced his retirement from the first-class game. He had been fielding there for more than a day before a bat-and-pad chance came, and he dropped it. Maybe he was as bored as the rest of us. There is little in cricket duller than a high-scoring draw.

At Old Trafford, Sidebottom's injury brought in Jonathan Agnew for his first Test of the summer. ('If Cowans is a bowler of occasionally devastating spells,' wrote Matthew Engel, 'then Agnew is a bowler of occasionally devastating deliveries.' Sidebottom, of course, would never be selected again.) Australia would have been unchanged, but Wood had been hit above his left eye in a county match at Northampton, and was replaced by Greg Matthews. Meanwhile my friend Brian, who had moved to

California a few years previously to become a theoretical physi-
cist, rang up and said he would be home (in the Wirral) for a
couple of weeks and did I fancy going to the Test match? I certainly did. It was the first Ashes Test match I had ever been to,
and a little disappointingly for this book, I can remember nothing of the game at all. I know we saw two days' worth, but I can't
even remember which two. I can't even ask Brian: he is long
dead. Memories shared count for nothing if there's no one left to
share them with. But I really should have been taking some
notes.

All I do remember is that the sun shone. Almost everyone I
interviewed remembered 1985 as a summer of unceasing warmth
and sunshine, when it was in fact one of the wettest summers on
record. About the only time it didn't rain, apparently, was during
the Test matches. The Old Trafford pitch was wet and slow. 'If
the wickets go on getting slower and slower,' wrote Engel, 'before
long the ball will just stop dead on pitching, like a deck quoit.'
Gower put Australia in, saw them reach 71 for no wicket just
before lunch, and started to wear his 'What? Me Worry?' smile.
Then the spinners took four wickets, which may not have been
part of the plan, and Australia were all out for 257. David Boon,
who had been hanging on to his place by fingernails, made 61,
and Botham and Edmonds each took four wickets. England then
took charge: Gooch (74), Gower (47), Gatting (160) and Lamb
(67) pummelled the bowling once more. Simon O'Donnell, it
was becoming clear, was never going to trouble Test batsmen on
a good wicket. Lawson was perpetually struggling with his fitness
and health (ricked neck and asthma attack in this match). Dutchy
Holland was tidy – that dismissive term for spinners who aren't
taking any wickets. Eight wickets fell in the innings to bowlers –
or rather, bowler, as McDermott took them all, eight for 141 in
36 overs. In nine Tests since being made vice-captain, Gatting
had scored 998 runs. This was his third Test century, but his first
in England.

So Australia batted again 225 runs behind. The pitch was slower than ever, and Border more determined than ever. In scoring 146 not out, his seventh century of the tour, he was supported in good stands by Wessels, Ritchie and Phillips, and the game was saved. England had looked by far the better side, but overall nearly a day had been lost to the weather. There were only two Tests left, at Edgbaston and the Oval, and the score was still 1–1.

For Edgbaston, Paul Allott and Jonathan Agnew were dropped: neither would play another Test. The selectors' revolving-door policy brought in Kent swing bowler Richard Ellison, who had played five Tests against West Indies and India the previous year, and Les Taylor of Leicestershire, a former miner who had only taken up cricket full time in his mid-twenties, and had gone to South Africa in 1982 with the rebels. For Australia, Graeme Wood returned from injury and Jeff Thomson was back for a final hurrah. Gower won the toss again, and put Australia in again. It was cold, damp, and Birmingham. The ball didn't swing at all and at the end of the first day Australia were 181 for two. Wessels was playing the innings we had been expecting from him all summer: ugly, stubborn, utterly effective. There was a theory abroad that Australia would go for the draw here and hope to sneak a win at the Oval, where the pace and bounce would suit their bowlers. But on the second morning the ball miraculously started to swing, Wessels went for 83 and Australia collapsed to 218 for seven, with Richard Ellison taking four for 12 in 43 balls. It was classic English swing bowling on 'the sort of day that made people want to emigrate to Australia in the first place', wrote Engel. After several stoppages for rain, the new ball was taken and Lawson, McDermott and later Thomson whacked the cover off it. Australia were 335 for eight at the end of the day, and I think we'd all given up.

In fact I know we had. On the Saturday I myself was playing

cricket for my team, the Captain Scott Invitation XI, on a council pitch in Ealing against a team of journalists called the Old Talbotians. What happened in the game I could not possibly tell you, although I am told we won. What I do remember was walking off at the end of the game and someone saying, I wonder what the Test score is, and no one knowing, because we had all forgotten about it. Someone had a transistor radio. We switched it on. It was close of play, and England were 355 for one, leading by 20. We all just stood there, our mouths open. One or two of us chuckled in disbelief. I had thoroughly enjoyed the afternoon – winning was a rare and beautiful experience for us – but the sense of having missed something infinitely more significant was overpowering.

Australia had lost both remaining wickets (Lawson for 53) in five balls without adding a run, and Gooch had been caught behind off Thomson (his 200th wicket in Tests, and his last). Five or so hours later, Gower was 169 not out and Robinson 140 not out. I watched the highlights again recently. It's true that the Australians bowled an awful lot of half-volleys on leg stump, but Gower was magnificent. He is the favourite player of an awful lot of men in their forties, but it's hard to imagine that he ever batted better, more effectively or satisfyingly than he did in this series. To show how far the balance had shifted, we saw him reach his century in the afternoon with a cover drive off Jeff Thomson, *while wearing a floppy sunhat*. Tell that to Dennis Amiss and Mike Denness.

Richard B: My almost carnal love of Gower. It's sad, it's obvious, it's a bit of a cliché, but there you go. The cover drive: made you purr. A friends of ours took my son on one side and said, does your dad always go on about cricket? And Alfie said, well, he does want me to play the cover drive all the time, and I don't know why.

You still might have put money on Australia escaping with a draw. There were two days left after the rest day, and the pitch was flatter than a very flat thing. Border had made only 45 in the first innings, so he was due a score. Remember Brearley's maxim: you must respect the opposition enough to finish them off when you have the chance. Clearly we needed to respect them more.

As it happened, this third day of the fifth Test was the turning point. Fortunately a sudden but severe gastric bug (symptomless, fortunately) compelled me to stay off work on Monday and watch it all on TV. Robinson played on to Lawson for a mere 148, but Gower went on to 215, off 314 balls in 451 minutes. Gatting walloped an unbeaten 100 and, best of all, we had the famous Botham cameo. It lasted seven balls. The first, off McDermott, he hit for six over long on into the pavilion. 'What about that?' said Jim Laker, chuckling. 'That is quite incredible, quite incredible.' The third ball also went into the pavilion, but a higher floor. The seventh was caught brilliantly inside the deep mid-wicket boundary by Thomson, who raised a finger to the crowd behind him. Botham had made 18 and it was, in some ways, the most joyous innings I have ever seen. My memory was that he grinned when he got out, but this is a false memory; in fact he looked rather narked. Maybe it was me who was grinning. In the third over of Australia's second innings, Botham dug one in short and Andrew Hilditch, who had been caught in the deep hooking at Lord's, did it again. At the close Australia were 37 for five. 'Real drama,' said Jim Laker. Ellison had taken the other four wickets in 14 balls. The big one, of course, was Border's: somehow Ellison had sneaked one through the tiniest chink in his defence to bowl him.

Day five: rain lashed down and play was delayed by three hours. I was so frustrated I seriously considered going into work. When the typhoon finally relented at 2.30 p.m., Greg 'Fat Cat' Ritchie and Wayne Phillips, the not-out batsmen overnight, seemed re-energised. Phillips played his favourite back-foot off-side shots with such aplomb that at one point Botham was bowling to an eight-one field, although admittedly, most of them were in the slips. Runs didn't matter. Wickets did, but we weren't getting any. After tea, with Australia on 113 for five, Gower turned to Phil Edmonds. As bowlers often did to Phillips, Edmonds bowled one a little short. Phillips middled it, straight on to Lamb's instep at silly point. The ball bounced up and Gower, at silly mid-off, took the catch. England appealed. Umpire David Shepherd, at the bowler's end, didn't have a clear view. He went over to David Constant at square leg. They had a little chat. Shepherd raised the finger. Phillips was 'distraught', said Richie Benaud. Television replays were, as they say, 'inconclusive'. Ask any Australian of 35 or over and he will assure you that the ball bounced before it hit Lamb's foot. England's fielders, David Constant, all my friends and I were certain it hadn't. Gower later called Constant 'courageous'. Border was 'very, very disappointed with the decision'.

Australia then collapsed. Fat Cat Ritchie gave a bat-and-pad catch *and walked*. The last five wickets fell in 47 minutes. England won by an innings and 118 runs. Richard Ellison's four for 27 gave him ten wickets in the match. Fred Trueman, a bowler, gave him the man of the match award. If England didn't lose at the Oval, the Ashes would be theirs.

Thomson was now dropped for the last time. Dutchy Holland and Simon O'Donnell, who would both make brief, unsuccessful returns to Tests in 1985/86, also went. The tour's three Lucans, fast bowler Dave Gilbert, slow left-armer Murray Bennett (who always wore sunglasses) and Oval specialist Dirk Wellham, replaced them. England won the toss, and Gooch and Gower put on 351 for the second wicket, the sixth best England Test partnership in history (pushing the previous week's 331 by Gower and Robinson down to seventh place). 'Golden days for English cricket this summer,' said Jim Laker when the 300 partnership came up. I was 25, impoverished, without a girlfriend, failing in a job for which I had not the smallest aptitude, and drinking too much in pubs with friends as prematurely washed up as I was; but for these few weeks I was happy.

Andy R: I remember going down the Oval without a ticket, getting in and watching Gower bat for a bit. It was sublime. It was dream cricket.

Tom H: It was Botham's last season as an effective bowler, so it has a slight feel of the Edwardian age for me. August 1914 – a slight bitter-sweet feel.

Andy R: What I also remember about eighty-five was the whole camaraderie of it. I remember Jeff Thomson with his son in the pavilion, watching the game; and the teams getting on really well.

Gower was out before the close for 157 and England were 376 for three, with Gooch 196 not out. They were the seventh and eighth centuries scored by England batsmen in the series, and discounting Gatting's 100 not out at Edgbaston (simply because it was not out), the lowest had been Tim Robinson's 148 in the same match. The following day, to keep us all honest, 11 wickets fell. Gooch added no more to his score, and England were all out for 464. But Australia were a beaten team. Yet again, Botham posted two long legs, and plugged in a short one to Hilditch the Happy Hooker. Yet again, he hooked uppishly and was caught. Emburey bowled Wessels ('The top-spinner,' said Richie) and the great prize, the captain, inside-edged Edmonds on to his stumps. At close they were 145 for six. Fat Cat Ritchie, Australia's best batsman after Border, went on to 64 not out on Saturday morning, but Australia were dismissed for 241, with a suddenly confident and effective England bowling line-up sharing the wickets. After a little more rain, in this soggiest of summers, Australia were batting again and, at close, 62 for four. 'The fight goes on,' said Border. 'But obviously we're not in a real good position. I look back on Headingley eighty-one and think maybe the good Lord will send something down for me one day.' He was right. The good Lord would send him down the 1990s.

On Monday a packed house saw 95 minutes of play, as Australia folded for 129, to lose by an innings and 94 runs. Ellison had taken five for 46, but Les Taylor took the final wicket, Murray Bennett, caught and bowled. It was the first time since 1956 that England had beaten Australia by an innings twice running. Gooch was man of the match, while Gower, with 732 runs, was man of the series. 'The greatest comeback since Charles II,' said the *Guardian*. On the pavilion balcony Gower held up the urn, or possibly a £3 plastic replica. An hour later it was raining hard.

Bill M: It was one of the most wonderful summers of my life. Totally because of that series. All my memories are of us bowling them out or scoring tons of runs. Everything was right with the world that summer. I think, out of all the series in my lifetime, that was the only one that felt like that because there wasn't any anguish. Because it just looked inevitable that we were going to win.

Ten

1986/87

Ian Botham would make a great Aussie.
                                        Jeff Thomson in 1986

In the press conference after the 1985 victory, David Gower said that the West Indies would probably be 'quaking in their boots'. Obviously he wasn't being serious: he wasn't Tony Greig. But like Greig, he was forced to eat these words, regurgitate them and eat them again, as his team experienced blackwash number two. What had appeared, to our innocent eyes, the most accomplished England team in a generation was demolished by one of the best teams that has ever played. 'In cold fact, England never had a hope,' wrote John Thicknesse in *Wisden*. Inadequate preparation and poor pitches set them up, and the West Indian fast bowlers knocked them down. What did become apparent, though, was how important to Gower had been Gatting's vice-captaincy. Being British we naturally see all this in class terms: Gower as the languid poshie, Gatting as the bustling NCO. But when Gatting had his nose crushed by Malcolm Marshall in the first one-day international and had to return to London to have it put together again, the heart seemed to go out of the team. Gower's 'inability to lift a beaten team's morale . . . was as apparent as in 1984,' said

Thicknesse. The captain was the only batsman to average even 30 with the bat; only Emburey of the bowlers averaged under 40. It was time to start afresh.

But obviously it couldn't happen right away. Like Denness in 1975, Gower was given the first Test at home against India, lost it and was sacked. (Peter May told the media first and the media told Gower.) Gatting inherited a team desperately low on confidence, with all memory of 1985 wiped clean as though it had never happened. Both home series that season, against India and New Zealand, were lost 1–0. Hundreds of players were used. Worst of all, the tabloids had been after Ian Botham again, and he was forced to confess that he had 'used' cannabis during the West Indies tour. The Lords blazers banned him for four Tests. His first match back was the last of the summer, the Oval Test against New Zealand, and the first one we had looked like winning for exactly a year. Unfortunately, it rained for two days and the match was drawn, giving New Zealand their first ever series victory in England.*

The squad that left for Australia in October 1986 was therefore given little or no chance by anyone. There were some notable absentees. Graham Gooch was worn out and needed a winter off. Tim Robinson had been found out in the West Indies; Richard Ellison had done his back in; Paul Downton had given way to Nottinghamshire's Bruce French. But an experienced core remained: Gatting (48 caps), Gower (86), Lamb (46), Botham (85), Edmonds (41) and Emburey (37). The extra middle-order batsman (i.e. the reserve) was James Whitaker of Leicestershire, while the three openers were Chris Broad of

---

* Years later Jeremy Coney, the New Zealand captain, told *The Wisden Cricketer*, 'We did believe that England would self-destruct. They had too many selectors, a tendency to amputate vital organs, in this case Ian Botham, and they were tinkerers, particularly at home. We knew if we got things right, we could take the tour.'

Nottinghamshire, who had played with moderate success against the Windies in 1984; Wilf Slack of Middlesex, who had ended the season festooned in runs; and Bill Athey, once of Yorkshire, now of Gloucestershire, admired by Gatting for his pure technique and sound temperament. The four pace bowlers were Graham Dilley, who, according to Gatting in his tour diary, 'had proved a hard-working, number-one strike bowler during the summer, much missed when injured for two Test matches'; Neil Foster, who despite yet another disappointing Test at Lord's, had taken a hundred wickets for Essex; Gladstone Small of Warwickshire, the neckless wonder, marginally less fast than the others but more reliable; and Phillip DeFreitas of Leicestershire, 20 years old, who had taken 97 wickets in his first full season. The big surprise was the second wicketkeeper: Jack Richards of Surrey, who barged in front of Downton, Steve Rhodes and Jack Russell because of his batting. Just as Slack was clearly a Gatting pick, so Richards may have gained the support of Micky Stewart, the assistant manager on tour, and a Surrey man through and through. These were not good years to be playing for Lancashire or Yorkshire.

Robin W: They were rubbished by everybody. I remember feeling really ashamed of that side when they went over there. I mean, Bill Athey . . .

What we needed, above all else, was a good, confident start. Instead, England were filleted by Queensland. Put in on a greentop, they were all out for 135 in the first innings, and although they managed 339 in the second (Botham 86, Foster 74 not out, Lamb 65) they lost easily by five wickets. At Adelaide against South Australia, Lamb and Whitaker scored centuries, Emburey took six wickets in the second innings and it was England's turn to win by five wickets. But the England batsmen were struggling against the left-arm over-the-wicket seamers they kept facing: in particular, neither slack nor Gower could buy a run. Bruce French had missed a stumping and dropped a catch, to universal shock, but it was the frailty of the batting that persuaded the selectors to replace him with Jack Richards for the game against Western Australia. This was drawn, just. England's first innings of 152 had not inspired much confidence. Martin Johnson, then of the *Independent*, made the comment for which he may always be remembered, that there was only one problem with this team: 'They can't bat, they can't bowl and they can't field'. Wrote Gatting: 'That provoked a "we'll show them" response from the lads. Perhaps it was just the thing to get us fired up.'

All this distracted us from Australia's problems, which may have been the idea. In 1985/86 they had lost 2–1 at home to New Zealand, a previously unimaginable humiliation, and drawn 0–0 with India. Then they went to New Zealand and lost 1–0. During these series new players did emerge: Geoff Marsh, Western Australia's limpet-like opener; Bruce Reid, six-foot-eight-inch beanpole left-arm paceman; and a 20-year-old bowling all-rounder called Steve Waugh. Graeme Wood and Andrew Hilditch had gone, the latter for good, and Kepler Wessels, less popular in person than his runs had been, had joined the Australian 'rebels' in South Africa, before re-emerging overnight as the true biltong-scoffing South African we had always known him to be. Wayne Phillips had had a go at opening the batting, and called the selectors 'idiots' when he wasn't selected for the 1986/87 tour of India, so that was the end of him. Punk off-spinner Greg Matthews had been given a run in the team, on the Geoff Miller basis that he also scored useful runs. David Boon was gradually making a reputation for himself, as was Dean Jones, the Victorian stropmeister who had been recalled for the tour of India and made a famous and courageous 210 at Madras in cruel heat. The Test had been tied, Jones had ended up in hospital on a saline drip, and coach Bobby Simpson said it was the best innings anyone had ever played for Australia. This tour too had been drawn 0–0, which meant Australia had won one Test in 12 and no series out of four. Rebuilding, after the Lillee-Chappell-Marsh retirements and the South African defections, was taking a long time.

For the first Test at the Gabba in Brisbane, Gatting and his fellow selectors decided on Athey rather than Slack as Chris Broad's opening partner, and DeFreitas as third seam bowler to partner Dilley and Botham. For Australia, McDermott was out after two poor tours in a row, and Geoff Lawson, recalled after a year out with a back injury, was surprisingly left out of the final XI. Believing the advance publicity that England were hopeless against left-arm seamers, Australia played two: Bruce Reid, already part of the furniture, and new boy Chris Matthews, who had taken a hatful against England for Western Australia. The third seamer, playing only his second Test, was the grunting Victorian, Merv Hughes, 'a player we knew little about,' wrote Gatting. It's hard now, years later, to imagine a point in your life when you didn't know anything about Merv Hughes. What a state of grace that must have been.

Gatting lost the toss. On television he looked a picture of misery. As he later admitted in his tour diary, he hadn't had a clue what to do and was quite relieved when Border asked him to bat. At the end of a rain-interrupted day, England were 198 for two and Gatting was a happy man. The Australian quick bowlers, with nine Tests between them, had been nervier than the England batsmen. Chris Broad edged Reid to the new keeper, Tim Zoehrer, for eight but then Athey and Gatting put on 116 for the second wicket. Gatting, who made 61, was impressed with Merv Hughes's aggression, especially his habit of glaring at the batsman when he bowled a good ball, walrus moustache quivering with rage and hands in double teapot formation. The following morning Athey (76) and Lamb (40) were both dismissed without adding a run. Gower, batting at number five, and Botham put on 118 for the fifth wicket. Gower's 51 was the innings of a man trying to play his way back into form. 'It was my most important innings of the tour,' he said later. Botham's 138 was of a different order of magnificence. Gatting said his concentration wavered only once, when Merv took the second new ball. Three of the first four balls were hit for four. The fifth ball he took a giant mow at, and missed by a whisker. Gower had a quiet word. Last ball of the over, Botham played with a straight defensive bat. Shortly before tea, Botham was on 96, DeFreitas was at the other end, and Merv was bowling again. The first two balls were hit for two twos, giving Botham his century. The third ball he hooked for six. Fourth, fifth and sixth balls were hooked or on-driven for fours: 22 off the over. 'Hughes simply glares down the wicket at him,' said Tony Greig on Channel 9. DeFreitas himself contributed 40, and England were all out for 456. Before the close DeFreitas also took his first Test wicket, when Boon obligingly pulled him to Broad at mid-wicket.

'It gets better every day,' wrote Gatting about the third day's play. The plan was to put the spinners on at one end to seal it up, and rotate the faster bowlers at the other, with the wind blowing over their right shoulders. Dilley was fastest and most ferocious and took five for 68, his first ever five-for in Tests. Emburey gave them nothing, conceding 45 runs off 22 consecutive overs. And when he needed a break, Gatting could bring on Edmonds. Border instantly sliced a catch to DeFreitas at backward point. Australia were 159 for five. With the second new ball, Dilley had Greg Ritchie caught at gully for 41 and Steve Waugh caught behind for 0, both to balls that lifted and moved away. Although the punk off-spinner withstood all to make 56 not out, Australia failed to save the follow-on by nine runs. Batting again the following day, Geoff Marsh, neat, balanced, playing late, hunkered down for a long stay at the crease. England managed only five wickets on this day, and a partnership of 113 between Marsh and Ritchie for the fourth wicket held them up for three hours. But the second new ball again saw off Fat Cat, lbw to DeFreitas, who

also bowled Marsh on the last morning for 113, his third century
in just ten Tests. Emburey scythed through the tail to pick up five
for 80. England needed 77 to win, and lost three wickets in
doing so. Says Gatting: 'Chris Broad produced the stroke of the
day, for me, when he stood up on his toes and cracked Merv
Hughes magnificently to the extra-cover boundary for the winning run.' Allan Border was too angry and upset to attend the
post-match TV interview, and sent his deputy, David Boon, in
his place. It was Gatting's first victory in his sixth match as
England captain, Chris Broad's first victory in his seventh match
for England, and Graham Dilley's second in his 22nd match.
(You may have some vague memory of the first one.)

Normal service was resumed against New South Wales.
England were all out for 197 and 82 and NSW won by eight
wickets. For the Perth Test England were unchanged, while
Australia replaced Merv Hughes with Lawson. Gatting called
'tails' correctly – he had no set policy for calling 'heads' or 'tails'
but, in this case, remembered that Perth was in the west and 'tails'
rhymed with 'Wales' – and Broad and Athey put on 223 for the
first wicket. The previous highest opening stand on tour had
been 16. There's more to good timing than hitting the ball with
the right bit of the bat. Admittedly, Lawson and Chris Matthews
bowled like drains. And the outfield was lightning fast. 'It was like
an upturned saucer,' said Chris Broad. He reached his maiden
Test century just after tea. Athey, dropped early at third slip by
Border, was less lucky on 96, when Reid bowled him with an
inswinging yorker. Lamb was instantly out for 0, but England
ended the day at 272 for two, no doubt feeling rather pleased
with themselves. Broad, wrote Christopher Martin-Jenkins, was
'pink with smiling glory'. Pride comes before a collapse: Broad
was out for 162, and Botham 0. But Gower and Jack Richards
added 207 for the sixth wicket. Richards said later that his best
stroke was the push back past Reid that got him off the mark.
Now he hit a belligerent 133, dominating the afternoon session.

Gower's 136 was his sixth century against Australia and 14th overall: anything even a fraction short was dispatched through mid-wicket. After four and a half hours he holed out to Steve Waugh on the boundary. 'And there's no way in the world he was going to drop that,' said Tony Greig.

John S: The great thing about 1986/87 was the Channel 9 coverage. The music, the commentary, and Tony Greig. Botham's hundred at Brisbane, I remember he called 'a great exhibition of powerhouse batting'.

Tom H: How different the television pictures looked from Australia: sort of bleached out. The umpires all wore different clothes. Daddles the cartoon duck when you were out for 0. And generally the television presentation seemed slicker and cooler.

But I always liked Jim Laker and Peter West. I found the sheen on Peter West's forehead comforting, somehow. I think if I was captured by al-Qaeda, that's one of the memories I would cling to.

Gatting could declare on 592 for eight. So who would win, England or the pitch? Boon was out cheaply, playing on to Dilley, and Steve Waugh came to the crease as nightwatchman. Imagine that. He scored 71 and Border, inevitably, made 125, his 20th Test century, constantly sweeping Emburey to disturb his line and driving Botham and DeFreitas in all directions. He was last out, just after Australia had saved the follow-on. Leading by 191, England had to bash quick runs, but Border set defensive fields and Bruce Reid and Steve Waugh bowled to them. Waugh took five for 69, and Reid three for 58. (CMJ had a lot of time for Reid: 'a bag of sticks to look at, but a fine bowler with an ideal body action.') Gatting himself made 70, but his declaration at the end of the fourth day was thought by some (notably Phil Edmonds) to be overly cautious. Australia needed 391, which they were never going to get, and a partnership of 126 between Geoff Marsh (49) and Dean Jones (69) sealed the draw. The pitch celebrated a famous victory. Chris Broad was named man of the match.

'Disaster, absolute disaster,' wrote Mike Gatting a few days later. 'And I was the cause of it.' What had he done? Pushed Botham under a train? Enjoyed the company of a barmaid in off-duty hours? No, he had overslept for the game against Victoria, and taken the field twenty minutes after play started. The press assumed he had been up to no good, but there was no evidence of that, and Gatting forcibly denied it. As it happened, England were bowling that morning and only had two seamers, so Gatting bowled a longish spell and took four for 31. But the press went to town on the incident. Wrote Gatting, 'I was surprised by the anger in some reports in English newspapers written by cricket writers, including one or two who frequently arrive late in the press box, particularly at home Test matches.' Go on, name names, Fat Gatt! I can see the headline now: 'Journalist Has Hangover Shock'. Australians renamed the errant skipper Rip Van Gatting. Out on the field, England completed an efficient win over the state side by five wickets. Athey and Bruce French scored fifties in the first innings, and Gladstone Small took five wickets in the second.

A more significant problem was Ian Botham's fitness. On the last day at Perth he had torn a rib muscle, and wouldn't be fit for the third Test at Adelaide. Gatting thought the pitch there was made for runs. So, slightly defensively, he went for the extra batsman (James Whitaker) rather than the extra bowler (Gladstone Small). Australia dropped Chris Matthews and Geoff Lawson, recalled Merv and, after a four-year gap, the South Australian leg-spinner Peter Sleep. Gatting was right about the pitch. Australia won the toss and scored 514 for five. England were all out for 455. 'There were four individual hundreds,' wrote CMJ, 'of which Broad's 116 was the most important for his side, Boon's 103 the most significant for his own career, Border's 100 not out the most predictable and Gatting's 100 by some way the most brilliant.' Broad and Athey's first-wicket stand of 113 and Broad and Gatting's second wicket stand of 161 meant that England were never in any real danger of following on. The pitch was too good and the bowling not quite good enough. According to the *Wisden Book of Test Cricket*, 'a female spectator set up an ironing board and attended to her laundry throughout the day's play'. James Whitaker went in at number seven, behind a nightwatchman, and scored 11. He never played Test cricket again.

Still, it was Christmas, and after victories over Tasmania and the Prime Minister's XI, England gathered for the annual fancy dress party. Bill Athey went as a schoolmaster, and his wife Janet as a naughty schoolgirl. Phil and Frances Edmonds were convicts, Jack Richards was an American Indian chieftain, and Phillip DeFreitas was Diana Ross, complete with moustache. James Whitaker's hotel chambermaid may be the reason he only ever played one Test. On Boxing Day the decisive Test began. Australia needed to win both remaining Tests to regain the Ashes.

As it happened, the first day at Melbourne went even better than Gatting or his team could have hoped. There was a brief moment of concern in the morning when Graham Dilley said his right knee wouldn't last the full five days. Gladstone Small played instead, and Botham returned for Whitaker. Australia had decided they needed another bowler, Craig McDermott, and so left out Ritchie. Gatting thought this an extraordinary decision, and it persuaded him to bowl when he won the toss. Small removed Boon soon enough, but it wasn't until Gatting made a double bowling change, bringing on Emburey and Botham, that things started to happen. Twice in his first four deliveries, Botham dropped short. Marsh didn't play a shot but after the ball had gone by he feinted the pull shot he obviously wished he had played in each case. Sure enough the next ball was just as short, but a bit wider and faster. Marsh would normally have cut it, one of his favourite shots. But he pulled it, got a top-edge and Jack Richards pulled off an acrobatic catch above his head. Clever bowling, which also looked completely innocuous, which I suppose made it even cleverer.

Border went soon after, to a fantastic low catch by Richards, and Australia were 80 for three at lunch. The other seven wickets went down between lunch and tea. Small bowled superbly, swinging the ball away and maintaining the perfect line on or just outside off stump. Botham winkled out batsmen with endless variation, changes of pace and general tomfoolery. In his own words: 'I was about 50–60 per cent fit but we felt like it might do a bit, so I waddled in off a few paces and the Australian batsmen obliged.' Botham took five for 41, Small five for 48 and Richards five catches, equalling the England record for an Ashes match. Maybe his best was the 30-yard sprint and dive to take McDermott's top edge over his shoulder. Only Dean Jones (59) stayed for any length of time. Australia were all out for 141. England were 95 for one at the close, for the loss of Athey. This was good news to wake up to on the morning of Saturday, 27 December 1986, with all day to mull it over and wait for the TV highlights.

(I watched the tape of this series recently with my six-year-old son, who has a surprisingly subtle appreciation of Test cricket for one of his age. 'There's always a fat one on each team, isn't there?' said James, as Gatting pulled a short ball murderously for four.)

The skipper was jubilant after day one, disappointed and frustrated after day two. England had scored 349, to give them a first innings lead of 208, but he thought they might have blown it. Chris Broad had scored 112, his third century in successive Tests, and only Hobbs (twice) and Hammond had ever done that before against the Australians. Thereafter England had given their wickets away, four each to McDermott and Reid. According to CMJ, 'once or twice McDermott behaved a little like McEnroe, which did his reputation no good'.

Mark McC: Billy Bloodnut. Because he's ginger, and always on the verge of exploding.

Gatting may have thought his team hadn't done enough, but

Melbourne's cricket followers clearly thought otherwise: attendance was well down on the first day. You have to admire Australians' capacity for ignoring defeat. Accentuate the positives. And pretend the negatives haven't happened.

Day three proved that Gatting had fretted unnecessarily. The pitch was turning and the Middlesex spin twins exerted total control. The top order batsmen – Marsh (60), Jones (21), Border (34), S. R. Waugh (49) – stayed for as long as they could. The middle and lower order didn't. Half an hour after tea Australia were all out for 194, and England had won by an innings and a handful. They shouldn't have left out Greg Ritchie. England had toyed with leaving out Edmonds, and thank heaven they hadn't: he had taken three wickets and had a part in two run outs. Gladstone Small, with seven wickets and 21 not out batting at number eleven, was named man of the match. 'In their present form and mood,' wrote CMJ, 'England would have been a match for all Test teams except the West Indies', and quite soon we would beat them too, albeit in a tinpot one-day tournament no one can now remember. England had the series and the Ashes. Much champagne was poured over young men's heads in celebration. Elton John joined the party in the dressing room, wearing one of his more sober hats and sunglasses indoors. It was the first Ashes match Australia had lost at home inside three days since 1901/02.

John S: It was Botham's extraordinary five-for that did it for me. He came on and bowled a heap of shit and managed to get Dean Jones caught down the leg side, and so on. And I think that made it all the more enjoyable, that we hadn't necessarily played that well and still we'd won.

There followed not the fifth Test in Sydney, but 'the Perth Challenge', a brief and gloriously pointless one-day series. As well as Australia and England, West Indies and Pakistan sent teams. Each played each other once, with the top two teams in the league table playing again in the final. England beat Australia by 37 runs, thanks to an opening stand of 86 between Broad and Athey and a wild, thumping 68 from Botham. England beat West Indies by 19 runs, and Pakistan by three wickets, and in the final they beat Pakistan again, this time by five wickets with nearly ten overs to spare. 'It was a good job thoroughly well done,' said Gatting. It was also the first time England had won a one-day trophy in which more than two teams had taken part.

For the Sydney Test, as so often, the losing team made several changes, at least one of them deeply eccentric. David Boon, Craig McDermott and Greg Matthews were left out; Fat Cat Ritchie came back to open the batting, no less; Dirk Wellham played the last Ashes Test yet again; and an unknown off-spinner from New South Wales, Peter Taylor, was called up. So fantastically obscure was he, this sandy-haired agricultural scientist, that at the age of 30 he had played just six first-class matches, only one of them this season. The selection was universally assumed to be a cock-up. Mark Taylor, of whom we would hear more, had been scoring tons of runs for New South Wales and would have been a like-for-like replacement for Boon. You can imagine the selectorial meeting.

'What about Taylor of New South Wales?'

'Good idea. Any more tea in that pot?'

England's only change was to bring back Dilley, whose knee was better, in place of DeFreitas who, for all his promise, had only taken nine wickets at 49. Allan Border won the toss at last and at the end of the first day Australia were 236 for seven. When he was on five, Dean Jones appeared to have given a straightforward leg-side catch to Jack Richards. Umpire Steve Randell said, 'Not out'. An action replay on the vast new TV screen showed beyond all doubt that Jones had hit the ball. At the end of the day he was 119 not out. Nonetheless, it's worth recording that Steve Waugh had been given out, caught behind for 0, when Gatting thought he might not have been. Swings, roundabouts etc.

Besides, it was day two that really made the difference. The tail kept Dean Jones company while he took his score to 184 not out, and Australia's to 343. Small had taken five for 75. England then lost their first five wickets for 142 runs. Defeat was in the air. But this was a more resilient England team than some. On day three they scrapped their way to 275. Gower hit 72, although the Australians thought he should have been out leg before on the second evening. When he saw the action replay on the big screen, Gower was inclined to agree. 'It must have been going under,' he told Tim Zoehrer. Emburey scored 69 and Richards 46. The accidental Taylor had taken 6 for 78, and 'showed a great deal of potential and maturity,' said Gatting. Emburey was also impressed by him. Indeed, he was bowled by him. 'What a sterling effort this is,' said Tony Greig. 'And the crowd here rising to their feet and applauding what has been a magnificent effort.' 'Certainly has,' agreed Bob Willis, studying the replay. 'Utterly dreadful stroke from Gladstone Small. Misjudges the length completely.'

This was the closest match of the tour by a distance. As Australia batted again, England's bowlers were showing signs of wear and tear. Dilley damaged a muscle in his right shoulder when throwing in from the deep and spent most of the day on the treatment table. Edmonds pulled a groin muscle, and so did Emburey (in separate incidents, fortunately), although it didn't stop either of them bowling more than 40 overs. Dean Jones and Allan Border put on 74 for the third wicket, before Border played on to Edmonds for 49. Half an hour later Australia were seven down. Emburey, bowling with wonderful loop, had taken all four wickets for 16 runs in 49 balls. With Australia on 145 for seven, and Steve Waugh and the accidental Taylor at the crease, Jack Richards made his only significant error of the series. Waugh charged up the pitch to a ball from Edmonds and missed. Richards fluffed the stumping. Two hours later, at tea, Waugh and Taylor were still there. Gatting 'had a few strong words to say in the dressing room'. Within an hour Steve Waugh holed out for 73, Taylor went bat-and-pad for 42 and Merv was bowled trying to hit Emburey to New Zealand. Emburey had his best Test figures, seven for 78. England needed 320 to win and had seven hours in which to get them.

And they were pretty certain they could do it. History suggested otherwise; indeed, history screamed in their ears that they should give up and go home right now. Only once had England ever managed to score as many in the fourth innings to win a Test, at Melbourne in 1928/29. On this occasion, soon after lunch on the fifth day, they were 102 for five. Botham had just been out first ball, chipping to mid-wicket. Jack Richards came out to join Gatting. 'Our position looked impossible, yet I still hadn't given up all hope of pulling it off even at that stage.' He felt in good form and neither Peter Sleep nor Taylor were bowling as well as Edmonds and Emburey had bowled the previous day. Border brought back Hughes for a short burst; Gatting edged but Zoehrer just missed a low chance. In the next over Richards edged Sleep but the ball was heading straight for Border's face, and all he could do was parry it away. It was like a rerun of the previous day's play: flurry of wickets in the morning, stout resistance in the afternoon. At tea they needed 133. With 20 overs to go, they needed 90. Steve Waugh came on to bowl. Gatting made to play his second ball through mid-wicket. The ball stopped on him, and Gatting proffered a return catch. He had made 96. 'And there was no way in the world that Steve Waugh was going to drop this one,' said Tony Greig.

Sleep then bowled Jack Richards. 'And what a beautiful wrong 'un!' said Max Walker in the commentary box. In the stands, two men in T-shirts danced around. 'The Australian crowds go berserk!' screamed Max. Richards had batted three and a half hours for 38. Edmonds was lbw first ball, and it was time for Emburey and Small to batten down the hatches. With three overs to go, and after a lengthy mid-pitch team huddle,

Border handed the ball to his bag of sticks, Bruce Reid. Gladstone Small edged his fourth ball to slip. An over later Emburey was bowled by Sleep, his fifth wicket in the innings. If they had survived six more balls, England would have squeaked the draw. As it was, Australia had their first win in 15 Tests. 'What a heart-stopper,' said Richie Benaud, wearing a blazer that has since been banned by the Geneva Convention. 'And what a marvellous approach to the game, when Mike Gatting continued to look for a win rather than a dull draw. I think that's an enormous credit to the England side.' In other words: suckers!

John S: I remember being infuriated that we lost the last Test. Two-one didn't do justice to England's dominance in that series at all.

But CMJ, not a friend of hyperbole, called it 'England's most successful tour for many years'. We won the Tests, we won the dinky 'Perth Challenge' and in the World Series ODI tournament, which sprawled over January and February, we won four of our eight group games, and became the first team *ever* to beat the Windies in three consecutive ODIs. Then we beat Australia 2–0 in the final. One particular six-ball over sticks in my mind. In their second group game against Australia, at Sydney, England needed 18 to win off the last over. Seven wickets had fallen, Bruce Reid was bowling and Allan Lamb was on strike. After a poor Test series – 144 runs at 18, top score 43 – Lamb had faced 97 balls for his 59 not out and hadn't hit a single boundary. First ball he managed two to deep extra cover after a wild throw. Second ball, four through square leg. Third ball, a vast six over mid-wicket. Third ball, guided to cover, but an overthrow gave him a second. Fourth ball, four through square leg again. Victory with a ball to spare. These days people seem to hit 18 off the last over at will, but in 1986/87 this was a bit special. And this was towards the end of a four-month tour whose itinerary, according to John Thicknesse in *Wisden*, 'could only have been devised by a group of men . . . who did not have to undergo it'. With three separate trips to Perth, England had flown, in internal air miles, the equivalent of a trip round the equator. 'England's genuine team spirit, sound and often brilliant catching, admirable professionalism and will to win, carried them through the last weary weeks of an excessively demanding tour,' said CMJ. We could never have imagined that this was the last time we would glean any enjoyment at all from an Ashes series for 18 years.

Eleven

1989

Border has not so much a style as a modus operandi. He is utterly practical.

John Woodcock in *The Times*

We have since called it the Tour of Gold.

David Boon

The 1986/87 tour was Ian Botham's last. Even though he had been reduced to a gentle medium pace by his rib injury halfway through the tour, he was a vital component of Mike Gatting's party. Indeed, England teams never seemed to know what to do without him. But he was tired of the hassle and the press harassment, and signed a contract to play for Queensland during the English winter. From now on we could have him for English summers only. With hindsight the 1986/87 series can be seen as the last flowering of that great talent. He was now 32 – incredibly, absurdly young, it seems to me now – but the next five years would see only decline and, finally, acceptance of that decline. And with Botham's decline came England's decline. There was no one to replace him.

In 1987 England hosted a five-Test series against Pakistan and lost 1–0. It was a bad-tempered series, mainly because the Lord's blazers ignored Pakistani requests to replace two umpires, David Constant and Ken Palmer, whose competence and impartiality they doubted. It's not as though we didn't have loads of good umpires, so replacing them wouldn't have been difficult. Whereas giving each of them two Tests to preside over could have been seen as arrogant and high-handed – which is how the Pakistanis chose to see it – as well as short-sighted, which it certainly was. (Nor was it fair on Constant or Palmer, whose every decision was then subject to the most intense scrutiny.) Just as 'can't bat, can't bowl, can't field' spurred England on, I always thought the umpires issue inspired Imran Khan's side to heights they hadn't previously been capable of. Pakistani captains had long struggled to unite their teams: in this case English officialdom did it for them. There were also rumbles about Gatting's captaincy. Although he didn't lose many matches, he didn't win many either. Allen Synge believed that 'he could not "pace" a game as Gower could' and that some of the draws 'could have been won with a little more bustle'. Still, the wheels truly fell off on the return trip to Pakistan in 1987/88. It seemed pure revenge, of course, with a little opportunism thrown in. Pakistan won the three-Test series 1–0 against a backdrop of what Martin Johnson in *Wisden* called 'some of the most shameful scenes witnessed in any sport'. In particular, the famous photograph of Gatting and Shakoor Rana screaming at each other at Faisalabad, beamed around the globe, played right into Pakistan's hands. Equally if more secretly pleased, I suspect, were the Lord's blazers who regarded Gatting as an oik, and wanted him replaced by some-one who had been to a proper school. This they were able to do after the first Test in 1988 against the Windies, in which Gatting did something Gower had never managed to do: get away with a draw. But Gatting had also done something else Gower hadn't done: engage in widely publicised late-night discussions with a barmaid in his hotel room. Gatting was booted.

But why should we fans always suffer for the misdemeanours of others? England lost all four remaining Tests under a busload of temporary captains, some of whom were not Peter May's godsons. In the summer's six Tests, England used 28 players. An efficient victory over Sri Lanka in September gave us new hope – false hope, as it transpired, but that's better than nothing. In October 1988, the winter tour fell apart. The Indian government refused to grant visas to eight of the England party, because of their previous connections with South Africa. It didn't help that the captain of the party was G. A. Gooch. The Indians probably thought we had done it just to annoy them. They couldn't have realised that there was no one else. Worse, Gooch had been planning to play for Western Province in South Africa that winter, and had had to be talked into captaining England instead. It was the usual shambles, in other words. Peter May insisted that the selectors' brief had been to pick the best available team, regardless of other considerations. So why had Gatting been sacked? Because of other considerations. After missing the second Test, the rotund one had played poorly in the third and asked not to be considered for the rest of the summer or the winter tour. His disillusionment was absolute. An important talent had thus been pathetically squandered.

In November Peter May resigned, 'the wintry-faced mandarin' as Frank Keating witheringly described him in the *Guardian*. He was replaced by Ted Dexter. We were out of the frying pan of bleak ineptitude, and into the fires of hell.

But at least the players had a winter off. Phil Edmonds had retired after the 1987 season, Jack Richards had played only three more Tests and lost his Surrey contract in 1988, and Bill Athey was gone too, having never quite fulfilled his potential. Or maybe he did fulfil it, in 1986/87, beyond which there was nowhere to go.

For the Australians, though, the long rebuilding process was nearly at an end. In 1987/88, New Zealand had been beaten at home 1–0 (despite Richard Hadlee taking 18 wickets at 19.6). Early the following season Australia had visited Pakistan for three Tests and lost 1–0, encountering many of the same stratagems as England had a year earlier. But they had also, vitally, won the World Cup, beating England by seven runs in the final in Calcutta. The West Indies had then visited for five Tests, and won the first three with their usual ease and ruthlessness. The fourth Test, though, was on a slow turner at Sydney. The West Indies quicks were unmanned, Boon scored a big century and Border, of all people, took 11 wickets in the match with his gentle left-arm tweakers. And then hit the winning runs. The Australians also had the best of the drawn fifth Test, in which Dean Jones scored 216. To lose only 3–1 against this incredible team – Marshall, Ambrose, Walsh and Patterson were the bowlers at this stage – was the corner that had long needed to be turned. England were next.

For Border, a vast amount was at stake. No Australian captain had ever lost three consecutive Ashes series. He had a young and supposedly inexperienced side: only Boon and Lawson survived from 1985 and only Alderman from 1981. But Carl Rackemann, of the 1982/83 side, was back after his South African adventure, and of the 1986/87 side, we still had Geoff Marsh, Dean Jones, Steve Waugh and big Merv Hughes, who had taken 13 wickets in the second Test against West Indies at Perth. Greg Ritchie had gone, maybe surprisingly given his record, but his lack of fitness had become an issue, especially with all the one-day cricket being played. Craig McDermott was out of favour – and probably furious about it – but would come again. The new batsmen were Mark Taylor, the non-accidental one, who had been blooded against the West Indies; Mike Veletta of Western Australia, who had hit 45 in 31 balls in the World Cup final; and a very tall man called Tom Moody. The new wicketkeeper, Ian Healy, had been fast-tracked into the team in Pakistan. The new bowlers were off-spinner Tim

May, leg-spinner Trevor Hohns and a young quick bowler called Greg Campbell, of whom no one can remember anything. Maybe he was the token Greg. These days Geoffs were in the ascendancy.

England won the first ODI easily, the second was tied very excitingly, and Australia won the third. Again, a pattern can be spotted. Lamb, Gooch and Marsh scored centuries; Alderman, Foster and Emburey took most wickets. But the revelation, according to the *Guardian*'s Mike Selvey in his tour book, was Steve Waugh, 'who was consistently able to come in when quick runs were needed and without resorting to anything other than pure strokes, provide them'. Waugh was only 24, but had already played 27 Tests and several million ODIs. The only thing he hadn't managed yet was to score a Test century.

So, to Headingley for the first Test, a ground where the Australians had not won since 1964. England, though, had been beaten in five of their last six Tests here, and this time would have to do without Mike Gatting, who had broken a thumb, and Ian Botham, whose latest comeback this was supposed to be. He had undergone an operation a year earlier to fuse two vertebrae, and hadn't played international cricket since. But in a county match against Glamorgan, he hooked a short ball into his face and fractured his right cheekbone. Australia were without Carl Rackemann, who needed keyhole surgery on a knee injury. (He insisted that he was not 'injury-prone' but 'injury-plagued'.) England called up Robin Smith and Kim Barnett, both of whom had made debuts during the West Indies nightmare the previous summer; and the new wicketkeeper was Gloucestershire's deeply eccentric R. C. 'Jack' Russell. Emburey was left out of the XI, and four seamers were used: Foster, DeFreitas, steady old Derek Pringle and horses-for-courses medium-pacer Phil Newport. It was the least frightening attack we had fielded since the Palaeozoic era. So obviously when Gower won the toss, he put them in.

Sorry, hold on a second. Gower? What's happening here?

Ted Dexter, dashing new chairman of selectors, had wanted Gatting as his captain. Ossie Wheatley, the TCCB's current chief blazer, vetoed this appointment on grounds of oikishness and barmaidery.* So it was back to Gower. He was told he would have the job for the summer, whatever happened. And we hoped for the best.

On the first day, Australia scored 207 for three. Marsh and Boon were out for buttons, but the new left-handed opener Mark Taylor stroked 96 not out, fed by dismal short and wide medium-pace bowling. Gower himself dropped Taylor at slip off DeFreitas with three overs left. But at least we had got Border out, for a mere 66.

On the second day, Australia lost three more wickets, and scored 373 more runs. Taylor was out for 136, a century in only his fifth Test innings. Jones made 79. Even Merv Hughes scored 63 not out. But overshadowing all this, wrote Selvey, was 'an utterly glorious maiden Test century from Steve Waugh, whose unbeaten 177 was compiled in less than five hours, and contained some 24 boundaries and not a sniff of a chance'. I was freelance by now, i.e. watching it all on TV at home, and I remember the grim misery of this innings with perfect clarity. The Dark Ages were about to begin. Selvey's report, written for the following day's newspaper, confirmed that A Star Was Born: 'His batting, demeanour and even appearance evoke Corinthian memories of old. He is slight of build, pale and slim as a celery stick, with chis-elled, angular cigarette-card features beneath the baggy green cap he favours rather than a helmet.' Yes yes, enough of that, thank you.

Australia declared at 601 for seven, which hadn't been the idea at all when Gower put them in. Foster was the only bowler

---

* According to Michael Parkinson in the *Telegraph*, Ossie was an abbreviation of his real name, Ossified.

to threaten at all, taking three for 109; the others, said *Wisden*, were 'horribly exposed'. England came in to bat and Gooch was soon lbw b Alderman for 13. Then Chris Broad missed Merv's slower ball.

Mark McC: That awful, very slow leg break. He just stared at it, mesmerised. He could have hit it about ten times.

But Kim Barnett made a chancy and unorthodox 80 (lbw b Alderman), while Allan Lamb held the innings together with 125, his first century against Australia in 12 Tests. Matthew Engel once described Border approvingly as 'a left-handed Lamb', but while Border scored all the runs expected of him, and many more, Lamb never quite seemed to. There seemed always a certain don't-give-a-monkey's quality to his batting, which may go some way to explaining why, despite making 14 Test centuries, he never passed 150. Still, this looked like a match-saving innings, and as Robin Smith (66) and Phil Newport (36) guided us towards the follow-on score, I think I may have breathed again. 'This Australian team look more determined and better organised than their two most recent predecessors,' Mark Ray (himself Australian) wrote in the *Daily Telegraph*, 'but the doubts about their ability to bowl England out twice, often enough to win the series, remain.'

Nonetheless, they led by 171 on first innings. Second time round, Australia declared on 230 for three, leaving England to survive five hours. We never seriously doubted that they would manage that. Until they were all out for 191, not long after tea. Gower's dismissal, glancing down the leg side, 'in many ways summed up the difference between the two teams,' according to *Wisden*. 'Australia had done their homework and knew exactly what they were trying to do, whereas England lived more in hope than expectation.' They had more in common with their supporters than they knew. Alderman, with five for 105 in the first innings, took five for 44 this time round. Bowling wicket to wicket, slower than he had been in 1981 but still moving it away late and only a little, he used the conditions to perfection. Five of his ten wickets were lbw. At such times you just have to be thankful that you can't see into the future. England cricket fans with clairvoyant tendencies could easily have been tempted to end it all.

On to Lord's, Australia's favourite ground. Lamb was the latest crock, with an injured finger, but Gatting's finger had healed, and he returned for his first Test in a year. Peter Deeley in the *Telegraph* warned us not to expect too much. 'Since scoring 150 not out at the Oval in 1987 and saving that final Test, Gatting has scored only 285 in 15 Test innings and only once passed the half-century.' DeFreitas, Pringle and Newport were replaced by Dilley (fit again), Emburey and Paul Jarvis of Yorkshire, playing his fifth Test. Australia made one change, bringing in leggie Trevor Hohns for Greg Campbell. Gower won the toss and decided to bat, on 'as near perfect a pitch as you are likely to get at Lord's,' wrote Selvey, who had played for Middlesex for many years and should know. Midway through the afternoon England were 191 for seven. They were scoring at nearly five runs an over and losing a wicket every half-hour. It was sheer crazed self-destruction, with the significant exception of Gooch, who batted in his new mature, less explosive style for 60. Gower made 57 at nearly a run a ball and, later on, Jack Russell restored a measure of order with 64 not out to bring the total to 286. A hundred or so more would have been useful, but we weren't out of the game yet.

Nor were we on the second day. Australia batted better than England had: well, it wasn't hard. But England bowled better than Australia had, and far better than the previous, now sacked bowling attack had at Headingley, to restrict them to 276 for six. Selvey called it 'a severe outbreak of Test cricket as she is meant to be played'. Taylor and Boon added 145 for the second wicket, but were made to work for it by diligent bowling and sharp fielding. I watched it on the telly: the following day I was going to my first Ashes day at Lord's with my friend Andy R, and I desperately wanted it to be a good day. Foster, in an unbroken 17-over spell either side of tea, finally trapped Taylor lbw for 62, reducing his average for the series to a modest 86. Even so, the Australians might have been expected to take advantage of a tiring attack in the late afternoon sun. Instead the England bowlers continued to harry and test them, and winkled out Boon (94), Border (35), Dean Jones (27) and Healy (2). Even Emburey was taking wickets. True, Steve Waugh was still there on 35 not out, but hey ho, with a bit of luck and a following wind, we might be able to get them out on Saturday for 300 or so, take advantage of a now perfect batting strip, and who knows what might happen?

Lucky old me. The third day of the Lord's Test is really where the tenor of this book changes. It's where English cricket changed, entirely for the worse. The third day of the Lord's Test was the end of one era, quite an enjoyable one in retrospect, and the beginning of another one, which, because we are masochists, we shall live through again in the next few chapters. Everyone who was there remembers the overpowering awfulness of it: it's indelible. What was noticeable was that however drunk you got that day – and I got very pissed indeed – the pain could not be relieved, or even moderated. And still we had to stay on until the end, laughing until we cried, to witness what we knew was going to happen, and what did happen.

The bare bones of it are that Steve Waugh batted for most of the day to make 152 not out. Hughes made 30, Hohns 21 and then, worst of all, worse than anything, Geoff Lawson scored 74 runs in 107 minutes. Australia were all out for 528. England had bowled as badly as it's possible to imagine three such talented bowlers, and Paul Jarvis, bowling. Gower kept putting them on at the wrong ends from the ones they had taken wickets at in the first innings. Selvey said it was 'as unhappy an exhibition of captaincy as those watching – and there were many who have seen an awful lot of Test cricket – can remember . . . it is possible that Gower's lack of leadership when the chips were down may already have cost England the Ashes.' But Waugh was magnificent. 'He has always looked like he learned cricket in an earlier life,' swooned Mark Ray. 'Now he is playing like it.' 'Australia's performance has been meritorious beyond all reasonable expectation,' intoned E. W. Swanton from Mount Olympus. England had 23 overs at the end of the day to survive.

Bill M: It was the day everything changed. We'd come there full of hope and optimism, expecting to see England bat. Not a bit of it. I have huge admiration for Steve Waugh, but I've always hated watching him bat. He just ground us down. It was so demoralising.

So I was down in the bar and England were just starting their innings. And there was this groan, this huge groan that we could all hear. There were no televisions in the bar, but I knew just from the groan that it was Gooch, lbw b Alderman for 0. You could tell from the timbre of the groan.

Gooch had gone second ball. Barnett was out for 3, Broad for 20. Andy R and I were in the Grand Stand. Every time an England wicket fell we all just laughed. What else could you do? By the end of the day the crowd had essentially disowned their team. They felt contempt for them. Mockery was all we had left.

England showed some resistance on the fourth day. Gower and Robin Smith put on 139 for the fifth wicket: Gower made 106 in an innings full of grit, and Smith a wondrous 96. But at 322 for nine, the game was effectively over. Alderman had taken another six wickets, for nine in the match, five of them lbws. Dilley and Emburey spanked a few extra runs on Tuesday morning to give Australia a target of 118. But there was no Botham in this England team, no Willis, and the Australians were altogether tougher than their 1981 counterparts. Boon, a completely different batsman from the shambling wreck we had seen in 1986/87, made 58 not out. Accompanying him at the end was

Steve Waugh, whose 21 not out gave him 350 runs for the series but no average, as he hadn't been out yet.

So, two-nil down, what could England do? Ted Dexter wrote a song. He said it was to lift the team's spirits. It was to be sung by them, to the tune of Onward Christian Soldiers, 'in the bath and at the top of their voices':

> Onward Gower's cricketers
> Striving for a score,
> With our bats uplifted,
> We want more and more,
> Alderman the master,
> Represents the foe,
> Forward into battle,
> Down the pitch we go.

How this man remained in employment was an impenetrable mystery to me.

Australia made no changes for Edgbaston: everyone was fit other than Tim May and Carl Rackemann, and we had long forgotten about them. England dropped Broad, for the last time. Lamb was still injured; Smith and Foster were newly crocked; Gatting's mother-in-law had died. Botham, his cheekbone healed, returned for his first Test in two years; Middlesex's metronome Angus Fraser made his debut; the Worcestershire opening batsman Tim Curtis came back, having played twice against the Windies the previous season; and most fascinatingly, Chris Tavare was recalled for his first Test since 1984. Tavare had moved to Somerset, thrown off the tortoise shell and reinvented himself as a middle-order hare. Could he transfer this form to the international stage? It was almost worth watching the match to find out.

Unfortunately it rained. At the end of the first day Australia were 232 for four; at the end of the second, 294 for six; at the end of the third, 391 for seven. Gower said he had no illusions about what England needed to do to win: bowl them out quickly on Monday, score 800 in four hours and put them under a bit of pressure. Australia's eventual total of 424 owed much to Dean Jones's 157, which itself owed much to wayward English bowling. 'Jones does not like being described as "cocky",' explained Mark Ray, 'preferring instead to describe himself as "arrogant at the crease".' Graham Dilley didn't look fully fit or strongly motivated; Jarvis had lost all confidence; Botham was now gentle medium pace, albeit with as much attitude as Merv Hughes. Without Fraser's four for 64 off 33 overs, we would have been sunk. At noon on the fourth day, Gooch and Curtis went out to bat. Gooch was out lbw yet again, this time to Lawson. We were 47 for two, then 75 for five. Curtis scored 41 and then hit around a straight ball. Tavare made two. Wrote Selvey, 'The old joke was that when the Mary Rose was raised from the Solent, a survivor was discovered, whose first words were to enquire whether Tavare had yet got off the mark.' Botham, batting in a helmet with grille, and Russell played with great common sense to add 96 for the sixth wicket, but both were out just before the close. England were 185 for seven, 40 runs away from saving the follow-on. They managed it on the last morning, with the last pair, Dilley and Jarvis, at the wicket, and guaranteed the dribbly draw. But it hadn't been their most convincing performance.

What made all this worse, if it could be worse, was the knowledge that the South Africans were sniffing around again. In fact more than sniffing: another rebel tour was being arranged, and it was just a matter of time before we found out which deadbeats and also-rans were taking the rand this time. For Old Trafford England made several more changes, some forced, some just desperately necessary. Dilley's suspect knee had flared up, so he was out. In fact he was one of three players who had just played their last Test, the others being Kim Barnett and Chris Tavare, whose recall had lasted ten minutes and nine balls. And Paul Jarvis, with two for 290 from his two Tests, was out as well. Back in were Tim Robinson, preferred to Gatting at number three; Robin Smith and Neil Foster, fit again; and the Leicestershire left-arm spinner Nick Cook.

And on a pitch Mike Selvey described as 'hard and dry as a ship's biscuit', England won the toss and were soon 158 for seven. Every single wicket was bowled or lbw, and not one went to Alderman; today was Lawson's and Hohns's day. 'Last home season, [Lawson] was rated by many Shield batsmen as the most accurate seamer in the country and a must for this tour,' wrote Mark Ray, and after three quiet Tests this faith in his talents seemed to have been justified. Left on the burning deck were Robin Smith and Neil Foster, who hauled the score up to 224 for seven by the close, with Smith unbeaten on 112. Selvey called it 'an innings full of skill, determination and good old-fashioned bottle, qualities not much evident in many other English batsmen so far this series'. Next day he extended it to 143 – more than Allan Lamb had ever scored in Tests, or would ever score – and England's total to 260. Such was our misery that we appreciated his innings less for what it was – not quite enough to prevent an almost certain Australian victory – than for what it promised. Better days, in short. This is the groundless, desperate optimism of the sports fan. Hope never dies. It would, however, spend much of the 1990s in a deep coma, with doctors hovering in the background, discussing among themselves whether it was time to switch off the machine yet.

Australia scored 447: Taylor made 85, Border 80, Jones 69, Waugh 92. England's bowling was 'steady rather than dangerous,' wrote Tony Lewis in the *Sunday Telegraph*, in an excess of generosity. England started their second innings promisingly, not losing Curtis until the second over. Lawson and Alderman sliced through a top order bereft of confidence and, in some cases, talent. At 59 for six, with all top six batsmen out, things had looked better. Peter Deeley wrote that 'they were like rabbits transfixed by the predator's hypnotic glare and went almost meekly to their execution'. We still needed 129 to make Australia bat again. But Jack Russell was still there. One notable feature of this series is that it was the youngest, least experienced players, the ones untainted by previous failure, who made England even faintly competitive. Robin Smith, Jack Russell, Angus Fraser – these were the players of the future. Some others were starting to look like players of the past. But Russell and John Emburey put on 142 for the seventh wicket. Emburey made 64 and Russell 128 not out – not only his first Test century, but his first century in all cricket. At Headingley the Australians had sensed his discomfort against the short ball and subsequently pummelled him with bouncers. Since then, Russell had practised assiduously in the nets. This was a magnificently gutsy innings, maybe the most memorable of the summer for an England supporter. And yet, and yet. If Russell and Emburey had lasted another hour, the match might have been saved. In the event, the Australians had more than enough time to score the 81 they needed, and lost only one wicket. Border was the first Australian captain to regain the Ashes in England since 1934. And Gower was the first English captain to lose them.*

All this was overshadowed, though, by the announcement after the match that a squad of 16 Englishmen, under the captaincy of Mike Gatting, would undertake an unofficial tour of South Africa during the winter. Because of new ICC rules, all would immediately be banned from Tests for five years. Three of the 16 had just played at Old Trafford: Robinson, Emburey and Foster. Another six had played during the series: Gatting, Broad, DeFreitas, Barnett, Dilley and Jarvis. (DeFreitas later changed his mind and withdrew.) The others were Bill Athey, Chris Cowdrey, Richard Ellison, Bruce French, Greg Thomas (who

* Mike Selvey's book had had a working title of *The Ashes Regained*. This now had to be changed to *The Ashes Surrendered*.

replaced DeFreitas), Matthew Maynard and two uncapped players, David Graveney and Alan Wells. What a bloody waste.
Recruitment had been going on since May. Wrote Selvey, 'One
cricketer, not one of the 16, has said that the dressing room has
been a dull, nervous place, totally lacking in spark or spirit. It's
not hard now to see why.' Parallels with the pre-Packer Australian
team of 1977 were obvious.

Gatting was going because he felt the cricketing establishment
had let him down. Most of the others were yesterday's men, but
the loss of Foster and Emburey, in particular, was hard to bear.
Such was the turnaround in players in those days that we had
never really had the opportunity to find out whether Maynard
and Thomas had the right stuff, and now we wouldn't. Still,
they had outed themselves now, so they could fuck off and leave
us alone. Gower, Dexter and 'team manager' Mickey Stewart
could start the rebuilding process that, in my lifetime at least,
would never cease.

(One subsidiary thought on this, though. Most of the press
were quite well disposed to this latest batch of rebels, accepting
the argument that they were professional sportsmen, their careers
were short and so on. But think back to Lord's for a moment.
The catastrophic third day that changed the course of the series.
Who was bowling, exactly? Dilley, Foster, Jarvis, Emburey. All
four went to South Africa. This is not to say that they bowled
badly on purpose: of course they didn't. But if recruitment had
started in May, it's possible that some, if not all of them had
already signed up. And how can you give of your best if you are
harbouring a secret like that one? I suspect that this South African
affair undermined the England cricket team far, far more deeply
than we realised at the time – and, oddly enough, more deeply
than the 1982 tour. I would have banned them all for life.)

But maybe it was all for the best. 'It means that Ted Dexter
can now clean the stables of the tired old failures who have
brought one victory in the last 24 Tests without being seen as a

hatchet man,' wrote Peter Deeley. For Trent Bridge, England made four changes. The three rebels had been sacked, and Gooch, whose technique had collapsed against Alderman, asked for time off to go and build it again. Martin Moxon came in at the top of the order; Michael Atherton and Devon Malcolm made debuts; and Eddie Hemmings, aged 40, was the second spinner. None of it made any difference. Border won the toss and Marsh and Taylor batted through the whole first day. *Wisden* dismally listed the records they ticked off: 89, Australia's previous highest opening partnership at Trent Bridge; 135, Australia's best opening partnership of the series; 170, the highest Australian partnership at Trent Bridge; 201, the highest Australian opening partnership in England; 244, the highest Australian opening partnership against England. They ended the day at 301, the first pair to bat through a full day's play in England, and only the ninth to do it anywhere.

Ben D: I watched that whole day on TV. It was like being tortured.

On Friday morning they passed 319, the highest partnership in any Test at Trent Bridge, and 323, the highest by two openers in Ashes history, breaking a record that had stood to Hobbs and Rhodes since 1911/12, before Marsh was out for 138, c Botham b Cook. Although Taylor went on to 219 – the first double century to be scored in an Ashes match since Keith Stackpole's in 1970/71 – England did well to restrict them to 602 for six declared. Good grief, Boon only made 73, Border 66 not out, and Steve Waugh was out eighth ball for 0. Were you watching? Me neither. I probably felt that it was a good day to get on with some work. Only afterwards did we search for what would come to be called 'positives'. Angus Fraser took one wicket (Jones for 22), but he conceded only 91 runs in 46 overs. 'Stupendous,' said Selvey, 'the very essence of Test cricket'. And Mark Taylor was stumped for the third time for four innings. At last England had found a weakness. The fact that, of Australians, only Bradman had scored more runs in a series against them was neither here nor there.

Obviously it got worse. 'Every Test match, it seems, a new low is reached,' wrote Selvey. 'Headingley . . . which at the time was regarded as a national disaster, is increasingly looking like a minor triumph by comparison with what has followed.' It had taken us seven hours and 744 balls at Trent Bridge to get our first wicket; Terry Alderman picked up his with his fourth ball, when Moxon edged to slip. Two balls later Atherton was lbw, playing down the wrong line. Tim Curtis got a brute that kept low. 'Oh dear me,' said Richie Benaud. 'That is as plumb as you are likely to see, ever.' Gower slashed at one outside off stump, and England were 37 for four. By this stage, we were beginning to feel a bit sorry for Gower. It wasn't his fault that he was unable to motivate the team at all. Well, not entirely. After all, it was a different team every week. Before the announcement of the South African tour, Gower had been the scapegoat, excoriated by the press, who were only really expressing the feelings of the rest of us. (It's not always the case.) But at least he was still there, enduring this hell, day after day. Gower *never* went to South Africa, and was rarely given enough credit for it.

Fresh minds, fresh talents, that's what you need. Robin Smith's 101, scored in 150 balls, was 'bracketed alongside Waugh's unbeaten 177 at Headingley as among the great innings in England v Australia Tests,' said Martin Johnson in *Wisden*. Smith hit the bad ball as hard as any England player can have done for years. He walloped Merv Hughes for five boundaries in ten balls. Tony Lewis compared him to Clyde Walcott. And it was all done with the tail, as Botham had dislocated a finger diving for a catch on the second day and batted at number 9 in some pain. Eddie Hemmings was second-highest scorer with 38 – after his nightwatchman gig in 1982/83, we would have expected no less – and England were all out for 255 (Alderman five for 69). Border imposed the follow-on. They needed to score 347 to avoid an innings defeat. They managed 117. It was the lowest score of the summer. It was the largest margin of victory Australia had ever inflicted in this country. It was the last Test for Tim Curtis and Martin Moxon. It was 4–0 with one Test to go.

The latest silver lining, though, was provided by Michael Atherton, who had stuck around for nearly three hours in scoring 47. He was one of five survivors in the team for the Oval. Botham, Malcolm and Fraser were injured, and Hemmings was left out on the day. Gooch returned, alongside his Essex opening partner John Stephenson. David Capel, Derek Pringle (who had been taking wickets for Essex at will) and Gladstone Small were recalled, while Alan Igglesden of Kent, away-swinging beanpole, received a first cap. This brought the number of players chosen this summer to 29, one more than the previous year against the West Indies, and one fewer than the all-time record. Not once had England been able to field the team originally selected: someone had always been injured in the interim. Australia had the same XI they had fielded since the second Test.

Let's race through this one. Australia intended to. On a perfect Oval batting strip, they scored 325 for three on the first day. Dean Jones was 114 not out. '[He] quite simply tore the England bowling to shreds,' said Selvey. Taylor's 71 took his series aggregate to 791; Boon made 46 and Border 66 not out. On day two, though, cloud cover gave the England bowling some teeth. Border was out for 76, Jones 122, Pringle took four for 70, Small bowled beautifully and without luck, Ian Healy smashed 44 from 44 balls, and Australia were all out for 468. Another record: it was the eighth consecutive first innings in which they had made more than 400. And Gooch was out third ball, lbw b Alderman. Five times this summer Alderman had taken a wicket in his first over. It was his 17th lbw. Sometimes you can have too many statistics.

Mark McC: The Smiling Assassin. There was an absolute inevitability about him getting England out that series. He was just unplayably

good. 'Thatcher out' was the famous graffito, to which someone added
'lbw b Alderman'.

On Saturday the rains came: only 38 overs could be bowled, the ball swung for everybody and England scratched out 124 for six. Gower was still there on 43. For the first time this summer he had played at his graceful best, possibly in the knowledge that freedom was only a couple of days away. But 145 runs were still needed to avoid the follow-on. Border had 5–0 within sight. No Australian captain had ever done that in England.

That England did avoid the follow-on was due first to a 71-run stand for the seventh wicket between Gower (79) and Pringle (27) and then, more astoundingly, to a 73-run stand for the ninth wicket between Gladstone Small (59) and Nick Cook (31), both of whom recorded their highest Test scores. Why wasn't Gladstone Small always playing for England? This was only his sixth Test in three years. He was certainly made of the right stuff. His regrettable shortage of neck didn't count against him, surely?

On the fifth morning, Australia were thinking about declaring and setting a target. Here, in effect, was where the 1990s were defined. While some players thought they should make a game of it, Carl Rackemann, who had barely played all tour, had different ideas. According to Gideon Haigh, Rackemann said that 'full mental and physical disintegration' could only come about 'if Australia batted longer than England expected, forcing them into the demoralising state of bowling and fielding in futility'. In short, beating England was less important than humiliating them. Border therefore declared with 67 overs left, giving England a notional 403 to win. They lost five wickets for 143 before bad light closed in. Smith again resisted for 77 not out, while Alderman took his wicket tally to 41, one short of his 1981 record. No bowler had ever taken 40 wickets in an Ashes series twice. My god, were we pleased to see the back of him, and of what *Wisden* called 'yet another English summer of despair and emphatic failure'. In a press conference after the match, Ted Dexter said, 'I am not aware of any errors I have made.' No, it was someone else's fault he had been given the job: no one could blame him for that at all.

Interlude
1989

Chris P: There was a three-day game, Middlesex versus Australia. I went with a couple of mates of mine — ground wasn't particularly full — and there we were, sitting in the Tavern Stand, in the front row, and Geoff Lawson is fielding right in front of us. I had the Sunday Times *in front of me, and Peter Roebuck, I think it was, had written this article saying, Australia will be lucky to get away with this series without being whitewashed. And I laughed, saying, 'What rubbish', and Geoff Lawson overheard. And he said, excuse me, can I just have a look at that? We spent the next hour or so having a chat with the bloke: a really, really pleasant man. And of course it wasn't a whitewash.*

Andy R: That was the year I went to every single Test match. My mate Geoff had long had an ambition to do this, and of course we picked this year . . . All I can remember is wherever we went, we watched either Steve Waugh or 'Tubs' Taylor scoring endless amounts of runs. They weren't even doing it with any style or grace, just that whole Aussie hat-screwed-down chewing-away accumulation thing. It had all been set up for me, this great summer of cricket, and everything was horrible, from start to blinking finish.

Poor Geoff. He's a really nice guy, and it was great, because he organised all the trains. I was spoilt. He did all the hard work. And I think it broke his heart. I can't remember one redeeming day. Just a blur of trains, and Steve Waugh and 'Tubs' Taylor.

Ben D: I was always a cricket fan but I became an obsessive cricket fan in around 1989, which was my disaster. I watched every ball, except when they cut to the racing. I was 15, and that was my adolescence. There were no girls involved; I was very late developing in that area. I remember many little things about this series. I remember the British press saying, is this the worst Australian team ever to come to our shores? I remember Graham Gooch falling over his front leg to Alderman. And then the opening day of the Old Trafford Test. He got ten off the first over from Lawson and I thought, Is Gooch coming back? Second over of the game, Alderman bowls, gets him. We'd had that moment of hope. It was like being tortured, that summer, it really was.

So what I did is I fixated on the 1986/87 series. I had only been 12, 13 then. I hadn't seen it on TV, hadn't even listened to it on the radio. But this became crystallised in my head as an era of great glory. I bought books and books on it, and I knew every session of every game, each one imprinted on my mind. To this day I remember that after Small got his five wickets at Melbourne, he went to some local restaurant and they gave him a standing ovation. And I became weirdly obsessed with Chris Broad. Because I hadn't actually experienced the series, it took on an almost mythical quality. To this day, I still look it up on YouTube when I'm at work. I've seen every clip, and you'd be amazed how much of it has survived.

Then Lord's 1989. That was my great obsession Chris Broad's last ever Test. Promise unfulfilled is something you experience a lot as an England fan. Someone who could clearly do it, and had done it in 1986/87, didn't do it, and they dropped him after two Tests.

I think I invested a lot of my frustrations as a young person in cricket. I wasn't a classic teenager. I didn't rebel against my parents and slam doors. No, I got angry with the England selectors. For picking Alan Igglesden, for example, or dropping David Gower, who was my all-time favourite player.

★

Tom H: It was when the vividness faded. England were expected to do well, and they got stuffed. Botham was a crock, and Steve Waugh scored all those runs. I've never felt the same intensity or enthusiasm since.

Twelve

1990/91

The other advantage England have got when Phil Tufnell's bowling is that he isn't fielding.

Ian Chappell

Since winning the Ashes in 1985, England had played 40 Tests and won three of them: the two in Australia in 1986/87 and the one against Sri Lanka in 1988. Of the other 37 they had lost 19. Gower had lost 10 of his last 12 matches in charge. Bangladesh would have fancied their chances against us.

But the loss of the Ashes – the worst thing that could happen to us, let's face it – and the defection of the South African turncoats gave Ted Dexter and Micky Stewart an opportunity to start again. Again. Their new captain was Graham Gooch, who took a squad to the West Indies formed in his own image: tough, uncompromising and liable to get out lbw. Fortunately the West Indian bowlers weren't bowling for lbws. England won the first Test and were robbed by the weather of winning another. Gooch was injured, the wheels fell off again and the series was lost 2–1, but confidence had been restored. At home in 1990, England beat New Zealand 1–0 in three Tests. Michael Atherton hit his first Test century and averaged 71; Devon Malcolm took

15 wickets at under 18. India were also beaten 1–0, in a famous runfest. Gooch made his 333, Smith averaged 180, Gower, Atherton and Lamb all averaged above 60, and Angus Fraser took 16 wickets at 28. And before we knew it, before we could even draw breath, it was time for another Ashes series. Surely we had a chance this time. Surely.

For once, many of the touring party picked themselves, and the rest were picked by Gooch. The batsmen were Gooch himself, Atherton (now usually opening), Lamb, Smith, Gower, John Morris of Derbyshire (who had played three Tests during the summer) and Gooch's lucky charm Wayne Larkins, of whom Andrew Miller has memorably written, 'he was invariably selected when he should have been ignored, and ignored when he should have been selected'. The quick bowlers were Malcolm, Fraser, Small, Martin Bicknell of Surrey (as yet uncapped) and Chris Lewis, who was classed as an all-rounder at this stage (i.e. saddled with the title 'the new Botham'). The real all-rounder in the team was Alec Stewart, who had gone to the West Indies as deputy wicketkeeper to Jack Russell, and played four Tests as a specialist batsman. And the two spinners were Eddie Hemmings, the great survivor, who had played all six Tests in the summer, and an uncapped 24-year-old larrikin named Phil Tufnell. We have sent weaker squads.

But I don't think Australia were too fussed. In 1989/90 they had drawn a one-off home Test against New Zealand, beaten Sri Lanka 1–0 in two Tests, seen off Pakistan 1–0 in three Tests, and lost a low-scoring one-off Test in New Zealand, their first defeat in 15 matches. Their squad was settled and confident, and really only lacked a decent spin bowler. (Trevor Hohns had played his last Test, as indeed had Geoff Lawson.) Allan Border was contemplating his fourth Ashes series as captain and eighth overall. 'Bring 'em on' might have been his rallying cry.

Some familiar faces greeted England in their first tour match against Western Australia. G. R. Marsh was captain, G. M. Wood scored 108 batting at number four and the opening bowlers were T. M. Alderman and B. A. Reid, who was back after 21 months nursing a back injury. According to *Wisden* he 'bowled brilliantly but unluckily'. England squeaked a draw, mainly thanks to Robin Smith's second innings 98 not out. Without their realising it, though, the single most disastrous event on the tour had already taken place. In an early practice game, while trying to take a caught-and-bowled, Gooch had gashed the fourth finger of his right hand below the lower knuckle. Although the bone was visible, the doctor decided stitches weren't necessary. Gooch had no reaction for a fortnight, and then started to feel intense pain. Not only had the finger gone septic, but the infection had spread to the palm of his hand. He was operated on that evening, and was out of action for a full calendar month. Wrote John Thicknesse in *Wisden*, 'The loss of the captain and main run-scorer, midway through the build-up to the Brisbane Test, was shattering, and had immediate and dire effects.' England duly lost to South Australia (though Bickers took wickets and Stewart scored 92) and drew against 'an Australian XI' in Hobart, with Lamb hitting 154 and 102, Stewart 95, and Malcolm picking up seven for 47. The captaincy had fallen on Lamb in the West Indies the previous winter, when Gooch had been injured, and both matches had been lost. For Brisbane he again took charge. Larkins would open with Atherton, Stewart would come in at number six, and the attack would be all seam: Fraser, Malcolm, Small and Lewis. The pitch was green, the weather was humid and Border put England in after winning the toss. Australia's only two changes from the Oval, 1989, were Greg Matthews for Hohns and Bruce Reid for Lawson. Well as the Australian open-ers bowled, with the ball swinging and seaming bounteously, England were not doing badly at 112 for two. But Allan Lamb fell to the punk off-spinner for 32, Gower 'used three innings' worth of good luck' (*Wisden*) in making 61, and England were all out for 192. Reid had four for 54 and Merv Hughes three for 39.

Conditions did not improve on day two and Australia were all out for 152. England's fielders took a succession of screaming catches, and Fraser, Small and Lewis each took three wickets. Game on! But Reid had Larkins (who had been off the field with an infected tooth) lbw for 0, Alderman bowled Atherton with an unplayable late outswinger and wickets never stopped falling. England were all out for 114. Alderman had taken six for 47, his best Test figures. Ten minutes later, when the Australians came out to bat, the pitch had miraculously calmed down. The sun came out, and Marsh (72 not out) and Taylor (67 not out) knocked off the 157 they needed without any bother. Game off.

Darrien B: It's my first memory of cricket, watching it on TV. The highlights were on BBC2 at teatime. Wayne Larkins was definitely playing. A duck going across the screen. I don't remember the scores – I'd never seen cricket before, let alone played it – but it was the duck going across the screen. Quite often. I was eight. I remember thinking that Wayne Larkins was a really silly name. He had a big curly mullet, and he wasn't very good, so I instantly liked him.

How had such a close game become so easy for Australia to win? It emerged that on the second evening, when England were tottering slightly at 56 for three in their second innings, Lamb (the captain, 10 not out overnight) and Gower (out for 27) had gone to a casino 50 miles away with Tony Greig and Kerry Packer. Lamb was out early the following morning and received the usual meaningless reprimand from tour manager Peter Lush. The incident probably didn't mean much in itself – although it did give a fascinating glimpse into the high-rolling, glamorous lifestyles of international cricketers (presumably Lord Lucan dropped by for a hand of *vingt-et-un*). And it did make us wonder. Was this a happy, cohesive touring side? And what was going to go wrong next?

We soon found out. After a month of brain-sapping ODIs, England had a four-day game against Victoria in the run-up to the second Test. Lamb scored 143 in three hours and, in an excess

of enthusiasm, jogged back to the hotel and tore a calf muscle
(injury number three). He would be out for two Tests, and would
presumably have to hobble to the roulette table. During the same
match Micky Stewart spent a night in hospital after complaining
of prolonged numbness in his leg (injury number four). England
just about managed to draw that one, thanks to another salvage
operation by Robin Smith. For the Melbourne Test, Gooch came
in for Lamb, Phillip DeFreitas, a 'reinforcement' to the tour party,
for Small (injury number five) and Phil Tufnell, winning his first
cap, for Chris Lewis (injury number six): one cat for another, as
it were. Australia, naturally, were unchanged. England won a
useful toss and scored 352. Gower made exactly 100, his eighth
Test century against Australia and 17th overall, despite a badly
bruised right wrist (injury number seven). Larkins, his place at
stake, scored a doughty 64 and Stewart ('impetuous but lucky',
said *Wisden*) made 79. So, game on again. Australia fought back.
Taylor and Border each batted more than four hours for 61 and
62 respectively, Jones had swatted 44 in 57 balls and, at tea on the
third day, Australia were 259 for four, contemplating a small first-
innings lead and the England collapse that would surely follow.
Fraser then took the second new ball, bowled Waugh with one
that straightened and then sliced through the tail, bowling
unchanged for figures of six for 82. He just kept on bowling, and
along the way sustained the hip injury (injury number eight) that
would cut short his tour and keep him out of Tests for two and a
half years. Excellent work, everyone.

The pitch was low and slow, and asked nothing of batsmen
other than unflappable patience and intense concentration. After
lunch on the fourth day, England were 100-odd for 1, with
Gooch at his most expansive and Larkins again working hard to
prolong his career. Bruce Reid got them both after they had
reached fifties, but just after tea, on 147 for four, and a lead of
201, you would still have put your fiver on England. And waved
goodbye to it for ever. Micky Stewart called it 'fifty minutes of

madness'. In twelve overs Reid and Matthews conceded three runs and took six wickets. Reid, who had never taken five wickets in a Test before this match, had taken six for 97 in the first innings and seven for 51 in the second. Marsh (79 not out) and Boon (94 not out) showed us how to do it, and Australia won by eight wickets.

No time for reflection, though, as the Sydney Test started five days later. Small came back for the injured Fraser and Hemmings was the second spinner, in place of DeFreitas, while Rackemann came in for Merv. Australia won the toss, Malcolm bowled fast to remove Marsh and Taylor, but this was now a very confident and talented Australian batting order, and England might have bowled a little too short. Boon made 97, Border 78, Jones 60, Steve Waugh 48 and the punk off-spinner 128, his fourth century in 24 Tests. Wrote John Thicknesse in *Wisden*, 'Only Malcolm's stamina and strength saved England from submersion.' Nor did the batsmen buckle. Gooch and Atherton put on 95 for the first wicket; Gooch edged Reid behind for 59 but Athers went on to his 105, his third hundred and, at 451 minutes, the new slowest in Ashes Tests. He was fourth out at 295, just before the follow-on was saved, but Gower and Stewart added another 99, Gower playing as sweetly as only he could for 123. Stewart made 91 and Gooch, amazingly daringly, declared at 469 for eight, still 49 runs behind. How long was it since anyone had put Aussie under any pressure, least of all us? The ball was turning, and again both openers went cheaply. For the first time in nine Tests against England, 'Tubs' Taylor hadn't scored a fifty. On the last morning, with Australia 38 for 2, nightwatchman Ian Healy gave a difficult chance to Gower at square leg off Hemmings. It didn't go to hand and Healy stayed until after lunch for 69. Although wickets fell all day, Rackemann survived 112 minutes and 32 overs of spin, before Gooch brought back Malcolm, who bowled him with his sixth delivery. England had to score 255 in 28 overs. The draw was a formality.

Two-nil down with two Tests to go, and a victory just missed: many of us will have switched off and given up then and there. But even in the direst circumstances, there's usually something to keep you watching, and in this case it was a lantern-jawed, chain-smoking 24-year-old left-arm spinner named Philip Tufnell. The Australians took to him immediately, partly for his larrikin tendencies, but mainly (it has to be admitted) for his pathetic fielding. According to Simon Briggs, 'No England tourist since Douglas Jardine has attracted more heckles from the bleachers.' (What, not even Mike Brearley?) But at Sydney, in only his second Test, Tuffers came good with five for 61 in the second innings. The crowd showed their appreciation by heckling him even more.

England's next game was against New South Wales, an extra fixture that had been crowbarred into the schedules when they failed to get into the ODI finals. Another weedy first innings lost it for them, but Hemmings took eight wickets in the match and Atherton scored a second innings century. Thence to the Carrara Oval in Queensland, and a much better performance all round. Tufnell took another five wickets as Queensland (without Border) were all out for 286. Gooch responded with 93, John Morris, in a rare innings, 132 and Robin Smith 108. Everyone was in a very good mood after weeks of misery, so, to celebrate Smith's century, Morris and David Gower popped over to Carrara airport and rented a Tiger Moth biplane. They asked the pilot to fly between the ground's floodlights, swoop down to 200 feet and pretend to strafe the playing area. Allan Lamb, then batting, machine-gunned his teammates down with his bat. All good fun. It's also the only thing anyone now remembers about this tour.

For this incident revealed, maybe as nothing else could, the vast cultural chasm that had opened up in the England party. On one side, the cavalier approach of Gower: casinos, Tiger Moths, flicks to the leg slip that had just been stationed there. On the other side, the strict dogma of Goochism, with its emphasis on non-stop physical jerks and naughty-boy nets. The following day Gower and Morris were summoned to a meeting with Gooch, Micky Stewart and tour manager Peter Lush. 'You can either be heavy about it, or you can treat it as a harmless prank,' said Gower.

'I don't think you enjoy this game very much, Lubo,' said Gooch. The two miscreants were each fined £1000; Peter Lush, in a statement, said the gag had been 'immature, ill-judged and ill-timed'. Outside Essex, and maybe the Stewart family home, you would struggle even now to find anyone who didn't think this an over-reaction that simply made the management team look foolish. John Thicknesse in *Wisden* called it 'a harsh penalty for an essentially light-hearted prank, reflecting all too accurately the joyless nature of the tour. Impressive as Gooch's captaincy was, a hair shirt was usually to be found hanging in his wardrobe.' In the event, Gower was probably lucky not to be sent home, had he not scored more runs than anyone else (347 at 57.83). But he would play only five more Tests and Morris would play none at all. Yet again English cricket would waste some of its finest resources, simply because Gooch and Stewart seemed only to accept a certain type of person in their dressing room. And did it do us any good? Did it usher in a decade of unstoppable success and triumph?

For the Adelaide Test Australia made a few intriguing changes: Merv Hughes and Craig McDermott (a.k.a. Billy Bloodnut) replaced Alderman and Rackemann (who had played his last Test), while Steve Waugh was dropped after 42 consecutive Tests, but only 82 runs in the last three. He was replaced, possibly uniquely in cricket history, by his twin brother Mark, who rubbed his nose in it with a quite breathtaking century. A timely one, too, for Australia were 104 for four when he came out to bat. Waugh (138) and Matthews (65) put on 171 for the sixth wicket, McDermott spanked 42 not out and Australia climbed

out of the hole once more to score 386. For England, Lamb and
Small returned for Larkins and Hemmings, and in another por-
tentous and far-reaching move, a fifth bowler, DeFreitas, was
included in place of Jack Russell. Micky's son Alec, with his
extra-clean kit, took up the gloves. I don't think it is overstating
the case to say that, for a lot of us, something important was thus
lost. Somehow Gooch's charmless, utilitarian England were less
easy to support than the teams who had gone before – and let's
be frank here, much easier to disown when they screwed it up
royally. Because that was the problem: marginalising Gower and
dropping Russell were what tennis players would call unforced
errors. How the Australians must have laughed.

England lost Atherton for 0 to a poor decision and Lamb
caught behind for 0. Gooch and Smith added 126 for the third
wicket, but the vital moment – the only other thing anyone
remembers about the tour – was Gower chipping the last ball
before lunch to long leg for an easy catch. It launched another
abject collapse, as the last seven wickets fell for 69 runs. Bloodnut,
playing his first Test in two years, took five for 97. Australia, with
the Ashes safe, and needing only a draw to win the series,
declared 45 minutes before the end of the fourth day, giving
England a target of 472 to win. At lunch on day five, England
were 113 without loss, and Gooch decided to go for it. In the
next hour he alone scored 58 before slashing Reid to gully for
117. Atherton went soon after for 87, giving Mark Waugh his
first catch in Tests, but at tea England were 267 for two. They
couldn't, could they? No, they couldn't, but Border was suffi-
ciently rattled by the assault to stay on the defensive even after
England lost a few wickets. Their final 335 for five was England's
highest fourth innings total since the 1977 Centenary Test in
Melbourne.

The fifth and last Test, at Perth, told a more familiar tale. Reid
was unfit and replaced by Alderman; Fraser's hip had gone and
Phil Newport played, having flown in three days earlier as cover.

England won the toss and, assisted by a fast pitch, wild bowling and billiard-table outfield, Lamb and Smith bashed 141 for the third wicket. Lamb's 91, off 122 balls, was his highest score in Australia, but his dismissal, mis-hooking Bloodnut to mid-on, sparked off yet another collapse, and McDermott suddenly had eight for 97. (The not-out batsman was David Gower, marooned on 28, but that was probably his fault as well.) England's 244 was hopelessly inadequate, but their bowlers strived to make amends, and at 168 for six Australia were also in serious danger of under-achieving. (Mark Taylor's last five scores had been 11, 19, 5, 4 and now 12. Yahoo!) Greg Matthews, the now balding punk off-spinner, then counter-attacked with 60 not out, Healy made 42 and Australia had a first-innings lead of 60. On day three, the ball started swinging as it almost never did at Perth. England were all out for 182 (Smith 43, Newport 40 not out). Australia lost Taylor for 19 (ha ha!) but won the Test by nine wickets and the series by three to nil. At home no one was listening; we were all asleep, possibly under the influence of drink or sleeping tablets. Gooch would later describe the tour as 'a fart competing with thunder'. Of our last twelve Tests against Australia, we had lost eight and won none. It wasn't funny any more.

Thirteen

1993

[Merv Hughes] could spit and snarl at you from 22 yards, but when you had a beer with him, you realised he was just a silly old poodle; after that, he didn't frighten you so much.

Michael Atherton

In the 1980s we had beaten Australia regularly and lost to everyone else no less regularly. In the 1990s we tried our damnedest to do the opposite. The West Indies came over in 1991 and we managed a 2–2 draw in a gripping series. Gooch's 154 at Headingley, on an inadequate pitch against Ambrose, Walsh, Marshall and Patterson, was one of the greatest innings any of us had ever seen. Gooch and Smith, according to Scyld Berry in *Wisden*, 'batted with astonishing consistency . . . and the utmost mental rigour. It would hardly be an exaggeration to say that they both batted virtually as well as humanly possible.' The following winter England won 2–0 in New Zealand and lost in the final of the World Cup in Australia. True, in 1992 Pakistan won 2–1 in a five-Test series, amid the usual bickering about umpiring standards and ball-tampering. I was sitting directly behind Waqar Younis at the Nursery End at Lord's as he roared in and bowled a succession of unseeable toe-crunchers. But the Gooch captaincy was running out of puff. In 1992/93 he took a team to India and Sri Lanka, but left Gower and Russell behind, to an extraordinary public outcry. (Gower had been left out because he was too old at 35. This didn't apply to Gooch himself, Gatting or Emburey, who were 39, 35 and 40 respectively. The latter two had been recalled at the first opportunity, after their South African bans lapsed.) England lost three Tests in India and a one-off Test in Sri Lanka, each by a huge margin: the perfect preparation for an Ashes series.

Australia's progress had been no more serene. After a 2–1 defeat in the West Indies, they had trashed India 4–0 at home. But in 1992/93 the West Indies came back and again won 2–1, and then Australia went to New Zealand and could only draw 1–1. (New Zealand hadn't lost a series at home to them for 16 years.) Maybe Border's captaincy, too, was reaching its natural end. Most observers had assumed that 1990/91 would be his last Ashes series, but no, here he was, still Captain Grumpy, fourteen years after his first Test and eight years after taking over as skipper. Still, at least no one was making the mistake of calling his squad the weakest ever to arrive on these shores. Gone since last time were Geoff 'Swampy' Marsh, Terry Alderman, Greg Matthews and Bruce Reid, either to age or injury, and Dean Jones, dropped in his prime.* But making second tours were Mark Taylor (now vice-captain), Ian Healy, Merv Hughes, Craig McDermott, Steve Waugh and the off-spinner Tim May, and making his third was David Boon. Among the newbies were NSW's 23-year-old opening batsman Michael Slater, fast bowler Brendon Julian (22), English conditions specialist Paul Reiffel (27), and a 23-year-old leg-spinner called Shane Warne, the newly enthroned young cricketer of the year.

* His personality may have had something to do with it. Most players are given nicknames by other people. Jones chose his own: 'The Legend'.

After beating nearly everybody in their early matches, Australia swept England aside in the ODIs 3–0. Both teams used the opportunity to blood young players. Opening for Australia was a 21-year-old hulk called Matthew Hayden, while England's middle order included the young Surrey left-hander, Graham Thorpe. In the second match Robin Smith hit 167 not out, 'one of the greatest innings ever seen in limited-overs cricket', wrote John Thicknesse in *Wisden*. Mark Waugh then scored 113, Border 86 not out, and Australia won with nine balls to spare. And so to Manchester for the first Test. England gave debuts to the Somerset fast-bowler Andrew Caddick and the off-spinner Peter Such, whose move to Essex might have been one of his smarter career moves. Graeme Hick also made his Ashes debut, having topped both batting and bowling averages in India. Australia's two debutants were Julian and Slater.

Call us foolish, call us worse, but there's something about the first day of a new Ashes series that stirs the blood and encourages unreasonable hopes. Maybe this will be the year. Five Tests to play, and none lost yet. Savour the atmosphere, enjoy the moment, feel the optimism in the air. And then switch off the television and go and do something more sensible instead.

As usual we started with an injury. Alan Igglesden, who had been damned in 1989 by Tony Lewis as 'no more than a good, honest trier', very nearly won a second cap, but sustained a timely groin strain. Phillip DeFreitas was recalled for the 673rd time. Gooch put them in on a soggy, marginally underprepared pitch and Taylor and Slater, who both came from Wagga Wagga, put on 128 for the first wicket. Off we go again! The big surprise was that the pitch was turning, and the even bigger surprise was that Peter Such (six for 67) outbowled Tuffers (two for 78). Taylor's 124 was his ninth Test century, but Australia's 289 looked below par. As Gooch and Atherton resumed their successful partnership – which had been interrupted by injury and prawns in India – 'England briefly looked like a team ready to compete for the Ashes,' in *Wisden*'s tremulous words. Atherton was out caught behind off Merv Hughes, Mike Gatting stomped out to the crease, and Shane Warne shuffled up to bowl his first ball in Tests in England.

If 1990/91 was the Tiger Moth series, so 1993 was the Ball of the Century series. It started on middle stump, drifted in, pitched outside leg stump, turned 18 inches and clipped the top of Gatting's off-stump. I watched it live on television. You wanted to see it again and again and again. (Thanks to YouTube, you still can.) Martin Johnson in the *Independent* put it into perspective: 'How anyone can spin a ball the width of Gatting boggles the mind.'

But imagine an alternative universe, in which Gower had not been fined £1000 for strafing the Carrara Oval, and had continued to serve England loyally and prolifically for another three or four years. He might have scored 10,000 Test runs. More pertinently, on a turning wicket and as a considerable player of spin bowling, he might have been batting at number three instead of Gatting. In which case that ball would have thumped into Gower's pads. Warne would have appealed, probably very throatily. The umpire would have said not out, and the game would have continued as normal. In this universe, however, England had picked eleven right-handed batsmen out of eleven. 'Never, perhaps, has one delivery cast so long a shadow over a game, or a series,' wrote Patrick Murphy in *Wisden*. Or a decade, we would now agree.

In fact Warne took only three more wickets in the innings, and not one ball turned as much. Merv took four wickets, as England conceded 79 runs on first innings. Gooch had been fourth out for 65, and played Warne better than anyone. The Australian batsmen cashed in. Boon got 93 (his fourth score in the nineties against England) and Mark Waugh 64, and then Steve Waugh (78 not out) and Ian Healy (102 not out) put on 180 for the sixth wicket. Healy's century was not only his first in Tests, but also his first in all first-class cricket, echoing Jack

Russell's achievement in 1989. (And where was he? At Tunbridge Wells, playing for Gloucestershire against Kent.) England 'looked depressingly pallid in the field during this partnership,' said *Wisden*. It was only the first Test, but they were a beaten team already. Border's declaration, timed to sadistic perfection, gave England a day and a half to survive, or 512 runs to win. Up to you if you want to go for it, mate. The pitch had dried out and slowed up: batting was easier, but that didn't mean it was easy. Every batsman got a start; none batted for less than half an hour; only Gooch went on to the century we needed from him and at least a couple of others. Half an hour after lunch, having scored 133, he instinctively flicked a glove at a ball from Hughes that was falling on his stumps, and was given out 'handled the ball', only the fifth batsman to be dismissed in this way in Tests, and the first Englishman. After that we were just waiting for the inevitable. Warne and Hughes picked up another four wickets each and Australia won by 179 runs.

For Lord's, their favourite ground, they left out Julian and gave off-spinner Tim May his ninth cap. England dropped DeFreitas (who, according to *Wisden*, had done 'little to justify his selection', as usual) and brought in Essex's Neil Foster, a wild hunch of England's latest manager Keith Fletcher, who might have seen him play once or twice before. Never mind that he was 31, had dodgy knees, and would actually be forced to retire after one more first-class match. Or that he hated Lord's, and had never played well there. The main thing was that he was the fourth of the 1989 rebels to play Test cricket after the end of his ban (Paul Jarvis had gone to India). Where were Matthew Maynard, Tim Robinson and Bill Athey? Presumably being saved up for Headingley.

Border won the toss. Mark Taylor scored 111, Michael Slater 152, David Boon 164 not out, Mark Waugh 99 (before Tufnell bowled him) and Border himself 77. It was so awful that when a ball finally beat the bat, there was a round of applause. England were all out for 205, a breathtaking 427 runs behind. Atherton was the star, as it were, with 80, while Robin Smith, stumped by Healy off Warne for 22, became the first England batsman ever to be given out by a third umpire studying TV replays. In the second innings Gooch was caught behind off Warne for 29, but Atherton and Gatting put on a hundred with great defiance. Atherton, on 97, clipped a ball from Border to mid-wicket. They took two, hesitated a moment on the third and decided to go for it. Gatting changed his mind, Atherton slipped and watched as Merv Hughes threw in the ball from the boundary. Run out for 99 at Lord's: no wonder he always looked as though the weight of the world lay on his shoulders. Hick (64) and Stewart (62) resisted for a while on the fifth day, but it was all over in time for HM The Queen's traditional teatime visit and handshake. She and Border must now have been old friends. Ted Dexter, meanwhile, was telling journalists that England would win the series four-two. The journalists were more interested in knowing when he would resign.

The only real problem for the Australians at the moment was the inability of the bowlers to take five wickets. Warne and Hughes had taken four each in the first innings, Warne and May took four each in the second. And this was without Billy Bloodnut, who had been carted off to hospital on the second day for an operation on a twisted bowel. His series was over, as was that of Neil Foster, Phil Tufnell, Chris Lewis and Mike Gatting. Graeme Hick was also dropped, despite his success in India and averaging 35 in this. But Merv Hughes had found his bunny.

Mark McC: Merv Hughes, the most unlikely selection in the history of Test cricket. This guy will never get anyone out. First Test at the WACA, 1986/87, got absolutely drubbed.

But look at Merv's record after that. He took 200 Test wickets faster than Curtly Ambrose. What happened was, he gave up the booze. Border made him stop drinking, get into the Mervaerobics, and his accuracy in that 1993 series – he was basically the only fast bowler they had – was extraordinary.

A famous photo exists of Hick walking off, head down, very recently dismissed, while an incandescent Merv screams abuse at him from a foot away. A brisk 'Fuck off!' would probably have done the trick, but Hick's passivity, rather than any lack of runs, probably cost him his place. Somehow I don't think Australia would have handled this delicate man-management issue quite so ineptly.

Still, the selectors were only reacting to universal public rage and contempt, which demanded sacrificial victims. The distracted air of Lord Ted, the dead hand of Fletcher, the hair shirt of Gooch himself: they weren't the most inspiring bunch. But for the third Test at Trent Bridge they took some serious punts. Gentle Mark Lathwell was called up from Somerset to open the batting, and Gooch dropped down to five to accommodate him, thus breaking up his opening partnership with Atherton, one of the few things that was working. Martin McCague, Kent's potato-faced emigré Australian, and Mark Ilott (from Essex) were the new seam bowlers; Graham Thorpe made his debut in the middle order and Essex's Nasser Hussain was recalled after three years. Only Atherton came from a county side north of St Albans.

But this strange multi-national hotch-potch of a team, with a New Zealander and an Australian opening the bowling, didn't start too badly. Robin Smith, who by making runs consistently for four years could probably count himself lucky to remain in the team, was promoted to number three and made 86 ('roistering,' said Greg Baum in *Wisden*). Hussain hit 71, his first Test fifty, batting at number seven, but others got in and got out, as they do. Merv Hughes took five for 92, his first five-for in Ashes Tests; England were all out for 321. You never felt it would be enough, especially when you watched Potato-Face run in, yet another 'good, honest trier' destined for failure at the highest level. Boon and Mark Waugh, the engine room, put on their third hundred partnership in successive Tests; Boon's 101 was his second successive century and 16th in all. (We hadn't thought much of him when he started either.) Waugh scored 70, but it needed a wag of the tail to bring Australia up to 373 and a relatively modest first innings lead of 52. At the close of the third day, despite 50 from Smith, England were 122 for four. If we lost this one, it would be the eighth Test defeat in a row. On Sunday morning the nightwatchman Andrew Caddick stayed for an hour. He had only taken two wickets in his first two and a half matches, but he had batted for nearly seven and a half hours. Gooch, meanwhile, stayed until an hour after tea to score 120, his 19th Test century and 11th as captain. When he reached his hundred, it was all he could do to lift his bat to acknowledge the cheers: this was serious and the job wasn't yet done. But this was England's best day of the series so far. Only the two wickets fell and, at close, we were 362 for six, with Thorpe unbeaten on 88 and Hussain on 16.

On Tuesday morning Gooch was able to declare and set Australia a target. I think I may have purred. Thorpe was still there on 114, as was Hussain on 47. How wonderful it had been to unearth new young batsmen who had immediately shown that they were equal to the challenge. Australia had 77 overs to survive – and, notionally, 371 to win – but Caddick suddenly made the ball swing and in the afternoon session Australia lost five wickets, as many as they had lost in the whole of the previous Test. At tea they were 115 for six. That was as good as it got. The ball grew soft, the pitch remained firm, the bowlers tired and Steve Waugh was at the crease. The seventh wicket never fell. Even so, it was the first Test England hadn't lost in nearly a year.

Before the fourth Test the Australians played Durham, and Ian Botham for the last time. He retired after the game, aged 38 and completely knackered. They had seen him off at last.*

---

* Now he is Sir Ian Botham. So why not Sir Michael Brearley? Baron Brearley of the Kirkstall Lane End? The Earl of Brearley, CH, OM?

Next up, though, was Headingley. Since the previous year the much-loved old Headingley Test pitch, which annually turned harmless English seamers into unplayable match-winners, had been dug up, apparently because Yorkshire feared losing their annual Test match. How could they? It was the only one we ever won. No one knew what the new pitch would do, but we soon found out. England left out Peter Such and gave Surrey's Martin Bicknell his first cap. Australia brought in Paul Reiffel for the injured Brendon Julian. Gooch won the toss, put them in under lowering skies and Australia scored 653 for four. Boon made 107, his third century in consecutive Tests, Slater 67 and Mark Waugh 52. That only took them up to 321 for four. The score was more than doubled by Allan Border (200 not out) and Steve Waugh (157 not out). It's like that warning they used to give on television programmes 35 years ago: if you are of a nervous dis-position, look away now. Gentle Mark Lathwell went third ball. England were all out for 200 and, following on, for 305. Reiffel took eight wickets in the match, Hughes six. Atherton – 'widely believed . . . to be batting for the captaincy,' said *Wisden* – made 55 and 63 in over seven hours at the crease. Alec Stewart had been aiming for an 'electioneering hundred' in the second innings – they are so cynical, these almanacks – but was caught in the slips for 78 and went off to clean his kit. In his post-match press conference, Gooch announced his resignation. He had captained England in 34 Tests and won ten of them, but nine of the last ten had been lost.

Michael Atherton, then, became England's 71st captain (and the fifth from Lancashire). For Edgbaston, gentle Mark Lathwell, a boy among men, was liberated of the burden of international representation, as was Andrew Caddick, whose five wickets had each cost 97 runs. Martin McCague had a back injury, which was a bit of luck. Back came Essex's Peter Such and, because the wicket was expected to turn, fresh-faced 41-year-old John Emburey, while shoring up the middle order was the fifth of the

South African rebels to be recalled, Matthew Maynard. It was a team, in short, that had defeat written all over it, although the absence of McCague probably ensured that it would just be comprehensive rather than ignominious.

Andy R: I'd been working in America for a year or so, and I'd only just got back. Someone had some tickets and we drove up to Edgbaston at extreme high speed. I didn't even know who was in the teams. So it was surreal to walk in and look and go, whoa! that's John Emburey! He even got runs. I can't remember who said this, but it was like watching a statue get down off its plinth.

England scored 276 (Atherton 72, Emburey 55 not out). It wasn't enough. Reiffel took another six wickets. Australia were 80 for four when Stewart failed to stump Steve Waugh second ball off Such. The Waugh twins added 153 for the fifth wicket. Steve made 59, Mark 137 and Ian Healy joined in with 80. M. E. Waugh's century was the tenth by an Australian in the summer, equalling the Ashes record. Bradman's Invincibles of 1948 had only managed eight. England made 251 in their second innings (Thorpe 60). Warne and May each took five wickets. Australia won by eight wickets, with Mark Waugh again so dominant against Such and Emburey that 'they seemed to be bowling on a different pitch to the Australians' (*Wisden*). Brings it all back, doesn't it. Really, by the end of the 1990s it's amazing that anyone in Britain was watching cricket at all.

Atherton was the seventh consecutive England captain to lose his first match in charge. (The last one to win his first had been Bob Willis.) Ted Dexter, in the meantime, had resigned as chairman of selectors, six months before his contract expired. When this was announced on the last day at Edgbaston, there was a round of applause. The team for the Oval was the last under his stewardship. Robin Smith, at sea all summer against Warne, was dropped after 45 consecutive Tests. Ilott went after three Tests, fresh-faced John Emburey's brief recall was over, and Bicknell had a dodgy knee. Back came Graeme Hick (who shouldn't have been dropped in the first place), Devon Malcolm and, intriguingly, Angus Fraser, who had only played two first-class matches since overcoming his long-term injury, while Glamorgan's Steve Watkin, the country's leading wicket-taker, finally got another chance (he had played one Test two years before). Then, an hour before play, Thorpe was hit on the hand in the nets, broke his thumb and passed out. The replacement had to be someone who was, literally, in the area. Mark Ramprakash was playing at Lord's and got the call. There are worse ways to renew your Test career.

Australia, of course, were unchanged. They were never injured, they never lost form. But, we soon realised, they were exhausted. Merv Hughes, in particular, had pushed his crumbling 31-year-old body to its limits. As Shane Warne noted, 'He said that if he ever needed five ice-packs instead of the usual four it was time to retire.' After Atherton won the toss, the England batsmen batted with greater ease than at any time that summer. Gooch made 56, Atherton 50, Hick 80 and Stewart 76 out of 380. Yet again, we thought, not enough. What we had forgotten was that England finally had a decent bowling attack. Malcolm was fast, Fraser was stingy, and Watkin was Welsh: you didn't mess with any of them on a hard, fast Oval wicket. Despite Taylor's 70, Australia were in trouble at 196 for eight. It needed all of Healy's grit – and 83 undefeated runs – to extend the innings to 303 all out (Fraser five for 87). England again started well, with Gooch scoring 79. Even in defeat, he had scored 673 runs at more than 56, and during this innings he passed Gower's Test aggregate to become England's highest scorer. Everyone applauded the moment, while all thinking the same thought: that Gower would have scored far more if Gooch had kept him in the team. After a middle-order wobble, Ramprakash, at number seven, scored 64, his first fifty in his tenth Test. England were bowled out for 313, leaving Australia 390 to win, or a whole day to survive.

It is a curious thing, but this series is regarded as less disastrous than 1989 primarily because of what happened here on the final day. The truth is that we needed quite a lot of luck. Slater was given out caught behind when the ball had only hit his arm-guard. Boon's lbw, first ball, wasn't plumb by any means. Border, given out caught behind just after lunch, stomped off in a rage. Reiffel and Warne put on 74 for the ninth wicket but for the first time all summer, in any match, no Australian batsman scored a fifty in a completed innings. Watkin took four for 65, Fraser three for 44, Malcolm three for 84 and England won by 161 runs. We had our consolation victory, the first of quite a few.

Interlude
1993

Andy J: You get there early — you're there by eight o'clock in the morning. Still half asleep. You jump out of bed, pick up your sandwiches . . . I was lucky enough to be a grass steward. So you just get there and you don't have to do anything until spectators start coming in. And you just make sure they don't put their coats over barriers or run on the pitch naked. That's your job. It's not too difficult. I wouldn't be a steward at Lord's now. They make you sit away from the cricket, facing the crowd. Before, you used to sit on a park bench, two of you to a bench, so there was someone to have a chat with. You'd watch the game, it was lovely.

So you'd be sitting there, reading the paper early doors, drinking your first cup of tea from the flask, and then you'd see the players come out for a little warm-up. The England players would come out, a couple of stretches, then go to the nets. Then you'd see the Australians come out, and they'd be running out, baseball mitts on, throwing it, diving around, a good warm-up, a good runaround, 45 minutes of it. It just seemed like a recipe for success. They had so much energy and enthusiasm. And I remember thinking, Blimey, they're looking hot, as opposed to, Blimey, they're looking relaxed and lukewarm.

Alan W: We are a generation that has been brought up knowing nothing other than horrific losses. My first Test series of all was 1992, which was a close-fought England vs Pakistan series. You had Wasim and Waqar, these amazing quick bowlers, and somehow we were able to compete with them, with the wiles of Neil Mallender and Tim Munton. England weren't as good as the opposition, and yet there was something of the wily old pro about them, even the young ones, and they could somehow compete. So that was my introduction, and then the Australians arrived the following year, and it was horrific.

And the stuff you remember, when you're getting to know the game: it's the completely inconsequential things that stick. For instance, it was Tim May's series for me, not Shane Warne's. All my memories are of Robin Smith storming down the wicket at Tim May, and being stumped. It just seemed to happen every time.

What else? There was a very fat man with a beard standing by the boundary rope, and I think it was Steve Waugh cover-driving Peter Such to the boundary, and this man stooping to pick up the ball, and the ball pinging up off the rope and hitting him in the face.

What was constant was the sense that the batting was flimsy – and not just flimsy technically or in terms of ability, but in terms of mental frailty. You'd look at Mark Ramprakash or Mark Lathwell coming out to bat, and even as a 13-year-old you could see the anxiety scrawled all over their faces.

And finally Atherton came in as captain and we won at the Oval, with a team of absolute no-hopers, as always. And we went off on tour and I really thought it was a bright new dawn. This is the very young cricket follower who knows no better. What I didn't realise was that this pattern was going to be repeated in every single Ashes series for the next ten years.

Jon B: My first experience of cricket was also my first experience of the word 'cunt'. I was 10. Devon Malcolm came into bat, and my dad threw the remote control at the television, and that's what he said.

Fourteen

1994/95

Man for man, on paper, the Australian side stand out like dogs' balls.

Greg Chappell

In 1993/94 England went to the West Indies, and David Gower wasn't invited. He took the hint and retired from first-class cricket. In the *Daily Telegraph*, his county captain Mark Nicholas acknowledged 'the end of [an] amazing career, a career in which he had never compromised, had always been himself: no posing, no con and few tantrums . . . In recent years nobody in a position of power has found it easy to cope with the Gower Thing. So dignified is his response to retribution that guilt overcomes the executioner.' In fact I can only think of one act of retaliation by Gower in all those years: he didn't invite Gooch to his wedding. 'He wasn't selected,' explained Gower. 'He's too old.'

The Gooch-Gower era was over, and the Atherton-Stewart era was about to begin. Atherton's young side – also lacking Gooch, Gatting and Lamb – lost 3–1 in a topsy-turvy series that took in a catastrophic defeat at Trinidad (46 all out) and an inspiring victory in Barbados immediately afterwards, the first time anyone had beaten the West Indies there in 59 years. And then, as an encore, Brian Lara scored his 375. Back in Blighty, Raymond Illingworth was appointed chairman of selectors. A man of strong views, some of them correct, he decided to dismantle the touring party when they came back and start again. The only five survivors in the first Test against New Zealand in 1994 were Atherton, Stewart, Fraser, Smith and Hick. The visitors, fortunately, were not at their strongest, and lost 1–0. South Africa's first series in England since readmission was tougher. Atherton's handful of dust overshadowed all else in a commanding South African victory at Lord's, Edgbaston was a run-heavy draw, and at the Oval Devon Malcolm took his nine for 57 ('You guys are history'), almost the most satisfying thing that has happened on a cricket field in my lifetime.*

In his six Tests in charge, though, Illingworth had already demonstrated that his legendary cussedness had turned into a sort of crazed and random dogmatism, almost as though he took delight in making decisions that everyone else would disagree with. For the 1994/95 Ashes tour, for instance, he chose to leave Angus Fraser behind. Pace, pace, pace was all that mattered in Australia, said Illingworth, and England's best bowler wasn't fast enough. The bowlers chosen instead were Malcolm, DeFreitas, Darren Gough of Yorkshire (who had taken 17 wickets in four Tests in the summer), Joey Benjamin of Surrey (who had played at the Oval) and potato-faced pie-chucker Martin McCague, who had taken 54 first-class wickets at 17 in the second half of the season. The batting combined promise, achievement and, that particularly English specialty, gnarled old age. As well as Atherton, Stewart, Hick and Thorpe, there were 23-year-old John Crawley, 41-year-old Graham Gooch and 37-year-old Mike

---

* I never could bear the South African team. Holier-than-thou crook Hansie Cronje, muscular Christian sledger Jonty Rhodes, humourless slab of beef Jacques Kallis ... and the fact that it was good old Devon, brave, big-hearted and extremely black, who destroyed them made it all the sweeter.

Gatting. There was no room for Ramprakash, Hussain or Robin Smith, who had lost his place before the South African series.* Yorkshire-born Steve Rhodes was the wicketkeeper (having played through the summer), Phil Tufnell and the uncapped Shaun Udal were the spinners, and Yorkshire's mild-mannered Craig White the all-rounder. Only six of these 16 had been in the West Indies a few months earlier. Keith Fletcher remained team manager, a miraculous survival that was ascribed by some to covert dealings with Beelzebub.

All began hopefully, though, with a non-defeat against Western Australia, during which Hick hit 172 and Malcolm nabbed six for 70. South Australia were beaten by four wickets, with centuries from Hick (first innings) and Gooch (second), and five-fors from McCague (first) and Gough (second). England didn't lose until the third match of the tour, against New South Wales.

Stewart had already broken a finger in a practice game, but returned for the draw against 'an Australian XI', in which Fletcher described England's batting as 'pathetic'. At home we tried not to read too much into this. It might all turn out fine. You never know.

If we had been paying attention, though, we might have seen that Australia were more vulnerable than for a while. Allan Border had finally retired, after 156 games, 153 of them in a row, 93 as captain, and 11,174 runs. The previous year, at home, New Zealand had been swept aside 2–0, but three-Test series against South Africa, home and away, had each been drawn 1–1. A quick trip to Pakistan had then been lost 1–0. Tubs Taylor was the new captain; Michael Bevan had replaced Border in the middle order. And Merv Hughes's knees had given way completely. It would

---

* Why was Smith not more appreciated? He was by us, the spectators, who remembered the countless times he saved his side's bacon and our sanity. And yet he only played 62 Tests: another criminal waste of talent.

have been pushing it a bit to say that Australia were there for the taking, but if everyone stayed fit and played out of their skins, we might have a chance.

And then Devon Malcolm got chicken-pox. Of course he did. Had he been inoculated for beri-beri? Was there anyone in the squad who hadn't had mumps? England's best bowler was in England, and their second best was in bed with a nasty rash. Step forward Phillip DeFreitas, serial underachiever, to bowl the first ball in the first Test in Brisbane.

Tom H: I'd got Sky specially to watch the Ashes series in Australia. Got all the cricket team around for the evening, including a couple of Australians who were playing for us at the time. Looking forward to a fair, hard contest. And the first ball was DeFreitas bowling a long hop, and Slater whacking it for four, and the palpable feeling of air going out of a balloon.

The ball would swing that morning, when bowlers came on who knew how to swing it. But the opening pair of DeFreitas and McCague conceded 26 off four overs and Australia were away. McCague usually ran in with a cartoon 'Grrrr' expression on his face, and walked back to his mark with his head down. Half an hour before the close, Slater chipped Gooch to Gatting at mid-off for 176. 'The two old men of the England side bring about the downfall of Michael Slater,' said Ian Chappell on Channel 9 with a chuckle. Gooch's moustache was now almost Victorian in its extent: he could have given Lord Kitchener a run for his money. Gatting's white beard suggested a lucrative future career as Santa Claus. Earlier in the tour Atherton had seen the two old blokes grazing in the outfield: 'I knew then it was going to be a long, long tour.'

The following morning, the agony continued. Mark Waugh shimmered on to 140, and Australia to 426 – less, maybe, than they had been expecting at 308 for two. Gough took four for 107. 'He's an impressive youngster,' said Chappell. England were all out for 167. Athers batted nearly four hours for 54 but only two other batsmen managed even 20. McDermott, his bowel twisted no longer, took six for 53. Taylor, aware that the ball would turn like a bastard on the fifth day, did not enforce the follow-on, and Australia piled on more runs. Tuffers bowled over the wicket into the rough, and took four good wickets for 79. Mark Waugh tried to reverse-sweep him, played on, looked a charlie. But after the declaration, England had 11 hours to survive, or not. (And 502 runs to win, or not.) At the end of the fourth day they were 211 for two, with Hick 72 not out, at his most authoritative, and Thorpe 66 not out, at his most fidgety. It was all an illusion. On the last day Warne took six for 27 in 25.2 overs. His eight for 71 in the innings would remain his career-best figures. England lost by 184 runs.

The next Test was a whole month away. Before then there were loads of ODIs to lose. Raymond Illingworth had insisted before the tour that his priority was the Ashes, which was why he had picked such a cumbersome and elderly squad for the ODIs. Their practice sessions, by all accounts, were unbearable to watch. 'England trained and grass grew at the MCG yesterday,' wrote Greg Baum in the Melbourne *Age*, 'two activities virtually indistinguishable from one another in tempo, but each with its own fascination.' Twice in December England played 50-over matches against the teens and tinies of the Australian Cricket Academy; twice they lost. There was only one escape from the nightmare: injury. Martin McCague incurred a stress fracture of the shin, and flew back home. (Well, back to England, anyway.) Illingworth, unabashed, called up Angus Fraser to replace him. McCague's Test career was over, although his finest hour was ahead of him: according to his teammate Steve Marsh's autobiography, he drank 72 pints of Guinness on his stag weekend in Dublin. Drinking to forget, maybe. The rest of us certainly were.

Each team made one change for Melbourne. Devon Malcolm's rash had gone, and his temperature was back to normal, while Australia's little-known new bowler, Glenn

McGrath, had made little impact at Brisbane, and was replaced by Damien Fleming. Atherton won the toss and put his hosts in on a damp pitch. Their 279, aided by 94 not out from Bloody Steve Waugh (as we all called him by this stage) and 71 from Mark, was probably 100 above par. Gough, with four for 60 off 26 overs, was again the outstanding bowler, although Malcolm also had his moments. One ferocious lifter hit Steve Waugh on the shoulder. 'Tell you what, he won't rub it,' said Tony Greig on Channel 9. 'No way in the world will he rub it.' And he didn't.

England then had some bad luck. Alec Stewart, opening with Atherton, broke his finger again, defending a short ball from McDermott. Hick was given out caught behind when the ball appeared to have only hit his thigh. Atherton went lbw to Warne for 44, another marginal decision, and Thorpe was given out bat-and-pad for 51, except without the bat. England were 148 for four at the end of the second day. First ball next day, Craig McDermott bowled a full toss and Gooch hit it straight back to him. *Wisden* acknowledged this as the turning point: 'From then until McDermott sealed Australia's victory, two days later, what was left of England's resolve and fighting spirit disappeared.' England were all out for 212 (Warne six for 46). Australia declared on 320 for six (Boon 131). With 120 overs to survive, England were dismissed for 92 in 42.5 overs. McDermott took five for 42. Warne's three for 16 came in successive balls. DeFreitas, Gough and Malcolm were the victims, and it was Warne's first hat-trick in any form of cricket. It was also the first in an Ashes Test since 1904, and the first in a Test by an Australian since, well, 9 October, when Damien Fleming got one against Pakistan. But that match was a dreary, high-scoring draw: this was an Australian victory by 295 runs. In his post-match interview with the England captain, Tony Greig was characteristically blunt. 'One would have to say that so far this tour is an ibsolute disAWSter from England's point of view. What can we do from here?' 'We've just got to pull our socks up and try and perform better,' said Atherton, looking very young. 'There's no miracles, just a bit of hard work and a bit of guts.'

At the Christmas Day fancy dress party, Graham Gooch went as Captain Hook ('without the hook nowadays,' he explained, 'too old'), Gatting was Henry VIII, with a rack of lamb in one hand and a roast turkey in the other, and Raymond Illingworth went as Fu Manchu.

For Sydney on New Year's Day, England brought in John Crawley for biscuit-fingered Stewart and Angus Fraser for Phillip DeFreitas, whose hamstring had gone. Australia were unchanged. It was humid and overcast, but the pitch looked good and quick, so Atherton had to bat. England were quickly 20 for three. It could have been even worse, had Steve Bucknor upheld an lbw shout against the captain by Damien Fleming. Instead Atherton and Crawley put on 174 for the fourth wicket, a battle won on the playing fields of Manchester Grammar School. But the second new ball accounted for them both, as well as Gatting, and Rhodes ran himself out. At the end of the day we were 198 for seven, staring down the usual barrel.

And yet this wasn't as bad a side as many we have put out. Robin Smith would have been useful to have around, and a couple of younger, more manoeuvrable batsmen instead of the oldsters, but the bowling attack for this Test was Gough, Malcolm, Fraser and Tufnell (with Hick and Gooch in support). In fact this was the only Test, against anyone, in which England fielded this bowling attack. What if they had had a couple of years together? What might they have done?

First, these four scored runs: Fraser, in a memorable sky-blue helmet, made 27 in two hours and 20 minutes, Gough 51 ('a jaunty innings of village-green innocence and charm,' said *Wisden*), Malcolm 29 (off 18 balls) and Tuffers four not out. England were all out for 309. Then it rained and rained, and when Australia came in to bat conditions were perfect for the seamers. Blam! 65 for eight. But Mark Taylor was still there. He and McDermott took a particular fondness to the bowling of Malcolm. On 107 for eight, a daft Malcolm bouncer sailed over Rhodes's head for four, and the follow-on was saved. Gough came back, caught and bowled Taylor with a slower ball, and yorked Damien Fleming first ball. Australia were 116 all out, 193 behind, and Gough had taken six for 49. Ray Lindwall sent him a note: 'Well batted, well bowled. Great effort. You will remember this match for ever. Keep up the great work and best wishes for the future.' They liked Gough in Australia, nearly as much as we liked him in England.

So, a new challenge: a chance to beat this team when the series was still alive. England batted with great care in their second innings. Gooch made 29 and Atherton 67, but it wasn't until Hick and Thorpe had both been in for a while that the run rate reached four runs an over. On 255 for two, Hick was on 98 and Thorpe 47. The last three balls of the 72nd over, Hick blocked. Everyone thought there would be another over before the declaration, but in an outbreak of irritability Atherton declared then and there and denied Hick his century. It was a mistake, as Atherton has been more than willing to admit ever since. It did nothing for team spirit and it can only have reinforced Hick's insecurity and self-doubt. Apparently he barely talked to his captain for the rest of the tour.*

Australia needed 449. Taylor and Slater began as though nothing could have been more straightforward. At the end of day four they had put on 139; both went on to centuries the following day, although Slater should have been caught by Crawley at mid-off ('Dear oh dear,' said Greg Chappell, 'when you can't take

---

* The TV commentators had another view. 'I agree with [Atherton], totally,' said Tony Greig. 'I think he's given him plenty of time.' Richie concurred. 'Some might think that's a harsh decision from Michael Atherton, but Graeme Hick had plenty of time out there for his hundred, and England's wishes and desires are paramount in this situation.'

catches as simple as this one, you don't want to win Test
matches.'), and on 175 Taylor was run out by a couple of inches,
but it wasn't given. A brief downpour settled the matter, anyway.
Taylor was persuaded that the win was no longer an option,
whereupon wickets immediately started to fall. Tufnell took a
brilliant catch – words we never imagined we would see in the
same sentence – off Fraser at deep square leg to remove Slater
(103). Malcolm bowled Taylor (113) with the second new ball.
The middle order fell in a heap, mainly to Fraser (five for 75).
England had spent all day trying to slow things down, to ensure
the draw. Now they were running between overs; even Gatting.
The last twenty overs started at 6.25, with seven wickets down
and Warne and May at the crease, but three overs later it was too
dark for Fraser and Gough to bowl. The two Australian spinners
negotiated the two English spinners without obvious difficulty,
and the match petered out. 'In the end,' said Ian Chappell, 'you'd
have to say it was their fielding that has cost them the opportunity to win this match.'

Let's catch up with the injury list for a moment. McCague
had gone, as had Craig White, with a torn side muscle. In an
ODI against Zimbabwe, Shaun Udal damaged a rib muscle,
which would also end his tour. Thorpe scored 89 and needed
hospital treatment for dehydration and heat exhaustion. Neil
Fairbrother had joined the tour and played in that ODI, but in
the next one he damaged shoulder ligaments as he dived in the
field, and that was the end of him. Gough broke down in the
same match with a stress fracture in his left foot, and was soon in
plaster and on a plane. Chris Lewis, playing club cricket locally,
was called up. In the four-day game against Victoria, Alec
Stewart returned, his finger healed. He was batting in the middle
order to avoid the new ball, but when he came in, the second
new ball was due. It hit the same finger and broke it for a third
time. End of tour. Hick made a century, but his four-hour
innings aggravated a back strain, which was rediagnosed as a

prolapsed disc. Bye bye, Hicky. Mark Ramprakash flew in from the England 'A' tour in India. Other players suffering injuries during the tour, but not allowed to go home, included Atherton (back), Thorpe (adductor), DeFreitas (groin) and Crawley (calf). Dave Roberts, team physio, broke a finger during fielding practice. And Tuffers, having heard that his latest marriage was in trouble, had a full-blown breakdown and checked into a Perth psychiatric hospital 'for observation'. An hour later, after the loony doctor had asked him about his childhood, he changed his mind and made a run for it. He was back in the team hotel, nursing a fag and a beer, before anyone had time to ring for another replacement.

Amazingly, though, England only had to make two changes for Adelaide. Chris Lewis and Phillip DeFreitas replaced Hick and Gough, which meant a five-man bowling attack and Steve Rhodes, not in the best of touch, batting at number six. Australia dropped Michael Bevan (81 runs at 13.5), who would return, and Tim May (one wicket for 219), who wouldn't, and gave first caps to South Australia's Greg Blewett and leggie Peter McIntyre. England won a useful toss, Atherton (80) and Gooch (47) put on 93, and then Gatting scored his first Test hundred since 1987, his tenth overall and, as it turned out, his last. A triumph of willpower over fading talent, it took him nearly seven hours, and Taylor made him fight for every run. He spent 77 minutes in the nineties, and half an hour on 99. The dominant Gatting of 1986/87 was a distant memory, but no more valuable innings had been played in the series. He was last out for 117, out of 353. Australia started well, as we had come to expect. Mystic Geoffrey Boycott came into the commentary box: 'Mark Taylor, the Australian captain and his partner at the other end, might be saying to Michael Slater, look, come on, just settle down a bit, you've got your half-century, you're playing very well, don't give it away.' Three seconds later Slater edged to second slip for 67. Taylor made 90, and then Blewett (102 not out) and Healy (74) put on 164 for the sixth wicket. Blewett, floppy-haired in the then-fashionable Hugh Grant manner, was the 16th Australian to score a hundred on Test debut. We hated every one of them.

England were 66 behind on first innings, and although Thorpe hit a fleet-footed 83, another defeat looked certain at 181 for six. Crawley and DeFreitas took the score on to 220 at the end of the fourth day: a lead of 154. But Australia were having an off-match. Fleming had a hamstring injury, Warne could find nothing in the pitch, and Australia didn't have a third seamer, unless you counted Blewett. In fact Mark Waugh was taking more wickets than anyone, and would end with five for 40, his best Test figures. On the fifth morning, DeFreitas was, in *Wisden's* words, 'seeing it like a football'. After Crawley was out for 71, he went on to 88 off 95 balls, with nine fours and two sixes. 'Absolutely superb knock,' said Geoffrey. Australia needed 263 to win in just over four hours. At lunch they were 16 for no wicket. Taylor edged Malcolm to slip for 13, and Slater mishooked to long leg. 'Tufnell!' screamed Bill Lawry. 'Tufnell! YEAH! TUFNELL!' He almost had time for a fag before it came down. Boon mishooked to the keeper, and Steve Waugh was bowled first ball. 'What a ripper!' yelled Lawry. 'Straight through him! Sheer pace from Devon Malcolm!' As ever, Devon looked modest and matter-of-fact about his achievement. 'That was a roaster,' said Ian Chappell. Australia were 23 for four. Tufnell took his only wicket of the match when Mark Waugh bashed a ball on to Gatting's toecap at short leg, and it lobbed up for an easy catch. After tea Australia were 83 for eight. Healy and Fleming now stayed for two hours and added an irrelevant 69, before Lewis got Fleming lbw with one that kept low. Moments later Malcolm had McIntyre lbw for 0 with a ball that looked as though it hit him outside the line and might not have hit the wicket. Malcolm ended with four for 39 and Lewis four for 24, and with 35 balls left, England had won by an unlikely 106 runs.

'Test cricket is alive and well,' said Bill Lawry. 'England hit back hard at the Adelaide Oval.'

So we were 2–1 down with one match to go. The Ashes were gone, forgotten; the series was rescuable. If we had forced a victory in the previous Test . . . well, it doesn't bear thinking about. If the Australians had been rubbish, that would have helped as well.

The fifth Test was at Perth, everyone's favourite trampoline. England left out Tufnell, brought in Ramprakash and reverted to a four-man pace attack. Australia had lost Fleming to injury and left out McIntyre for a third seamer. Glenn McGrath returned after several matches as 12th man, and Western Australian quickie Jo Angel came in to supply a little local knowledge. Australia won the toss and made 402. Slater's 124 was his fourth century in 11 Tests against England. Mark Waugh made 88 and Steve Waugh 99 not out. (Ha ha, sucker!) Gooch had dropped Slater early on; Malcolm dropped him on 58 and 87 (the latter a shocker at long leg); Crawley dropped Steve Waugh on 18; and when he reached 35, the same Waugh slashed DeFreitas between Thorpe and Atherton in the slips. Thorpey looked at Athers, Athers looked at Thorpey. The ball went to the boundary.

England were five for two and 77 for four. Thorpe (123) and Ramprakash (72) added 158 for the fifth wicket. With 444 runs at 49, Thorpe was the batting success of the tour, and Ramprakash showed why he should have been there from the beginning. But a second collapse left England 107 behind on first innings. Again Australia wobbled. At 123 for five (two each for Malcolm and Fraser) we had a sniff of hope. Which was gradually obliterated by the stench of failure and disappointment. Dropped by Thorpe in the slips, Bloody Steve Waugh hit another 80 and Greg Blewett (115) became the third Australian (after Bill Ponsford and Dougie Walters) to score hundreds in his first two Tests. England, set 453 to win, had 104 overs to survive. By the close of the fourth day they were 27 for five. Ramprakash (42) and Rhodes (39) were what my grandmother would call 'pissing in the wind'. McDermott took six for 36, England were all out for 123, Australia won by 329 runs.

There's a sort of consensus that in the 1990s Australia simply got better and better, and while we were compelled also to get better just to compete with them at all, the gap remained vast and unbreachable throughout. I'm not so sure. In 1994/95 Australia showed a vulnerability that, tragically, we were unable to exploit. They really had only two bowlers – McDermott (32 wickets at 21) and Warne (27 at 20). They had lost Border, who they would struggle to replace for years, and David Boon was ten Tests from the end of his career. We, on the other hand, were a potentially better team than we allowed ourselves to be. Raymond Illingworth wasn't entirely a bad thing: he would be proved right about Craig White, and Darren Gough (20 wickets at 21) was an inspired choice. But the initial decision to leave out Fraser was incomprehensible, and the selection of Gooch (245 runs at 24.5) and Gatting (182 at 20) didn't really work. (Hilariously, the two oldsters were two of only four squad members who remained fit from first to last. The other two were Steve Rhodes, who could only average nine with the bat and never played another Test, and Phil Tufnell, padded-cell excursions notwithstanding.) Gooch later talked of 'a tour too far' and both of them retired from international cricket at the end of it. We all felt for Atherton. Illingworth's need to dominate, to be in charge and to be seen to be in charge, clearly needled him intensely, and may have contributed to what *Wisden* called 'his lack of drive and urgency as captain'. The declaration at Sydney revealed a man under immense pressure, and itself put him under even more pressure. But he never buckled. Lancashire's Sisyphus would be pushing the ball up the hill for several years to come.

And there were one or two 'positives' to be taken away from the tour. Not only were there the form and promise of Thorpe,

Gough, Fraser and Ramprakash, but also team manager Keith Fletcher got the sack. A few friends and I thought of having a street party to celebrate. But we changed our minds when we found out who had got his job: Raymond Illingworth himself.

Fifteen

1997

He borders on being obsessive compulsive. He knows every
Test wicket he's ever taken, how the batsman was out and
what number victim they were.

Steve Waugh on Glenn McGrath

When I was interviewing my fellow cricket tragics for this book,
it struck me how few of them realised how inviolable the Ashes
itinerary is, or at least has been since the Packer circus was
wound up. Eighteen months after the series in England comes
the series in Australia. Two and a half years after that, another
series in England. 'But that's not fair,' said one. 'I mean, we're
more likely to win in England than over there, aren't we? So if
we win, we get to keep the Ashes for eighteen months, whereas
if they win they get to keep them for two and a half years.
Typical lowdown Australian trick.' Somehow I doubt that this
disparity has never occurred to Steve Waugh.

If you keep them permanently, of course, none of this matters
at all. Immediately after their 1994/95 triumph, Australia went
to the West Indies and beat them 2–1, the first team to win there
since 1972/73 and the first to beat the Windies anywhere since
1980. The following year they overcame Pakistan 2–1 and Sri
Lanka 3–0 at home, and in 1996/97, a busy season, they lost a

one-off Test match in India, beat the West Indies at home 3–2 and then went to South Africa and won 2–1. Along the way they mislaid David Boon (retired) and Craig McDermott (ravaged by injury), but discovered a world-class fast bowler in Glenn McGrath, a very good one in Jason Gillespie and another useful opening batsman in Matthew Elliott. But there was still that bedrock of experience: 1997 would be the third Ashes tour for Mark Taylor, Steve Waugh and Ian Healy, and the second for Shane Warne, Michael Slater, Mark Waugh, Paul Reiffel and Brendon Julian. Even the future was well cared for: the reserves on this trip, neither of whom would play a Test, included Adam Gilchrist and Justin Langer. As Chris Broad would later tell *The Wisden Cricketer*, 'The one thing we took an age to realise, and that Australia had started doing [in 1986/87], was to pick players who they thought would be very good and stick with them and make them better.'

Whereas for poor old England it was the usual rollercoaster: triumph, despair, absurdity, humiliation, and back to triumph again before you know what has hit you. In 1995 West Indies were the visitors and an intense, fluctuating six-Test series was drawn 2–2, an incredible achievement for Michael Atherton and his team. In South Africa, though, they lost 1–0, having held off the bull-necked ones for four Tests, and collapsed in a pitiful heap only on the last two days of the fifth, which by terrible coincidence I was there to watch. In 1996 the Indians were beaten 1–0 in early-season chill, and Pakistan won 2–0 when the sun came out. From there it was off to the World Cup with the usual ill-chosen squad of bits-and-pieces players. 'Hapless, Hopeless, Humiliated,' read the headline in the *Independent on Sunday*. 'We Must Get Rid of Lord's Losers,' said the *News of the World*. 'The England team and the system which produces it is a heavy lorry in the slow lane being passed by a succession of sports cars,' wrote CMJ in the *Telegraph,* narrowly avoiding being run over by his own metaphor. Fortunately we visited some even slower-moving vehicles in the aftermath, Zimbabwe and New Zealand. The series in Zimbabwe, treated too lightly by everyone, was drawn 0–0, but at least New Zealand were beaten 2–0. By now Raymond Illingworth had had enough and drifted off to his retirement villa in Spain, David 'Bumble' Lloyd was the new coach, the TCCB had become the ECB and Lord MacLaurin of Tesco was its chairman and new broom. 'Illingworth's three-year reign as chairman of selectors, and briefer period as all-purpose supremo, will not be remembered kindly,' wrote Matthew Engel in *Wisden*. 'He had no long-term strategy, merely faith in his own instincts.' The throughput of players, needless to say, had been astonishing, although it calmed down somewhat after Illingworth's departure. And, amazingly, Michael Atherton was still captain, worn down to premature old age by the job, but determined to go on, because that's what you do. All of us could identify with his suffering. He knew, as we knew, that international cricket wasn't just a game. It was unending punishment for a crime we hadn't known we had committed.

Nonetheless, the summer began promisingly with a 3–0 victory for England in the one-day series. The third, at Lord's, was the scene of a wondrous debut by 19-year-old Ben Hollioake, whose open-hearted 63 thrilled the nation. Could this be our year? Australia's greatest problem, curiously, was their captain. Mark Taylor was so out of form that he dropped himself from the one-day team. Since hitting 96 against Sri Lanka at Perth in December 1995, he had scored 360 runs in 11 Tests at an average of under 19, with a top score of 43. Poor man: whenever anyone engaged him in conversation, it was to ask him when he would resign. You are the weakest link, Mr Taylor: goodbye.

Curiously, though, the Australian opener who couldn't get a game was not Taylor but Michael Slater, who had lost his place to lantern-jawed left-hander Matthew Elliott. His apparent crime was 'impatience', but never mind, because the sight of 'Slats' smacking the first ball of the series for four was one we were happy to avoid. At Edgbaston Taylor chose to bat, took the first ball himself from Gough, and watched it zip past the outside edge. Gough was opening the bowling with Devon Malcolm, recalled by new chairman of selectors David Graveney, with Andrew Caddick first change. The great new bowling find of the previous summer, Dominic Cork, who had taken 26 wickets against the West Indies, including a hat-trick, was crocked. The current favoured spinner was Robert Croft of Glamorgan, who had topped the averages in New Zealand. He didn't get a bowl in this first innings. After 20 overs Australia were 54 for eight. It was dazzling stuff. 'The sheer drama of it all scrambled the senses,' wrote John Etheridge in *Wisden*. Shane Warne and, in his third Test, pace bowler Michael Kasprowicz doubled the score. Warne was last out for 47 and Australia had made 118. Caddick had five for 50, Gough three for 43, Malcolm two for 25. It was the first time these three had bowled together. The second and last time would be the next Test.

Alan W: There was a great moment when Darren Gough bowled someone with a no-ball, and he was already celebrating when he realised, and he walked back to his mark, ran in and bowled him again. Which was just fantastic.

Andrew N: When England got Australia to 54 for eight, I went to the Ladbrokes portakabin and saw Brian Close sitting on one of those plastic seats, having a bet on all-weather racing at Wolverhampton. And he walked over and said, how did Lord Scrap do in that race? And someone said, third. And he said, oh, all right, and sat down again. And here's this hero of the sixties and seventies sitting on a plastic seat in a Ladbrokes portakabin, and you want to say, get out there! Go! Get out there!

Chris D: In the crowd there was a man in front of us who sat there doing his Guardian crossword all day. He was on his own, and he had his sandwiches and his thermos of tea, and he didn't speak to anybody, just sat there, very quietly. And then at about five to six, he put his thermos and his rucksack down, stripped off and underneath he was dressed as Superman. And he ran across the pitch.

There was, of course, much discussion about the pitch. The 1995 and 1996 Tests at Edgbaston had finished in three and four days respectively. England's latest batting line-up started with Mark Butcher, recent graduate of a highly successful England 'A' tour of Australia,* and had Alec Stewart keeping wicket again and batting at number three. Neither lasted long, as England struggled to 50 for three. But Nasser Hussain and Graham Thorpe dumbfounded a nation, maybe even two nations, with a record fourth-wicket stand against Australia of 288. (The previous record had survived just 59 years.) Hussain's 207 was the innings of his life: 'Touched by genius,' said Etheridge. The frailties in his game seemed to have been excised with Gooch-like single-mindedness.

Andy R: I was there and I watched him get it. I liked Nasser anyway, but I thought that double ton . . . the fact that he got it against the Aussies and the way that every run really mattered to him, it was just fantastic. I think, in a lot of ways, that Test set Nass up for what was to come.

Thorpe's 138, dare one say it, was less of a surprise, and his third century in four Tests. Like Robin Smith before him, Thorpe's consistent excellence had been taken for granted by some, and grievously underestimated by others. (He, Malcolm and Fraser had all failed to impress Illingworth at various stages, making one wonder, even now, exactly what did impress him, other than his reflection in the bathroom mirror.) Thorpe's 'cutting and sweeping of Warne were crucial in seizing the initiative', said Etheridge. I remember the wonderful mental strength of the two batsmen, blossoming into genuine confidence and even,

* Unlike most such squads, this one was made up almost entirely of former and future Test players. Among the future internationals were Dean Headley, Ashley Giles, Michael Vaughan and 18-year-old Owais Shah.

towards the end, a sort of light-headedness. It was Glenn McGrath's first Test in England, and he hadn't got his length right. But even Warne was hit for more than a hundred runs, and took only one wicket – Hussain's. Later on Mark Ealham, the latest applicant for the long-unfilled post of England all-rounder, hit a merry 53 not out, allowing Atherton to declare on 478 for nine.

One thing was certain: Australia weren't going to cock it up again. At first scratchily, and then nearly as scratchily, Mark Taylor batted from memory to put on 133 with Matthew Elliott (66), and nearly as many with Blewett. I was at the wedding of one of my oldest friends: in an ante-room in the hotel, I found a telly mounted high on a wall. 'Why do you keep disappearing?' asked my girlfriend suspiciously. But every time I escaped into the back room, Greg Blewett would smash a good length ball through the off side for four. I reacted in the only way I knew how: drink far too much and dance very badly to dismal disco favourites from the late 1970s.

At close, Australia were 256 for one. They added another 71 in the morning as Blewett became the first man ever to score a hundred in his first three Ashes Tests. But then Robert Croft caught and bowled Taylor for 129 and nipped out Blewett for 125. Gough worked through the middle order and Ealham did for the tail. Australia were all out for 477. England needed 116 to win and if they got a move on, they could do it before close on the fourth day. Butcher hit 14 off ten balls, and then Atherton (57 not out) and Stewart (40 not out) took over. Victory came in the 22nd over. 'The adrenaline was flowing so much that I couldn't stop myself playing attacking shots,' said Atherton. It's amazing what the prospect of a day off will do for you.

Better days to take off would have been June 19th to 23rd, the Lord's Test. After the first day had been lost to rain, Taylor put England in and, when it wasn't bucketing down, his bowlers bowled them out for 77. Glenn McGrath, who had done some serious fine-tuning since Edgbaston, took eight for 38. Paul Reiffel, replacing the injured Gillespie, took two for 17 in 15 overs. Taylor played on to Gough in his third over, but Elliott was dropped three times on the way to 112, his first Test century. 'England were suddenly unrecognisable from the competent unit of a fortnight earlier,' wrote David Frith in *Wisden*. After Blewett went for 45, Mark Waugh was dropped at slip by Hussain and went unstumped by John Crawley, standing in as wicketkeeper for Alec Stewart (back spasms). Going for everything, throwing away wickets with crazed abandon, Australia declared at 213 for seven on the fourth evening, but the pitch had calmed down, the sun came out, and Butcher (87) and Atherton (77) made the game safe. One-nil up, with four matches to go. We had been lucky.

Alan W: Lord's showed the Australians that we're not that good, actually. As if they hadn't known it already.

After brushing Hampshire aside, Australia made one change for Old Trafford. Jason Gillespie, his hamstring healed, replaced Kasprowicz. England dropped Devon Malcolm and gave a first cap to Kent's Dean Headley, grandson of George, son of Ron, and therefore the third member of his illustrious family to play Test cricket.* On a green pitch with bare patches at either end, Taylor chose to bat and England couldn't believe their luck. Just before tea, Australia were 160 for seven. But Steve Waugh was still at the crease, with that expression on his face. (It may have had something to do with the fact that England were certain they had had him plumb lbw when on 0.) Paul Reiffel, as useful a number nine as ever played Test cricket, joined him. After a break for bad light, Stewart dropped Reiffel behind the stumps off Headley. Sorry, but where was Russell? Had we not learned this lesson by now? This drop 'could be construed as the turning

---

* Ron played only two Tests for the West Indies in 1973, but no one who saw his extravagantly flared trousers will ever forget them.

point of the entire season,' said *Wisden*. A switch is flicked, and thereafter Australia will not be denied.

Waugh scored 108, and said afterwards that it was the best of all his millions of centuries. Reiffel contributed 31 to an eighth wicket stand of 70. Headley took four for 72 and Gough three for 52, but the significance of the Waugh-Reiffel partnership was made clear by England's first innings of 162. For the third time in three first innings, Atherton was dismissed for buttons by McGrath. 'In the end, I don't think it mattered what I bowled, he seemed to get out to it,' the old bastard said years later. 'I got him out caught behind, caught in the slips a lot – he probably played at the ball occasionally when he didn't have to. But other times when he decided to leave it, it seamed back and got him lbw. It became a mental battle more than anything else.' Warne, getting vicious spin, took six for 48 off 30 overs; Butcher's 51 was top score and sealed his place for a while. Headley took out both openers, and Blewett blew it, but the Waughs responded to the circumstances in their contrasting ways. Mark played the connoisseur's innings, the one even we would pay to see, before Ealham bowled him for 55. Steve, his right hand badly bruised, gritted it out for 116 in more than six hours. He was only the third Australian batsman to score a century in each innings against England, and the first since Arthur Morris in 1946/47. Then Healy scored 47, Warne 53, Reiffel 45 not out and Gillespie 28 not out. England had the usual unreachable target – 469 runs – and far too many overs – 141 minimum – in which to survive. They were all out before lunch on the final day for 200. Crawley made 83, and also sealed his place for a while.* The series score was only one-all, with three Tests to go, but all our hope and optimism of a few weeks earlier had been squished like an ant under a jackboot.

---

* 'Australians play for national pride. Englishmen play for their place in the next Test.' Discuss.

Give David Graveney some credit, though: unlike some of his predecessors, he resisted the temptation to sack half the team and replace them with people who were even worse. For Headingley he made just the one terrible decision, to call up Mike Smith, the Gloucestershire medium-pacer, as a horses-for-courses selection. Caddick was dropped, and on a pitch of uneven bounce (which would have suited Caddick perfectly) Smith took no wickets at all, and never played a Test again. Taylor won his fourth toss of four, put England in, and they were all out for 172. Gillespie took seven for 37. Australia were 50 for four with two young players at the crease: 25-year-old lantern-jawed Matthew Elliott and bustling 22-year-old Ricky 'Punter' Ponting, who had come in at number six for Michael Bevan. Elliott immediately edged a ball from Smith to Thorpe at first slip. He dropped it. Elliott scored 199 and 'Punter' 127. Australia declared on 501 for nine. In their second innings, Hussain made 105 and Crawley 72, but 222 for four became 268 all out, in familiar fashion. Reiffel had five for 49. In other news, two men dressed as a pantomime cow were crash-tackled by stewards, and the rear end needed treatment in hospital. And a university lecturer dressed as a carrot was ejected from the ground for 'drunken and abusive behaviour'. He denied these allegations. Apparently the turnips had started it.

For England, it was time to panic. Ealham, Smith and Butcher (unluckily, I thought) were dropped, and Gough had a sore and inflamed knee. Back in were Malcolm and Caddick (who should never have been out) and the Hollioake brothers, Adam and Ben. You've got brothers? We've got brothers. Ben, at 19 years 269 days, was the youngest England debutant since Brian Close in 1949*. His selection for the Trent Bridge Test was not so much a measured response to desperate circumstance, as a wild

---

* When presumably he had some hair. Maybe this is just me, but I don't recall ever seeing a photograph of Brian Close in which he had hair.

punt conducted with a manic giggle and fingers crossed. Taylor
won the toss and batted on a shirtfront. I was there. I wish I
hadn't been. Headley, Caddick and Malcolm did their best on a
baking hot day, and the fielders let no one down, but Australia
were just a much better side. Elliott, Taylor, Blewett and the two
Waughs all scored fifties out of 427; Headley had the best figures
once again with four for 87. There was an air of inevitability
about it. As I wandered around the ground, I kept bumping into
people I knew, which was strange, and not just because I don't
know anyone who lives in Nottingham. But no one wanted to
watch it. It was miserable.

Batting at number three, and keeping wicket, Alec Stewart
had so far scored 126 runs at 18. Now, opening again, he and his
heavy bat cracked a spectacular 87 runs.* Thorpe made 53 and
Adam Hollioake 45 not out, but McGrath and Warne each took
four wickets, Australia led by 114 and everyone on both sides,
and everyone listening on the radio, or watching it on TV, or
trying to ignore it completely, could see where the match was
heading. Even when Australia stuttered a little in their second
innings at 171 for five, Healy and Punter smacked 105 at a run
a minute in what Peter Johnson in *Wisden* called 'one of their
familiar spirit-crushing routines'. England were set a target of a
vast number of runs in a very long time. Despite Thorpe's
unbeaten 82, it was all over before the end of the fourth day and,
wrote Johnson, 'one of the more lifeless and misguided England
innings of a dark decade passed quietly into history'. Journalists
asked Michael Atherton whether he would resign now or later.
He presented a slightly straighter bat to that than the one he had
been using for McGrath.

---

* Boycott later told Stewart, 'If you'd been able to open ... all the time,
rather than getting distracted by your wicketkeeping, you'd have gone
down as one of England's greatest openers.' Stewart averaged 34.92 when
keeping wicket, and 46.90 when he wasn't.

The Ashes were gone, the series was gone and, at the Oval, several England players had gone. John Crawley, averaging 30 for the series, got the heave-ho, as did Robert Croft, whose eight wickets had each cost 54, and Ben Hollioake, who had looked every minute of his 19 years at Trent Bridge. Headley was injured, which meant recalls for Butcher (who again shouldn't have been dropped), Tufnell (on his favourite ground), Mark Ramprakash (the enigma) and Peter 'Digger' Martin of Lancashire, who had been in the wickets recently. Australia had lost Reiffel (who had flown home for the birth of his child) and Gillespie to injury, so Kasprowicz was back, and the Tasmanian all-rounder Shaun Young had a surprise call-up, having scored heavily for Gloucestershire. Mark Taylor lost his first toss of the summer and England decided to bat in steamy south London heat. They must have been thinking of 500. They scored 180. Matthew Engel in *Wisden* called it 'a total only useful at darts'. McGrath just did what he always did – bowl very straight, and sledge remorselessly – and took seven for 76. Caddick and Martin each hit a six, and England were bowling before tea.

So we settled back for the usual. Tufnell took out both openers, but at the end of the day Australia were 77 for two. And then on day two, things began to happen. The pitch, too dry from the beginning, started to wear and Tufnell bowled with patience and aggression, mainly over the wicket, in an unbroken spell of 35 overs. I think it was one of his ball-on-a-string days. He removed M. E. Waugh (19), Blewett (47), Healy (2), Young (0) and finally Ponting (40) for figures of seven for 66. Caddick took the other three, including the vital wicket of S. R. Waugh, lbw for 22. Australia led by only 40 on first innings. At close on the second day, England were 52 for three, and Hussain cut the second ball of the third day straight to Matthew Elliott at gully. But Warne was in trouble. Some-where along the line – maybe when slogging Tufnell – he had incurred a groin strain.* Thorpe and Ramprakash put on 79. Thorpe's 62 was 'an innings of exceptional quality and tenacity,' said Engel. Ramprakash's 48 was 'worth at least double'. (We were always amazed when he showed what he was capable of at Test level. Perhaps we should have noticed that it was always against Australia. He should have played every Test against them and none against anyone else.) Unfortunately the tail crumbled, and Kasprowicz became the third bowler in the match to take seven wickets in an innings, this time for 36. Australia needed 124 to win.

It was, of course, a dead rubber. Twice before in 1997, Australia had lost the last Test of a series they had already won. And tiny targets had tripped them up in the past. It was probably this last fact that inspired the Oval crowd to roar Malcolm in with every ball, and his fourth delivery had Elliott lbw. Taylor and Blewett looked comfortable enough, so Atherton brought on Tufnell and Caddick to bowl in tandem. Both were magnificent. Caddick had Taylor lbw and Blewett caught behind. Matthew Engel described this latter as 'a quaint decision' by umpire Lloyd Barker. Each bowler got a Waugh, and Australia were 54 for five. Oh yes. We were all watching now. Ponting and Healy fought back. At 88 for five they were just 36 short. But Tufnell had Ponting lbw on the back pad, and Healy thumped a caught and bowled back to Caddick, which he nearly dropped, twice. Warne was batting with a runner, tried to hit Tufnell over the top, and found Digger Martin. Digger had dropped Warne 24 hours earlier and might have been feeling a little trembly as the ball swirled down. But he caught it, the last two didn't hang around and England won by 19 runs. Tufnell had taken four for 27, Caddick five for 42. It was the first time an Oval Test had finished in three days since 1957.

* It seemed to have got worse overnight, which amused us all immensely.

So one of the oddest of modern Ashes series had ended in a 3–2 defeat. At Edgbaston we had caught them unprepared; at the Oval they were mentally on the plane home. In the interim they had demonstrated an unquestionable superiority: when they made the one change in their top six, it was to bring in someone who would go on to score 10,000 Test runs. But that last game gave us hope. Cruel, really. We would have been much better off without it.

Sixteen

1998/99

*Despite the fact that it was a day off, seven of us –
me, Chalky, Gus, Tudes, Ramps, Suchy and Nass –
turned up for a session in the nets along with Bumble and
Fizz.*

Alec Stewart in his book *A Captain's Diary:
The Battle for the 1998/99 Ashes*

Even the strongest men run out of puff in the end. For
Michael Atherton the last straw was a series in the West Indies
that we should have won but lost 3–1. The Windies were in
decline and Brian Lara was captain, usually a recipe for
disaster. And after the Oval, England knew they had the
potential to do the job. With three Tests to go, the teams were
one-all. At Guyana Lara won the toss, enabling him to bat
first before the pitch fell to bits: 2–1 to the Windies. In
Barbados England set a target of 375, more than the West
Indies had ever scored in a fourth innings to win. It hadn't
rained there for five months. On the morning of the fifth day
the skies opened. By lunchtime people were building arks.
Still 2–1 to the Windies. Then at Antigua Lara won another
decisive toss, and bowled on a pitch so damp that three divots
came out of it in the first over. Atherton resigned in despair.

He had borne the burden for too long. It was someone else's turn.*

The someone else, of course, was Alec Stewart, who had been patiently waiting his turn for as long as the rest of us had been dreading it. Fine, attacking batsman, fair if reluctant wicket-keeper, Stewie had always appeared to ally himself with the Gooch school of England skippership – lead from the front, best foot forward, 50 press-ups before breakfast, leave the talented mavericks behind. And so it proved. Neither Andrew Caddick nor Phil Tufnell played a single Test under his captaincy. Nonetheless, all started promisingly. England beat South Africa at home 2–1, the first 'big' series they had won since 1986/87 (before Atherton had played first-class cricket). The stars were the experienced players: Butcher, Atherton and Stewart himself, who all averaged over 50 with the bat, Fraser (24 wickets at 20.5) and Gough (17 at 23). Unfortunately the summer was marred slightly by defeat in the one-off Test against Sri Lanka, who pulled off an amazing smash-and-grab raid courtesy of Jayasuriya (213 runs at top speed), Muralitharan (16 wickets) and Ranatunga (captaincy and outrageous chutzpah). England looked dim and stolid in comparison.†

For Australia, then, Stewie was backed up by new team manager Graham Gooch and coach David 'Bumble' Lloyd. Hussain

---

* 'I did one tour too many,' Atherton told Stephen Fay in the *New Statesman* in 2001. 'I knew instinctively I should have packed it in when we beat Australia at the Oval in 1997 . . . The more you think about it, the more you get talked round to a thing you don't want to do.'
† Alec Stewart, by coincidence, was born on the same day of the same year as Julian Lennon, another son of a famous father. Michael Atherton was born on the same day of the same year as Damon Albarn, of Blur. Here are a few other notable twins. Chris Old, Noel Edmonds. Dickie Bird, Jayne Mansfield. Matthew Hayden, Winona Ryder. Mike Gatting, Javed Miandad. Mike Denness, Richard Pryor. Geoffrey Boycott, Manfred Mann. Keith Fletcher, Joe Cocker. And my personal favourite: Eddie Hemmings, Ivana Trump.

was vice-captain, and the other batsmen were Atherton, Butcher, Thorpe, Ramprakash and Crawley. (Hick and Crawley had both scored first innings centuries against Sri Lanka, in what was widely seen as a play-off for the final place.) The faster bowlers were Fraser, Gough, Corky, Dean Headley, left-armer Alan Mullally (who had played nine Tests in 1996 and early 1997) and Surrey's Alex Tudor in the young tyro slot. Robert Croft and Peter Such supplied spin, Ben Hollioake was the all-rounder and Lancashire's Warren 'Chucky' Hegg the spare wicketkeeper. (Jack Russell had played his last Test, as had Devon Malcolm.) For Stewart, Atherton and Fraser, it would be a third tour to Australia; for Crawley, Gough, Thorpe and Ramprakash, a second; and four others had been there on England 'A' tours. Alan Mullally had grown up in Western Australia, and Ben Hollioake had been born in Melbourne and grown up in Perth. Previous experience would not be a problem for this team.

Present incompetence, though, might yet be. In the second first-class match, against South Australia, England trailed by 138 runs on first innings, and were 80 for four in the second when Ramprakash joined Thorpe. They put on 377, unbeaten, the highest partnership by any touring team in Australia, the best for an English team overseas in 45 years and the best by any representative England team since 1957. Thorpe's 223 not out was a career best, Ramprakash's 140 not out was another century of many and the game was saved in style. A mood of cautious optimism infused the squad, in between all the cross-country runs. Even so, the first injuries had already been sustained. Stewart had tweaked his back and missed the first match, during which Mark Butcher ducked into a good length ball, which meant ten stitches above his left eye.* Atherton's by now chronic back problem had worsened: as usual he was playing through the pain. Ben

---

* But he also won a Corby trouser press, for being 'the best dressed player'.

Hollioake had pulled a groin muscle, and during the Queensland game John Crawley was set upon by a local drunk while walking back to the team hotel. The drunk asked him if he was Irish, called him a wanker and punched him so hard he was momentarily knocked unconscious. Crawley was badly cut and bruised about the face. Graeme Hick flew in as cover for Atherton, but would stay for the rest of the tour. Everyone was trying their hardest not to trip off kerbs, or type too vigorously.

For once, though, the Australians also had injury worries. Shane Warne was still recovering from a shoulder operation in May, and Jason Gillespie hadn't played a Test since the Oval. The 1997/98 season had been frantically busy: three Tests at home to New Zealand (won 2–0), three more against South Africa (won 1–0), the usual absurd burden of ODIs and finally, exhausted, three Tests in India, which had been lost 2–1. By then McGrath and Reiffel had also been injured (Reiffel had played his last Test); Matthew Elliott had lost his place to Michael Slater after a poor series against South Africa; while Greg Blewett had averaged 21 against South Africa and eight in India, and also disappeared from view. This season Australia had already nipped over to Pakistan for three Tests, and won 1–0, with Mark Taylor hitting his record-equalling 334 not out (the record being Bradman's). And now came their favourite bunnies of all, against whom they had won 17 Tests in the past ten years and lost four, only one of them before the Ashes had been decided. And Brisbane, with a fine sense of occasion, was also Mark Taylor's 100th Test.

England, then, left out Crawley and Hick of their eight batsmen, and played a five-man bowling attack: Gough, Fraser, Mullally, Dominic Cork and Robert Croft. (After three years in and out of the side this would be Cork's first Test against Australia.) The home side had Justin Langer at number three (he had batted there with distinction in Pakistan), McGrath, Fleming and Kasprowicz to bowl fast, and the crazed Stuart

MacGill to bowl leg-spin. In his first two Tests, against South Africa and Pakistan, MacGill had taken 14 wickets and thus begun what must be one of the most frustrating Test careers of modern times. If he had been a few years older or younger or not Australian at all, he might have played 100 Tests and taken 400 wickets. As it is, he would spend the next decade as Warne's understudy. No wonder he was such a basket case.

Taylor won the toss, batted on a Brisbane beauty and Australia scored 485. It could all have been so different. Steve Waugh and Ian Healy came together at 178 for five and put on another 187. On 29 Waugh should have been run out by Stewart, but Mullally had already knocked off the bails by mistake. At 68 he was dropped by Hussain at second slip. At 36 Healy mis-pulled Gough to third man where Fraser dropped it. At 62 he played on to Gough, and the bail didn't come off. Gough ended with one for 135, a travesty. Mullally had five for 105. Waugh made 112, Healy 134 and Damien Fleming one of those heartbreaking lower-order 71 not outs of which England players are so rarely capable. Atherton was caught in the slips off McGrath in the fifth over, for 0. I was listening on the radio in the early morning. I switched off, and ate three bowls of Shreddies in incoherent rage.

Alan W: My single overriding memory of the Ashes is of Glenn McGrath bowling a ball to Mike Atherton on or around off-stump. The ball itself doesn't do anything at all. It's straight up and down, and Atherton finds himself in a convoluted position, with the bat coming across slightly, and the ball ends up in third slip's hands. And the thing that was always really annoying about it, beyond the fact that it happened every single fucking time, was that Richie Benaud would always describe it as 'a good leg-cutter', when it had never done anything. That used to make me really cross.

Darrien B: Atherton went to my school. It was drummed into you: Atherton, England captain. And then you think, Is he actually that good? This bloke [McGrath] keeps getting him out every time. I used to consider it a triumph if he was second man out.

The third day was better. Mark Butcher scored a wondrous, aggressive 116, 'a great innings', according to CMJ in the *Telegraph*. 'He proved himself again to be not only a top-class opening batsman but also a man of exceptional character and the soundest temperament.' Hussain made 59, Thorpe 77 and Ramprakash 69 not out, but England lost their last six wickets for 60 and conceded 110 on first innings. McGrath took six for 85, as you might expect. Slater then hit a dazzling 113, his ninth Test century (and fifth against England), and Langer 74, allowing Taylor to declare on the evening of the fourth day. England needed 348 to win. Twenty minutes before tea on the final day they were 179 for six, with Croft and Cork hanging on desperately, when it began to rain. Alec Stewart reckoned it was the first time in his 82 Tests that England had been saved by the weather. But CMJ pointed out that they had made the same old mistakes: 'They dropped catches, batted on the fourth morning as though the game was safe when it was not and proved vulnerable once more to the two types of bowler they do not themselves possess: a leg-spinner and a match-winning fast bowler.'

For the Perth Test, Australia brought in Gillespie for Kasprowicz and omitted MacGill, because leg-spinners had never flourished there, even Warney. In came Colin Miller, a journeyman off-spinner who had started out as a right-arm swing bowler. Nicknamed 'Funky' because of his earrings and predilection for multi-coloured hair, he always reminded me of a bloke in my local pub we called 'the world's oldest punk'. England left out Angus Fraser (who had also never flourished on this ground) and Robert Croft, while Thorpe's back had seized up after the twelve-hour flight from Brisbane. This latter was the crucial loss. Still recovering from an operation in the summer to remove a cyst from a facet joint, England's best batsman (with an average against Australia of 49) would soon be flying home. Crawley and Hick came into the side, as did Alex Tudor to make his debut on the notorious WACA trampoline. The local equivalent of the Tote put an ad in the paper, exhorting readers to 'Do Something Nobody's Done for Years – Bet on the Poms' in vast letters. What, at five to one? You've got to be kidding. Only one England side had ever won here: Mike Brearley's 20 years before.

Stewie lost his second toss of the series and England were all out for 112 in three hours. The world's fastest pitch had wreaked its usual havoc. Mark Taylor then showed how it should be done, leaving countless good length balls that bounced harmlessly over the stumps. His 61 took marginally longer than England's entire innings. Gough took three wickets and Tudor four to limit Australia to 240, although again, catches were dropped. 'Taylor and Mark Waugh had made similar chances look easy,' wrote CMJ. After five wickets in the first innings, Damien Fleming took the first four in the second innings, bowling a good length into the wind. England were 15 for three, 40 for four, 67 for five. Ramprakash, who had batted longest in the first innings for 26, was looking Ken-Barrington-tough, while Hick, coming in at number seven, suddenly cast off all doubts and inhibitions. Gillespie, bowling short and fast, was pulled over square leg for six, square cut for four and pulled again for an even bigger six. But he got his man on the morning of the third day for 68, and all the other wickets as well. Gough lasted one ball, Tudor two and Mullally four. Ramprakash was left on 47 not out. Australia needed 64 to win. The match was all over before tea on the third day. But at least England's debutant, with match figures of five for 108, had acquitted himself. 'Tudor's emergence as an opening partner for Gough has long-term significance,' wrote CMJ, 'if England can somehow keep them both fit.'

It was Adelaide next, and while several of the England squad played themselves into and out of contention in a first-class match against Victoria, Australia was gripped by the revelation that Mark Waugh and Shane Warne had taken cash from Indian bookmakers a few years earlier for 'information on pitch and weather conditions'. Not only that, but the Australian Cricket

Board had found out, fined them both several thousand dollars and then kept it all secret. No one suggested for a moment that Warney and Waugh-y had fixed matches (actually, that's not true – we all did in the pub) but it was the ACB's cover-up that really attracted the attention. Just when you think that administrators can't do anything more stupid, they up the ante once again. And the big question was: would the scandal undermine the Aussies' team spirit and give us victory in the third Test? To which the big answer was: no.*

Australia made one change, leaving out Gillespie for MacGill and playing two spinners. England dropped Cork and Tudor and recalled Dean Headley and Peter Such. The main problem for both sides was the heat: roughly gas mark three, according to local sources. It was therefore vital that Stewart won the toss. Australia chose to bat and scored 391. Justin Langer made a dogged 179 not out, thus cementing his place for the next decade. Players consumed, on average, six litres of energising drinks each in temperatures exceeding 40 °C. England's bowlers were superb: tireless, brave and staunch. Yet more catches were dropped. Mark Waugh was booed to the crease and scored seven. A banner read, 'I DON'T HAVE TO PAY $6000 TO KNOW HOW HOT IT IS TODAY'. But the weather forecast was for cooler weather halfway through the second day. As Matthew Engel wrote in *Wisden*, 'Australia were able to run England ragged in the heat, and then wait for the batting to collapse – which it duly did, twice.' At the end of the second day England were 160 for three, with Hussain and Ramprakash going well. At 187 Ramprakash edged to second slip for 61, and 'the rest strode

---

* Google 'Barmy Army Songbook' and you'll come up with this, sung to the tune of 'My Old Man's a Dustman': Mark Waugh is an Aussie/ He wears an Aussie hat/ And when he saw the bookie's cash/ He said, 'I'm having that'/ He shared it out with Warney/ They went and had some beers/ And when the ACB found out/ They hushed it up for years.

on and off again as fast as models on a catwalk'. England were all out for 227, with Hussain stranded on 89 not out. Some Australian commentators started talking about giving England just a three-Test series in future. Slater hit another century, 103, as Australia moved serenely to a declaration. A banner read, 'IN THE CITY OF CHURCHES, ENGLAND DOESN'T HAVE A PRAYER'. Stewart and Ramprakash made fifties, but no one really expected England to save the game. Hick's first-ball 0 was the eleventh by an England batsman in 1998. This time the last five wickets fell for 16 runs. Australia's margin of victory was 205 runs. 'I just don't think they are as good as we are at the moment,' said Mark Taylor. The Ashes were Australia's for the sixth successive series.

What was going wrong, other than everything? Christopher Martin-Jenkins counted 15 catches dropped by England so far: 'The bowling has been excellent, by and large, but the batting and catching hopelessly inconsistent.' Butcher had faded after his century in the first Test; Atherton was McGrath's bunny; Stewart averaged only 22 against Australia; and Crawley's unfortunate mugging seemed to have obliterated all form and confidence. For Melbourne Crawley and Such were dropped, Fraser was reinstated and the idea was to field a five-strong seam attack, until Alex Tudor reported a sore hip on the morning of the match. This actually enabled Stewart to do what he had probably been wanting to do for a long time: give up the gauntlets and go back to opening the innings. So a wicketkeeper, Warren 'Chucky' Hegg, replaced a bowler, and for the first time in ages the batting order looked right to my eyes. Australia always have a proper wicketkeeper batting at number seven. Why couldn't we?

Melbourne began on Boxing Day. (I can find no record of the usual fancy dress party on Christmas Day, so either it didn't happen any more, or they were keeping it very quiet.) Taylor won his usual toss, inserted, and it rained all day. Ponting was injured, so Darren Lehmann was given his fourth cap; Gillespie was to have replaced 'Funky' Miller, but he too was crocked, so Western Australia's raw fast bowler Matt Nicholson made his first appearance. McGrath dismissed Atherton and Butcher for ducks, but Stewart had the bit between his teeth, and dominated a 77-run partnership with Hussain. Stewart and Ramprakash then added 119, before the skipper was bowled by MacGill for 107, his first century against Australia in 23 Tests. Ramprakash went next over for 63 and 200 for three became 270 all out. From topsy to turvy and back to topsy: no one would ever pretend that watching England is a stress-free experience. England needed to bowl well and they did. Gough regularly hit the late eighties mph – faster than anyone else on either side – and took five wickets to limit the Australians to 252 for eight by the close. Needless to say, though, Bloody Steve Waugh was still there. In *Wisden* Simon Briggs pointed out that Stuart MacGill had come in at number ten for Devon in the 1998 Nat West Trophy and scored 0. Now he scored 43, and added 88 with the flinty-eyed one. Waugh finished on 122 not out, his 17th Test hundred and seventh against England, and his team had a first innings lead of 70. Before the end of the third day England had lost two more wickets: Atherton for a pair and Butcher a little unluckily, when he swept a ball from MacGill straight into Slater's armpit at forward short leg.

The following day, Stewart (52), Hussain (50) and Hick (60) hauled England up to 221 for nine, and Fraser and Mullally added 23 priceless runs for the last wicket. Australia needed 175 to win. The wicket had had some variable bounce since the first day, but hadn't deteriorated any further, and at 103 for two, words like 'plain sailing' were beginning to be used. Then Ramprakash took an astonishing diving catch at square-leg to remove Langer. (He had started off nearer mid-wicket.) Headley now bowled the spell of his career. Mark Waugh was caught by Hick in the slips for 43, Lehmann caught behind for four, Ian Healy snaffled by Hick for 0, Fleming lbw for 0. Score: 140 for seven. Who was at the other end? The flinty-eyed one, of course. Matt Nicholson was the partner he had been waiting for. Slowly, inexorably, they wore down the England bowlers and moved ever closer to the target. An extra hour had already been added to the playing time to make up for time lost, and at 7.22 p.m., at 161 for seven, and 14 needed, the batsmen claimed the extra half hour. Headley and Gough had bowled the previous 16 overs, but Stewart kept them going. Finally Nicholson edged Headley to the keeper. Waugh took a single off the first ball of Gough's next over. Gough bowled MacGill with an inswinging yorker, and had McGrath lbw second ball. England had won by 12 runs. Dean Headley, with six for 60, was man of the match. 'The series was not merely vibrant again,' wrote Simon Briggs, 'but set for a tumultuous finale at Sydney.'

The SCG, though, presented different challenges. Expecting the usual Bunsen, Australia left out Fleming and Nicholson (a one-Test wonder), and recalled Funky Miller and Shane Warne himself, convalescence apparently completed. England brought back Such and Crawley, their best player of spin, but ignored Croft, and omitted Mullally and Fraser, who had also just played his last Test. (It hadn't been a happy series for him: soon the word would go out that his 'nip' had gone.) Atherton also dropped out, the back pain too much to bear. Taylor won another priceless toss, and thus inflicted a 'coinwash' on his opposite number. He had won 11 out of his last 12 Ashes tosses – terribly unfair, given that he had the better team as well. That day *The Australian* newspaper announced that he was 1998's Australian of the Year. Inevitably, he was out in the fourth over, caught Hick bowled Headley for two. England's good start was maintained as Slater and Langer both fell inexpensively, but the Waugh twins put on 190 at nearly a run a minute. Mark's 121 was his 16th Test hundred; Steve's 96 was his ninth Test ninety, another new world record. It was batting of the highest quality, said Gideon Haigh in *Wisden*: 'Enterprise without recklessness, power without force'.

And where was Tufnell? As Scyld Berry wrote in the *Sunday Telegraph*, 'To turn up for a Sydney Test without anything but off-spin is such a culpable mistake that the present selection panel do not deserve to survive in their current form.' Especially as the mistake had been made more than once before.*

When the second new ball was taken, Australia were 319 for five. Mark Waugh edged Headley behind. In the next over, Healy tried to withdraw his bat from a short ball from Gough, but didn't quite manage it: caught behind. Next ball, Gough yorked Stuart MacGill. Colin Miller had to face the hat-trick ball, and Gough said later that it was the best ball he had bowled all series. This yorker swung out rather than in: 'I'm not one of those bowlers who pretends he always knows which way it's going to go.' It was the first hat-trick by an Englishman in an Ashes Test since 1899. Australia had lost their last five wickets for three runs.

England, though, floundered against Australia's three spinners. Crawley made 44 and Hussain 42 out of 220, and MacGill took five for 57. And now it was time for some genuinely bad luck. Australia were 60 for two in their second innings, with Slater on 35. A direct hit from Dean Headley appeared to run him out, but umpire Steve Dunne wasn't sure, so he referred it to the third umpire, Simon Taufel, then at the very beginning of his career. Taufel had three camera views on which to make his judgement, but Peter Such, the bowler, obscured the most important one, so he felt he had to give it not out. Slater went on to make 123. Not only that, but of the other batsmen only Mark Waugh, with 24, scored more than eight. Slater's runs represented 66.84 per cent of the innings score, 184, the second highest proportion in all

---

* On Sky Sports in early 2009, I heard Stewart (in pundit mode) say that he didn't think Monty Panesar was 'a thinking cricketer'. He went on to compare him unfavourably to Phil Tufnell. No need to tell you what I shouted at the screen.

Tests. Such had taken five for 81 and Headley four for 40: heroic performances. But England still needed 287 to win. Despite 53 from Hussain and 42 from Stewart, they lost by 98 runs on a typical Sydney crumbler. Stuart MacGill took seven for 50, improving his best figures for the second innings in a row. 'Some abominable strokes were played against him,' wrote Haigh. Australia had won 3-1, as usual.

A few statistics. Of the 16 Australian batsman who reached 50 during the series, eight went on to centuries. Of the 15 England batsman who reached 50, only Mark Butcher at Brisbane and Alec Stewart at Melbourne went on. Only Nasser Hussain of England batsmen scored 400 runs; Steve Waugh, Michael Slater and Justin Langer did so for Australia. England made 22 ducks and dropped 22 catches; Australia made 15 ducks and dropped nine. The only English bowler to average under 25 was Dean Headley; five Australians did.

A month later Mark Taylor retired from international cricket. He had captained Australia in 50 games and won 11 series out of 14. The flinty-eyed one stood waiting to take over. And we had thought things couldn't get any worse.

Seventeen

2001

Perhaps the most ruthless cricketer I've ever played with.
Shane Warne on Steve Waugh

He would be unbackable favourite, were there such a reality television show as Celebrity Lifeboat.
Gideon Haigh

The Alec Stewart captaincy didn't last long. Abject failure in the 1999 World Cup saw to that. 'We've been found wanting when it really mattered,' said David Lloyd.

'Let's get things fully in proportion – this was only the most catastrophic day ever for English cricket,' wrote John Etheridge in the *Sun*. As it turned out, it wasn't even the most catastrophic day of the summer. Several worse were to follow as England lost 2–1 in four Tests to New Zealand. Nasser Hussain's first series as captain hadn't really panned out as he might have wished. There was no coach (Bumble had gone after the World Cup). Selection was muddled (no shocks there). But Andrew Caddick was back, with 20 wickets in the series at 20.60. He said, 'It was just like playing for Somerset.' Hussain 'felt that his predecessors had been guilty of ostracising complex or awkward characters rather than making them feel part of the team,' according to Simon Briggs in *Wisden*. As a complex or awkward character himself, of course, Hussain should know. Nonetheless, the defeat sent England to the bottom of the new *Wisden* World Championship league table, below even Zimbabwe. This, I would suggest, was the nadir that the previous fifteen years had been preparing us for. Blackwashes, relentless Ashes humiliation, repeated World Cup failure: all of it had led to this day.

Once the worst has happened, though, there's no longer anything to fear. The new coach for the tour of South Africa was the taciturn Zimbabwean Duncan Fletcher. Among his first hunch-picks was a young Yorkshire batsman called Michael Vaughan, who hadn't done anything very much, but had a lovely cover drive. We lost 2–1, a flattering scoreline, for the one victory was the single innings farrago at Centurion cooked up by Hansie Cronje at the behest of his bookmaker chums. Hussain led the way in the series with 370 runs at 61.66; Caddick took 16 wickets and Gough 14. In 2000 there was genuine achievement, as England beat West Indies at home 3–1, and regained the Wisden Trophy after 27 years. Atherton and Stewart both played their 100th Tests; Marcus Trescothick, in his first series, averaged 47; while Caddick, Gough, Dominic Cork and Craig White all took heaps of wickets for very little. (Dean Headley had gone, his career wrecked by injury.) In the winter England went to Pakistan, their first tour there since Shakoor Rana, and won 1–0, the first Test (let alone series) they had won there since 1961/62. Atherton, Thorpe and Craig White were pre-eminent with the bat – Atherton batted nearly 23 hours in three Tests and averaged 68 – while a young left-arm spinner named Ashley Giles had a useful first tour, with 17 wickets at 24. Sri Lanka was even better: a 2–1 victory, after losing the first test, with epic performances from Thorpe, Trescothick, Caddick and, particularly, Gough, who in the two victories took a wicket every 26 balls. We had won four series in a row (if you count a dinky Zimbabwe win just before the West Indies), and were now up to third in the world rankings. Surely we had a chance in the Ashes. Surely?

The Australians, though, were now under the control of Steve Waugh, the Dalek who could actually go upstairs. Nothing less than victory over the entire galaxy was enough for him. Teams couldn't just be beaten, they had to be crushed. After drawn series in the West Indies and Sri Lanka, Australia beat Zimbabwe in a one-off Test, walloped Pakistan and India at home, both 3–0, and went to New Zealand and won 3–0 there too. In 2000/01, the West Indies were the visitors and lost 5–0. 'The series was so one-sided as to be dull,' wrote Greg Baum in *Wisden*. They extended this winning streak to 16 consecutive Tests when they won the first Test in India, but then lost the last two. They always struggled in India. They never struggled in England.

The astonishing strength of Australian cricket at this stage was reflected in the smooth efficiency of their selection policy. Ian Healy retires, Adam Gilchrist takes his place. With Mark Taylor gone, Matthew Hayden gets a second chance, knowing that if he fluffs it, there won't be a third. He doesn't fluff it. This battle-hardened squad, average age 30, with 665 Test caps between them, were the oldest to tour England since Bradman's Invincibles. Steve Waugh was on his fourth tour; Warne, Slater and Mark Waugh were on their third; McGrath, Gillespie, Langer, Gilchrist and Ponting had been here last time, while Hayden and Damien Martyn had been here in 1993 without playing a Test. The only new faces in the Test squad were 'Funky' Miller, spare batsman Simon Katich, spare wicketkeeper Wade Seccombe, young tyro fast bowler Nathan Bracken and seven-Test veteran Brett Lee, who arrived with the unofficial title of Fastest Bowler in the World, having recently been clocked at 96 mph. Stuart MacGill, scourge of England in Sydney, was surplus to requirements. Everyone wondered idly whether this was not, in fact, the greatest cricket team of all time.

England had two Tests against Pakistan early in the season in which to hone their talents. The first they won, easily, at Lord's in 'English' conditions; the second they lost, rather feebly, at Old Trafford on a dusty turner; and the momentum they had been building up for the challenge ahead instantly vanished. In a triangular ODI tournament, England played three games against Pakistan and three against Australia and lost the lot. Injuries now denied them the services of Thorpe (calf strain), Michael Vaughan (knee surgery) and Ramprakash (hamstring). For the first Test at Edgbaston the selectors called up Mark Butcher, who had lost his place 18 months earlier, and Nottinghamshire's Usman Afzaal, who had done well on an 'A' tour of the West Indies. Craig White and Ashley 'Wheely Bin' Giles were also back, having missed the early season Tests, while the only previously unfamiliar face in the middle order was Ian Ward of Surrey, later Sussex (and now Sky Sports 2, usually in the middle of the night). Australia left out Langer, who hadn't missed a Test since we last saw him, but had lost form. Ponting the Boy Wonder was promoted to number three, and Martyn, who seemed to be scoring a century every time he reached the crease, was brought in for his 12th Test in nearly nine years. And we held our breath.

Waugh won the toss and inserted. Trescothick, Atherton's latest opening partner, went for 0 – the Australians boasted that they had 'worked him out' – but Athers and Butcher put on 106 in no time. For the last over before lunch, Waugh tossed the ball to Warne. Second ball, Butcher gloved a catch to Ponting at silly point. It had only taken two hours, but our hopes had already been dashed. Now they were to be pummelled into a soggy pulp. Atherton's 57 was his first Ashes fifty in 16 innings, but 106 for one soon decomposed into 191 for nine. Stewart, back keeping wicket and batting at six, hit 65 and Caddick a career-best 49 not out in a last-wicket partnership of 103. (Caddick's score was the highest by an England number eleven in Ashes history.) But we all knew it meant nothing when Michael Slater hit four fours in the first over.

Australia scored 576. Slater made 77, Steve Waugh and
Damien Martyn 105 each, and Adam Gilchrist announced himself to the British public with 152 in 143 balls, including 20
fours and five sixes, and 22 off an over by Mark Butcher, who
appeared to be the fifth bowler. Half a dozen catches were
dropped. After a diverting flurry of lower-order wickets to
Butcher, who ended with four for 42, Gilchrist and McGrath put
on 63 for the last wicket, of which McGrath scored a single.
McGrath then had Atherton edge to second slip for four. I have
tried so hard, harder than you can ever know, not to use the
words 'Groundhog Day' while writing this book, but really. The
uninterrupted success of McGrath blighted an entire decade for
England followers. Just the thought of his smug, unchallengeable
grin makes the bile rise in my throat.

*Bren S: My favourite player. Just to watch him bowl ball after ball,
over after over . . . He was something special. And I loved his capacity for
wind-up. Even if there were only two Tests in the series, he'd still say
we'll win five-nil.*

There was brief resistance. Trescothick (76) and Butcher (41)
put on 95 for the second wicket. But then Jason Gillespie broke
Nasser Hussain's little finger and the highest score thereafter was
Caddick's six not out. Australia won by an innings and 118 runs.
'Even if [England] lose all five Test matches, it is not the end of
the world,' wrote Michael Henderson in the *Telegraph*. 'These
tourists have stretched the game beyond what was thought possible and they are such an extraordinary side, from number one to
number eleven, that all cricket-lovers should rush to watch them,
and cheer them on their way. We may never see their like again.'
Well, not for eighteen months or so, anyway.

For Lord's, England needed a captain. Alec Stewart and Mark
Butcher both said no. Steve Waugh was amused. 'I don't think
you'd find anyone in the Australian side saying, "I don't want to
captain",' he mocked. Michael Atherton said, oh all right, I'll do
it. Back into the side came Thorpe and Ramprakash, Afzaal the

deputy was left out, and Corky replaced the Wheely Bin for an all-seam attack. Australia were unchanged, and at full strength.

Of the game, little need be said. Nasser Hussain, unable to play, was turned away three times on the first day by the Lord's gatemen. England were all out for 187: McGrath took another five wickets. During the tea interval the Queen presented the *Test Match Special* team with a Dundee cake baked in the royal kitchens. Australia scored 401: Caddick also took five, more expensively, while Mark Waugh scored 108 and Adam Gilchrist, dropped four times off Gough, made 90. When England batted again, Thorpe was hit on the hand by a Brett Lee bouncer, and broke a bone. It was the end of his summer. Butcher and Ramprakash put on 96 for the fourth wicket, during which the eternally optimistic and the mentally disadvantaged began to dream of 1981-type reverses. Pah. Gillespie took five wickets, McGrath slashed through the lower order, and Australia needed 14 to win. 'The fielding was the difference between the two teams,' said Steve Waugh, momentarily forgetting the batting and the bowling.

(Two days after the Test, the Gloucester *Citizen* reported that Vicky Ball, aged 12, had taken five for 30 while playing for Stone CC 3rds against Frampton-on-Severn. Asked about the England bowlers playing in the Ashes, she said, 'They bowled rubbish. They need to pitch the ball up and bowl straighter.')

Trent Bridge had slightly more drama. Thorpe was gone, and Cork was dropped: he had been picked for Lord's more on his past record there than on anything he had done recently with the ball. Alex Tudor, the Chris Old *de ses jours*, played his first Test for two years, and only his fourth overall. With Giles still unfit, Robert Croft took the spinner's place in a five-man attack. Atherton won the toss, and was given out for 0 when the ball looped up off his armguard to gully. The crowd booed the replay and then went off to get drunk. Trescothick scored 69 and Stewart 46 out of 185, on a recently relaid pitch offering bowlers bounce, sideways movement, all sorts of goodies. Gough and Caddick were a little ragged to start, and Hayden and Slater whacked 48 in 55 minutes. Then Tudor came into the attack and got Hayden lbw with one that pitched marginally outside leg stump. It was the first of seven wickets to fall for 54 runs in 20 overs in 93 glorious minutes. But Gilchrist's was now the wicket England wanted above all others, and the one they didn't have. From 122 for eight, the Australians counterpunched their way up to 190 all out (Gilchrist 54, Gillespie 27 not out). Despite Tudor's five for 44, England's bowling was 'spasmodic rather than systematic', according to Gideon Haigh in *Wisden*. Several observers racked their brains, trying to remember in which decade it had last been 'systematic'.

Trescothick and Atherton now compiled their first half-century opening stand of the series. On 32, Trescothick swept a ball straight on to Hayden's leg at short leg, and it rebounded up to Gilchrist for the catch. Bad luck has a tendency to come in threes: the TV replay showed that Warne had overstepped the front line; and seconds later rain started to fall and everyone left the field. Nonetheless, late on the second day England led by 110 runs with eight wickets left. The game was in the balance. In Haigh's careful words, Atherton 'may or may not have touched the ball he was judged to have edged to Gilchrist'. It was the turning point. The most memorable dismissal was that of Ramprakash, who after two hours of superb concentration went for a huge heave and was stumped. Warne had apparently been taunting him for ages: 'Come on, Ramps, you know you want to! That's the way, Ramps, keep coming down the wicket!' And eventually he cracked. England were all out for 162 (Warne six for 33) and Australia won with seven wickets and two days to spare. The winning run was a Caddick no-ball. They had retained the Ashes almost at the earliest possible moment, in fewer than 4000 deliveries, very few of which, I have to admit, I could bear to watch.

For Headingley, England dropped Ian Ward (for the first and

last time), Robert Croft (for the last time) and Craig White (not for the first or last time). Nasser Hussain was fit again, Usman Afzaal got his second cap, and Alan Mullally was also recalled as part of the usual Headingley four-man seam attack. Steve Waugh's calf muscle had gone 'ping' at Trent Bridge, so Adam Gilchrist was captain, and Simon Katich played his first Test, batting at number six. On the first day, rain delayed play until 2.15 p.m., but Australia still managed 288 for four. Ricky Ponting scored a lightning 144, Mark Waugh hit 72, and on Friday Damien Martyn joined in with 118. Australia were all out for 447 (Gough five for 103). England's response was more robust than usual but still not robust enough – thirties and forties but no fifties from the top five batsmen – until Alec Stewart, batting at number seven for the first time in 114 Tests (and thoroughly cheesed off about it), biffed 76 and helped avert the follow-on. For the first time all summer Australia had to take a second new ball. McGrath still took seven for 76. With a first innings lead of 138 the Aussies went on the rampage, led again by Ponting, with 72 at a run a ball. But weather was on its way. 'The static in the air was clearly visible in Alan Mullally's hair as he prepared to bowl,' wrote Jonathan Rice in *The Fight for the Ashes 2001*. 'Wisps of his blond locks were standing on end as the electrical storm drew closer.' Between lunch and 5.30 p.m., there was only half an hour's play. At 5.35 p.m. Gilchrist ran out of patience and declared. England needed 315 to win, and after more rain and bad light, they only had Monday's statutory 90 overs in which to get them.

Bren S: Gilchrist's Gift. He gave them a chance. Steve Waugh would have piled it on, just kept going. He wouldn't declare until it was frightening, like looking at a cliff face.

Not that England had shown the smallest sign that they would be capable of chasing such a target. The 'greenwash' – 5–0 – was a real possibility, and in order to win, Gilchrist needed time to bowl them out. 'One would have to say that, if the Australians

get 90 overs in, they will expect to win,' said Michael Henderson
in the *Daily Telegraph*, and this was the majority view. When
Atherton and Trescothick fell for eight and 10 respectively, it
looked a good call. Butcher and Hussain survived, just about,
against McGrath and then, on 60 for two, Hussain hooked a
short ball from Gillespie out of the ground. The ball was lost, and
the replacement didn't move around as much. The Headingley
pitch, of which much was always expected, settled into quiet
somnolence, the last thing anyone expected. And Mark Butcher
launched one of the greatest of all Ashes innings, as thrilling a display as we could have hoped for. For one day, and one day only,
England ran this Australian side ragged. I particularly remember
the ferocity of his cutting, the crisp clips off the legs for four, and
the growing sense that this obviously impossible target might
just be gettable after all.

Hussain, back as captain, was an essential foil. He and Butcher
put on 181 for the third wicket, of which Hussain made 55. Most
impressive was the matter-of-factness with which they went
about the job. It was almost Australian in its intensity. You never
had the sense that Butcher would throw it away. When he
reached his century Headingley almost exploded with emotion,
and at home I admit I wiped away a manly tear. (The Australians
made a point of congratulating him. 'We could see it was something special,' said Gilchrist.) But to Butcher the century was
merely a milestone on a longer journey. His lunch, famously,
consisted of 'coffee and a couple of cigarettes'. And afterwards, as
Jonathan Rice put it, he 'carried on exactly as before, not so
much playing each ball on its merits as dominating the bowlers so
that each ball was of less merit than it might otherwise have
been'.

Hussain was out with 101 still needed. Ramprakash, though,
helped Butcher add another 75, and when he was out for 32, victory was no longer in doubt. Because it was at Headingley and
against the Australians, people would compare Butcher's innings

with Botham's 149 not out in 1981. *Wisden* looked back a little further: 'A fairer parallel would be the fabled 1902 innings of Gilbert Jessop, whose attacking shots and endless verve inspired a remarkable Test victory no one thought possible.' Like Jessop's innings, Butcher's 173 not out didn't turn the series on its head: it was too late for that and Australia were far too good anyway. But it did provide us with an afternoon of memorable pleasure in yet another season of misery and failure. I bet Butcher quite enjoyed it too.

Normally we would have had a week to bask in the glow of this extraordinary victory. As luck would have it, this was the first of two back-to-back Tests, and the second started at the Oval two days later. England lost the services of Alex Tudor (hip) and Alan Mullally (rib), gave a first cap to Leicestershire's hungry fast bowler Jimmy Ormond and finally responded to the nationwide clamour for Tuffers, who had taken his 1000th first-class wicket earlier in the season. For Australia, Katich made way for Steve Waugh, as expected, but more ominously, Michael Slater was left out for Justin Langer. Slater's 'understanding of the Australian team ethic had been rather sketchy of late,' wrote Jonathan Rice in lawyer-proof code. 'Being dropped by Australia is always a more fearful and sometimes final blow than being dropped by England,' said Matthew Engel in *Wisden*, and indeed, Slater had played his last Test at the age of 31. Like Brearley, they weren't just ruthless with their opponents.

(But consider this. In the first three Tests of the series Ricky Ponting had scored 60 runs at an average of 12 and looked as though he was next for the drop. In the first innings at Headingley, still on 0, he edged his third ball from Caddick to Ramprakash at third slip. Although it appeared to have carried, Ponting stood his ground and the umpire referred it to the third umpire, who said the TV replays were inconclusive, and gave him not out. Even at the time, he was thought to have been very lucky. In the second innings, when on four, he edged to

Atherton at first slip, who dropped it. Punter went on to 144 and 72, kept his place and eventually succeeded Steve Waugh as captain. How narrow is the gap between success and failure.)

Australia won the toss, their fourth out of five this summer – Hussain had now lost nine in a row – and declared on 641 for four. Only Gilchrist of the recognised batsmen scored less than 62. Justin Langer scored 102 before being hit on the helmet by Caddick and retiring hurt. Mark Waugh made 120 and Steve Waugh, flinty-eyed with pain on this occasion, made 157 not out despite barely being able to walk. England missed the follow-on target by ten runs. Trescothick made 55, Usman Afzaal 54 (his wild celebrations when he reached 50 and his weedy exit a handful of balls later effectively ended his Test career) and Ramprakash 133, only his second Test century after all this time. As the ball started to bite, Warne took seven for 165. Second time round, we looked to the heavens for inspiration. Sunday was almost washed out; Monday's skies were blue and clear. England were all out for 184. Atherton announced his retirement. Tufnell might well have done: it was his last Test too. Australia had won 4–1. Glenn McGrath (32 wickets at less than 17) was Australia's man of the series; Mark Butcher was England's. 'I have been very proud of my team in the last couple of games,' said Nasser Hussain, 'and even before then they have showed a lot of character. As Duncan Fletcher said to us in the dressing room, we have got some young lads that have come in and there is no point looking anywhere else apart from Australia for the standards that are required.' In other words, sledging training starts tomorrow.

Andy R: The significance of Nasser isn't just that he was a very good captain. I can remember you saying, 'Cricket's dead on its legs, that's the end of it, it's the knockings.' And poor old Nass, with no support from anyone, dragged that whole team up by the bootstraps.*

Alan W: We seem to keep getting gradually slightly better, and the

* It is just possible that I did say something along these lines.

Australians get much better. The year 2001 was hilarious because we came in with a lot of hope. And a lot of that hope centred on Darren Gough, whose greatest talent was for propagating the lie that he'd get into the Australian side, on the basis of the fact that they liked drinking with him. I also think that taking three wickets at the end of the innings, and having tattoos, doesn't automatically make you 'lion-hearted'. I wanted him shot by the end of his career.

I think there are adults who sit in that crowd and go, it's a privilege to see Shane Warne in my lifetime. They are able to see it objectively. I can't do that. Steve Waugh I can't appreciate. I can't appreciate Ricky Ponting. I can appreciate a really gutsy 30 from Nasser, because I can see how much he's putting in to get those 30 runs. Imagine the rage that's behind every single shot. He's drawing on everything. People who've bullied him in the past, some off-kilter comment that someone made in the dressing-room, it's all going in there. But I can't appreciate skill for skill's sake. What's the fucking point of that?

Eighteen

2002/03

The first Steve Waugh medal for the outstanding New South Wales player of the season was won by Steve Waugh. Reported in *Sydney Morning Herald*, March 2003

Skating over tumultuous world events as we must, we arrive in India in late 2001 for an England tour more onerous than most. Alec Stewart wanted a winter off (not least from the words 'Indian bookmakers'), Darren Gough too, and Andrew Caddick and Robert Croft pulled out of the tour for 'security' reasons. Nasser Hussain's young side lost the three-Test series 1–0 but did not disgrace themselves. In New Zealand Thorpe scored another double century, the returning Caddick took 19 wickets at under 20, and Yorkshire's mop-headed seamer Matthew Hoggard 17 wickets at under 24. (Hungry Jimmy Ormond made the error of taking his shirt off near a photographer, and never played Test cricket again.) But England only drew 1–1 after losing the plot in the final Test. A lack of ruthlessness was deemed to be undermining their game. At home in 2002 Hussain and Fletcher attempted to address this. Sri Lanka, playing their first three-Test series in England, were beaten 2–0, with big runs for Trescothick, Butcher, Vaughan and Thorpe.

India, rather tougher than before under Sourav Ganguly, drew
1–1 in a four-Test series. Vaughan hit three hundreds, Hussain
two, and useful debuts were made by Stephen Harmison and
Simon Jones. But the consistency was still lacking, and a colum-
nist with the same name as me and roughly the same height and
weight asked whether England were a good team that sometimes played abjectly, or a useless team that occasionally played
above itself. It strikes me now that we could have asked this
question at almost any time since 1972. We are still asking it.
Maybe we always will be.

Once again, England's squad for the 2002/03 Ashes leaned
towards experience. Stewart would be on his fourth tour; for
Crawley, Thorpe and Gough it would be the third; Butcher and
Hussain had been there last time, as had Ashley Giles, in the ODI
squad. Marcus Trescothick and Michael Vaughan were the new
batsmen, augmented by Kent's Robert Key when Thorpe
dropped out of the tour for personal reasons. (Mark Ramprakash
had played his last Test, as had Dominic Cork and Alan Mullally.)
The other fast bowlers were Caddick, amazingly making his first
tour of Australia, Harmison, Hoggard and Simon Jones. Jamie
Foster of Essex was the reserve wicketkeeper (having been the
incumbent the previous winter when Stewart didn't play),
Yorkshire's Richard Dawson the second spinner, and Andrew
Flintoff the all-rounder. In between injuries Sir Freddie had
played 21 Tests, with one century and best bowling of four for 50
against India, but as yet he hadn't played Australia. Nor would he
on this tour. Bits still kept dropping off him when prodded. And
he wasn't the only one.

Australia, in the meantime, had played host to a determined
New Zealand, whose artful skipper Stephen Fleming had mis-
chievously played for three draws and got them. No visiting team
had played two or more Tests in Australia without losing at least
one of them since 1985/86. South Africa were then crushed
3–0. Bedding down nicely was the new opening partnership of

Hayden and Langer, who by the end of 2001/02 had an average opening stand of 117.9. Great: the one tiny weakness in their game – the relative fragility of the opening partnership – had been ruthlessly eradicated.

As it happened, the selectors had already identified the next potential problem. The Waugh twins were 37. In 2001 Mark had scored 430 runs at 86, and Steve 321 at 107, with two centuries each. (England had managed only two between all of them.) But the twins had started to look vulnerable against New Zealand and South Africa. You couldn't sack them both at the same time, not least because Steve was the captain and a particularly good one at that. But two Waughs, it seemed, was one too many. As England arrived, Mark was dropped after 107 consecutive Tests, and instantly retired. Brett Lee, still promising more than he delivered, was sent back to state cricket to sort himself out. Darren Lehmann (for his sixth Test) and Andy Bichel (for his ninth) took their places.

England, though, were already assailed by injuries. We had known beforehand of Darren Gough's troublesome knee, but he was the only bowler in the original party who had ever taken a wicket in Australia before, so you can see why they persevered with him. But Vaughan was recovering from a knee operation, Trescothick had a dicky shoulder, Simon Jones had a rib injury and so it went on. Craig White turned up as cover for, well, everyone. Harmison's sore shins ruled him out of the first Test at Brisbane, which at least prevented him from bowling the first over. England played five bowlers, with White batting at seven. Nasser Hussain won the toss, his first against Australia since anyone could remember, and invited the opposition to bat first.

Alan W: The decision to bowl, that everyone goes on about. That's a decision born of ten years of getting humped. That's what being constantly beaten down does to you. You take the most defensive option possible.

At the end of the first day Australia were 364 for two. Our new young fast bowler Simon Jones bowled seven overs, and dismissed Langer in his second. Then he ruptured knee ligaments while fielding at fine leg, and was stretchered off. He would soon be on the plane home. Dropped at 40, 102, 138 and 149, Hayden ended the day on 186 not out. Ponting was out shortly before the close for 123. England did well, on day two, to bowl them out for 492, with Giles taking four wickets and Caddick three, and score 158 for one. Trescothick and Butcher both went early the next morning, for 72 and 54 respectively, but Hussain and Crawley put on another 97. Then came the collapse. Crawley was left on 69 not out as England conceded 167. Hayden scored another century, his seventh in ten Tests, leaving England 464 to win. They managed 79. 'It was one of the worst England batting efforts since Tests began,' wrote Scyld Berry in *Wisden*, pulling his punches as usual. It was also Alec Stewart's 50th defeat in his 123rd Test, in which he had recorded his first ever pair.

Ben D: I think we play Australia too often. It's too painful. Why can't we play them every five years, as we do India or the West Indies? Fine, we'll get whacked, but . . . At least when you're playing South Africa or whoever, you feel you've got a chance.

Back to the injuries, which in this series are often more entertaining than the cricket. Darren Gough had broken down again, and flew home. 'With him went England's only hope of dismissing well-set batsmen with a soft ball on flat pitches,' wrote Berry. A bruised hip ruled John Crawley out of the second Test. Harmison, at least, was back: we knew he was fit when he broke Ashley Giles's hand in the nets. (Farewell, Wheely Bin, with his wheely suitcase.) Alex Tudor, Yorkshire's Chris Silverwood and Adam Hollioake joined the party. For the second Test at Adelaide England brought in Robert Key, Richard Dawson and Harmison to replace Crawley, Giles and Jones respectively. Australia were unchanged.

England won another toss. This time Hussain batted. Before the 90th and last over of the day, England were 295 for three. Michael Vaughan had made a sublime and life-enhancing 177 not out, his fifth Test century of 2002. Trescothick (35) and Hussain (41) had provided stalwart support, and Butcher was 22 not out. Andy Bichel, whole-hearted trier with a face like a squished tomato, ran in to bowl the last six balls. Vaughan edged his third ball to Shane Warne at slip and everyone trudged off. The following day England were all out for 342. Another advantage had been squandered. Ponting made 154 and Damien Martyn 95 out of 552 for nine. England were all out for 157. Merv Hughes said Hussain should be sacked at once. England's captain had a clearer vision: 'They want to beat us 5–0. They'll be completely cut-throat. They'll show no mercy at all.'

People who don't understand cricket – the countless millions of savages and barbarians out there who wouldn't dream of reading this book – almost always say the same thing about the game. How can you enjoy a game that goes on for five days and still ends as a draw? You might as well try explaining evolution to a fundamentalist Christian. What they don't understand, what they can never understand, is that when they think cricket is boring, it often isn't, whereas a series like this, where the result is pre-ordained by the absolute superiority of one side, can be mind-wipingly tedious – boring to watch, boring to write about, boring to read about. Utterly miserable to play as well, I would have thought: you have to take your hat off to Nasser Hussain and his men, who never did less than their best. At around this time the Australian side began to wonder why they weren't, well, more popular. Greatly respected, vastly admired, they were nonetheless a team created in the harsh glare of Steve Waugh's personality. Neil Harvey, Australian hero of the 1940s and 1950s, told a reporter, 'As far as I'm concerned, they are the greatest bunch of sledgers there's ever been. These boys get into a bit of trouble and it all comes out, every bit of badness in them. All I can say is I'm disgusted and the sad thing is I'm not the only one.'

By the third Test, in Perth, England were in disarray. Crawley was still unfit, and a sore back took Caddick out of contention. Hoggard was dropped for reasons unknown, so the opening bowlers were Silverwood, who hadn't yet bowled a ball in the middle, and Tudor, who had managed 19 overs a fortnight earlier without once getting injured. For the fastest wicket in the world, now apparently even faster, Australia recalled Brett Lee in place of Bichel. England won the toss for the third time, and were dismayed to discover that it only gave them the option to bat or bowl, not to go home. They scored 185, with Robert Key's 47 the top score. Australia were in just after tea. Chris Silverwood conceded 29 off his first four overs, then his ankle gave way. 'This is a new injury,' said the ECB press release, 'and not related to the joint inflammation he experienced in the same ankle at the end of the English season.' Of course not. Perish the thought. Australia's 456 featured not a single century. 'White snaffled five wickets, which flattered him,' wrote Vic Marks in *Wisden*, 'Harmison just one, which didn't.' He bowled fast and usually short, and Stewart leaped around like a 39-year-old salmon behind the stumps. England made 223 in their second innings (Hussain 61, Stewart 66 not out). The Ashes had been lost in eleven playing days, faster and earlier (1 December) than ever before.

Three weeks of one-day internationals followed, during which England broke another record: the fastest ever injury. Jeremy Snape was one of seven players to supplement the party for ODIs: in his first warm-up game against New South Wales, he went into bat, and first ball Brett Lee broke his thumb. Another flight home. Boom time for travel agents.

For the fourth Test at Melbourne, starting on Boxing Day,*

---

* Again, no fancy dress party. These modern cricketers have no sense of history.

both sides had injury problems. Shane Warne had dislocated a shoulder during an ODI; Stuart MacGill returned. And Darren Lehmann's poisoned leg – presumably a botched assassination attempt by MI6 – brought in Queensland's Martin Love, who had scored two double centuries so far against the tourists, and played a record 129 first-class matches before his call-up. Alec Stewart, meanwhile, had a bruised hand, so James Foster came in at number seven, John Crawley was back at six and England played four bowlers. Caddick was fit again so Silverwood and Tudor were edged out. Australia won their first toss and scored 551 for six. Langer made 250, Hayden 102, Steve Waugh a fast and mocking 77, and Martin Love 62 not out. England were soon 118 for six. 'Spineless,' said *Wisden*. John Crawley and Craig White remained. Crawley, conscious of his weakness outside off stump, had altered his technique to bring his bat down straighter, but in doing so had lost the ability to score a run. Craig White hit 85 not out, including three sixes off MacGill. This was the ground where he had cheered England on as a schoolboy. England were all out for 270 and followed on. They had never lost by an innings in three consecutive Tests before.

Alan W: I was at uni and I used to watch it in the TV room at two in the morning. But this was the series where I gave up on cricket, really after watching Richard Dawson bowl. I've never felt such a sense of impotence. He wasn't even doing anything wrong. I mean, someone like Martin McCague gets splattered everywhere, and everyone goes, what a disgrace. But I'd rather they got splattered everywhere than tugged along at five an over, looking as though they haven't a prayer of taking a wicket. For me it was as though the rage of the previous ten years had to be expressed, and if there's one thing that sums up all those shit years, it's that quasi-professionalism. The fitness regimes of the Stewart and Gooch eras. And Richard Dawson, a good honest pro. I just remember this incredible rage when he was bowling. And I walked out of the TV room and said to myself, let it go. I don't care. And apparently Michael Vaughan scored loads of runs and I never saw a single one of them.

England started brightly enough, with Marcus Trescothick scoring his second 37 of the match, until given out lbw to MacGill by umpire Russell Tiffin, The Man The Players Fear. But Michael Vaughan was now at the peak of his game, pulling short balls with what seemed like minutes to spare and caressing those cover drives through the off-side field, inch-perfect every time. He scored 145 out of 236 for four, his sixth Test century of 2002, and finished with 1481 runs for the year, beating Dennis Amiss's long-standing record for England. At last, we thought: the world-class batsman we have been waiting for all our lives. As Steven Lynch wrote in *Wisden*, 'The Australians paid him their highest compliment: they stopped sledging him.'

Even so, it took a maiden half-century by Robert Key, and more obdurate strokelessness by Crawley, to drag England into a small lead, and even then we lost the last five wickets for 45. Australia needed 107 to win.

And now Caddick woke up. Or rather, Second Innings Caddick, one of the greatest bowlers ever to don whites for England, took over from feeble, whining First Innings Caddick, who might struggle to get a game for a club side. On the last morning Hayden hit his first ball down the throat of substitute fielder Alex Tudor at long leg. Then Harmison took two wickets in his sixth over: Ponting for 30, Martyn for 0, both caught behind. Steve Waugh came in with a migraine. He was immediately beaten outside the off stump, and then caught behind. But the Barmy Army were so loud that no one heard the noise of the ball hitting the bat, and so no one appealed. In the same over he was caught behind off a no-ball. That would have been 58 for four. Even so, Second Innings Caddick had him glove to second slip on 83, and seven runs later had Langer lbw, courtesy of another shocker from The Man The Players Fear. Australia won by five wickets and went 4–0 up, for sure, but England had finally shown some character and guts.

For Sydney, Stewart was back, while Matthew Hoggard replaced Craig White, who had torn an intercostal muscle at Melbourne (and, as it happens, played his last Test). Australia made one change, but it was a crucial one. Glenn McGrath had a side strain: it was the first Test both he and Warne had missed since November 1992. Bichel joined Gillespie, Lee and MacGill: a good attack, not to be underestimated, but while compiling a record third-wicket stand of 166 with Mark Butcher, Nasser Hussain was occasionally seen to smile. Australia were also beginning to miss Mark Waugh, maybe the best slip-fielder of them all: a number of catches were dropped. Butcher hit 124, Hussain 75 and Stewart passed Geoffrey Boycott's aggregate of 8114 during his 71. England's 362 was their highest first-innings score of the series; that Australia should score 363 seemed appropriate, even inevitable. Steve Waugh, needing a score, made an uncharacteristically frisky 102 in just 130 balls, and passed 10,000 in Tests. Adam Gilchrist needed just 94 balls for his century, and got there with the strangest of shots, lifting the bat over his head to intercept a Harmison bouncer and then forehand-smashing it through mid-on for three. But Hoggy cleaned up the tail for four for 92, Harmison took three for 70 and First Innings Caddick three for 121.

So England came to bat again. Call it a dead rubber if you will. Excuse the absence of Glenn and Shane. But if England cocked this up, they would become the first side to suffer the greenwash since 1920/21. More than pride was at stake. Fortunately we had Vaughan. With Hussain (72) he put on 189 for the third wicket and was eventually dismissed for 183, lbw to Bichel thanks to an umpiring decision *Wisden*'s Christian Ryan called 'recklessly idiosyncratic'. (Guess who?) Stewart and Harmison added 43 for the last wicket and Hussain declared on 452 for nine. Australia needed that same number to win. Langer, Hayden and Ponting all went lbw on the fourth evening. Langer's pitched eight inches outside the leg stump: the Tiffinator raised the finger. Second

Innings Caddick continued taking wickets on the last day, taking advantage of some uneven bounce, as the Australians succumbed to pressure they simply weren't used to. Top scorer, with 49, was Andy Bichel, who had been sent in as night-watchman and given it some welly. Caddick took seven for 94, which gave him ten wickets in a match for the first time. Australia went down by 225 runs, their first defeat since England had beaten them last time. The greenwash was averted. And, according to Christian Ryan, Nasser Hussain 'had glimpsed a new world, a brighter world, a world without McGrath and Warne. It was hard to shake the feeling that, after 14 years of ritual Ashes humiliation, the worst for England might finally be over.'

Nineteen

2005

If any of our batsmen get out to Ashley Giles in the Tests they should go and hang themselves.

Terry Alderman

Hoggard's like a net bowler when you compare him to McGrath and Kasprowicz.

Jeff Thomson

It was real grandchildren stuff. 'Gather round and I'll tell you about that innings I played with Pietersen, with the white stripes and the earrings.'

The Wheely Bin, after the Oval

Gradually, and wonderfully, everything started to come together. First under Nasser Hussain, and then under Michael Vaughan, with Duncan Fletcher loitering ominously in the background, a squad of strong-minded characters was formed, who could give pretty much anyone a decent game of cricket. At home in 2003, Zimbabwe were brushed aside 2–0 and a resurgent South Africa were somehow held 2–2, despite two huge double centuries from new chipmunk-cheeked skipper Graeme Smith. A bruising 1–0 defeat in Sri Lanka followed, with Murali back to his wild-eyed best, but England then went to the West Indies and won 3–0, 'a united team playing harder, more disciplined and more thoughtful cricket,' wrote CMJ. In 2004 England won every Test of a seven-Test summer, three against New Zealand and four against the West Indies, and then went to South Africa and won 2–1. This was now, by most standards, a good team. The only trouble was that only one standard mattered to anyone. Could we beat Australia? Could we overcome two decades of dismal submissiveness to the Baggy Green Bastards? As Primo Levi might have said, if not now, when? Although, admittedly, he was talking about taking up arms as Jewish partisans behind the German lines in the Second World War, and not a silly game of cricket.

His point, though, may have been that to defeat your enemy you have, in some way, to become more like them. The central contract system, still disliked by some county cricket zealots, had given the England team a continuity they had never had before and an intensity they had only ever enjoyed on tour. To some extent they had become tourists in their own country. Several would say they identified more with England than with their counties, who were full of South African journeymen anyway, all talking in Afrikaans at 'their' end of the dressing room. Even with continuity, though, changes had been made. By the time Bangladesh were given the treatment in early summer 2005, Stewart and Hussain had retired, Darren Gough and Andrew Caddick had been superseded, and Thorpe was hanging on by his fingertips. Mark Butcher had cricked his neck in a car accident, and then damaged his wrist lifting weights in South Africa, and by the time he recovered from all these ailments, his place was gone for ever. Andrew Strauss was opening the batting with Trescothick, cheeky nipper Ian Bell was getting a run in the middle order, while Kevin Pietersen, newly qualified for England, had hit astonishing runs in ODIs in South Africa and was next in line for a Test place. Andrew Flintoff was the crux of the side at number six and first change, and Geraint Jones, once of Papua New Guinea and an enthusiast for the square cut, was behind the stumps. And Michael Vaughan had acquired immense authority as England captain, even if his batting had never recaptured the majesty of 2002/03.

Australia, of course, maintained their policy of evolution over revolution. Steve Waugh had finally been hauled off into retirement, but all the other principals were present. This would be Shane Warne's fourth tour; number three for Ricky Ponting (the new captain), Matthew Hayden, Justin Langer, Damien Martyn, Adam Gilchrist, Glenn McGrath and Jason Gillespie; and number two for Brett Lee, Simon Katich and Michael Kasprowicz. Of those who would play a Test, only Michael Clarke and Shaun Tait had never been here before. They might have been getting on a bit, but this was a team accustomed to easy dominance, with nothing to prove and less to fear. Glenn McGrath predicted they would win 5–0. When would the fucker retire?

The run-up to the first Test was endless but informative. In a Twenty20 international at Southampton, England won by 100 runs, having reduced the tourists to 31 for seven in the sixth over. That was fun. Somerset then beat them by four wickets in a 50-over match, courtesy of those legendary West-Countrymen Graeme Smith (108) and Sanath Jayasuriya (101). In their opening match of the one-day tournament, Australia then lost to Bangladesh. My, how we laughed. This was jitteriness beyond all expectation. Ten days later I went to the day-nighter against England at Edgbaston with my friends Nick N and Chris D, and before the rain slashed down and we fled for a curry, there was a memorable incident involving beetle-browed playground bully Matthew Hayden. Simon Jones was the bowler, Hayden played the ball back at him, and Jones threw it at the batsman's stumps. But he missed and hit Hayden on the shoulder. Hayden was apoplectic. Even though Jones had raised his hand to apologise, he gave him a mouthful. But instead of letting him get away with it,

Durham's Paul Collingwood (by this stage a one-day regular) and Michael Vaughan came over and gave him a mouthful back. The umpires had to intervene. It was great to watch, and Hayden was so taken aback he was lbw to Jones a handful of balls later. Drunk with optimism and beer, we gave him a rousing send-off. You really sensed there was something in the air that night, beyond the aromas generated by 20,576 slightly sweaty England supporters.

At Lord's, the queue of members – all guaranteed admission to the ground, but not necessarily a decent seat in the pavilion – reportedly started to form at 3.30 a.m. The players couldn't park in the ground because the space was needed for an extra hospitality area. Taxi-drivers said the journey was impossible, so most of the England team had to walk a mile to the ground from their hotel. 'Oddly,' wrote Ashley Giles in his column for the *Guardian*, 'this restriction did not affect the MCC committee, which drove in as usual.'

On a glorious sunny day, Ricky Ponting won the toss and decided to bat. Stephen Harmison, our Genuine Fast Bowler, roared in from the Pavilion End for that crucial first over that, we hoped or feared, would define the contest to come. His second ball was short and quick and smacked into Justin Langer's elbow, just above the armguard. The batsman needed treatment. Hayden tried to hook his 16th ball and missed: the ball dented his helmet grille. Harmison's 34th ball clanged Ponting's grille into his right cheek and drew a decent amount of blood. Through all these interruptions the England players offered no words of sympathy, but just chatted among themselves.

Andy R: You knew that suddenly the whole thing had gone up several levels. The whole attitude was right.

And wickets fell. Hayden went first, bowled by Matthew Hoggard. (We had become so used to Hoggard taking an early wicket with the new ball that we almost took it for granted. Fools!) The pitch was hard and responsive – according to Mike

Gatting on Channel 4, it 'had had too much hot weather' – and our four-man pace attack – Hoggard, Harmison, Flintoff and Jones, possibly the best we had ever fielded – ran through the Australians. At lunch they were 97 for five, and just before tea 190 all out. Harmison had five for 43 off 11.2 overs.* The *Independent's* Stephen Brenkley has since nominated this as one of his favourite passages of play: 'At the time it seemed momentous and its meaning has not diminished with the passing of a few years.' As Tony Greig would say, all we wanted to know was, would England come to the party? On this evidence they had not only turned up on time, they had brought crates of extra booze and were currently setting up the turntables in the front room.

What we had forgotten was that Glenn McGrath had also come to the party. Indeed, it was his house. England were quickly 21 for five. McGrath landed the ball exactly where he wanted it to land, and the batsmen played it exactly as he wanted them to play it. He had five for two in 21 balls. 'Vaughan fought and fought, but he couldn't keep out the master!' yelled Mark Nicholas. Kevin Pietersen, controversially preferred to Graham Thorpe, came in and went on the attack. He smacked McGrath for 4,6 and 4 off successive balls, whacked Warne into the crowd and was brilliantly caught at cow corner by Damien Martyn when he tried to do it again. Harmison and Jones added 33 for the last wicket to haul England up to 155, just 35 behind.

England now needed to bowl brilliantly and luckily and hold every catch. David Frith, who has seen a few of these matches, identified the turning point in *Wisden*. Australia were 139 for three just before tea on the second day. Damien Martyn and Michael Clarke were 24 and 21 respectively. The lead was 174.

---

* There is an argument that Steve Harmison is England cricket's Corporal Jones. 'They don't like it up 'em!' could be his motto, or, when things aren't going so well, 'Don't panic! Don't panic!'

Clarke gave Kevin Pietersen an easy catch at short extra cover. But not easy enough, it seemed. Clarke went on to score 91. Other catches were spilled, as they had been by so many other England teams when it had mattered most, and Australia were able to set 420 to win. Vaughan was bowled for a second time. 'I think he just played down the wrong line,' said Geoffrey Boycott in the commentators' box. 'He played down Piccadilly and it was on the Bakerloo line.' Ian Bell fell for Warne's straight ball. 'That was the slider to end all sliders,' said Richie Benaud. Rain was forecast and wiped out two-thirds of the fourth day but then, cruelly, it stopped. England were bowled out for 180, with Pietersen again outstanding on 64 not out. 'That's a biggie!' said Mark Nicholas of one of his sixes. 'That's straight into row 32,' said Richie of another. In *The Times* Simon Barnes suggested that Pietersen's innings was 'like the v-sign you give the headmaster ten minutes after you left school', making you 'feel a bit better without affecting the balance of power'. 'We have put ourselves in a position of real strength and can push on to fulfil our goal of winning this series 5–0,' said Matthew Hayden. 'They're getting on a bit,' said Matthew Hoggard. 'We've got back-to-back Tests, so it'll be interesting to see if they can put in the consistent performances for 25 days.' 'It's not been a very good couple of days for me,' wrote Simon Jones in his internet diary. 'Not only did we lose the first Test but my girlfriend has left me.'

Before Edgbaston, some tragic news. During practice Glenn McGrath had trodden on a cricket ball and torn his ankle ligaments. O woe! Michael Kasprowicz replaced him; otherwise both sides were unchanged. A week earlier Birmingham had been battered by an unseasonal tornado and the ground had been underwater. On the morning of the match it was cloudy above. Ponting won the toss and put England in. It was a catastrophic error. The pitch was a beauty and the best opening bowler in the world was on crutches. England scored 407 in 80 overs. It was the highest number of runs Australia had conceded on the first day of a Test for 67 years. Marcus Trescothick's 90 set the tone. They bowled it, he hit it for four through the off side. So wonderful and inspiring was his performance that, perversely, it didn't much matter that he didn't get a hundred, because other batsmen could come in and take over. Pietersen hit 71, his third fifty in three Test innings, and Flintoff an amazing and chancy 68 out of 103 added, with five sixes and six fours. 'You don't understand this, do you?' said Tony Greig on Channel 4. 'You're right, I don't,' said Geoffrey Boycott. 'It's fun, though.'

(The commentators were on good form this day. 'Gorgeous shot,' said Boycott as Vaughan cover drove for four. 'Now that's footwork, that's quality, that's class.' Pietersen pulled Lee over mid-wicket for six. 'Crikey O'Reilly!' said Mark Nicholas. Harmison mis-hooked Lee down to fine leg. 'Ah, that'll be out,' said Boycott. Pause. 'Out of the ground. Top edge for six.')

By this time we had grown used to Vaughan's mantra whenever he won the toss and chose to bat: 'We'll try and score some runs and put them under some pressure.' It shows either that cricket is a very simple game indeed or that he never tired of saying the same thing over and over again. And yet this is exactly what happened. For Hoggard's first ball to Hayden, Vaughan had positioned Strauss at short extra cover for the uppish bullying drive. Hayden hit the ball straight at him. Myself, I think this was the moment when I first thought overall victory was possible. One, they had done their homework. (And it became apparent over the course of the series that the Australians often hadn't done.) Two, the shackles of self-doubt had been shed. Three, the bully could himself be bullied. (Indeed, there's no one in the world more vulnerable to it.) Four, we were starting to make our own luck. Flintoff's 68, undeniably spectacular, had also been quite fortunate. Swatting Brett Lee's well-directed bouncer for six without looking at it or having any idea of where it's going . . . well, that needed guts and a four-leaf clover in your back pocket. Now England were bowling with the same ferocious concentration.

Ponting was batting superbly: amazing straight drives, cuts, clips off the legs when anyone erred even slightly in line or length. But as Gideon Haigh pointed out, one of the few shots he wasn't that good at was the sweep. The Wheely Bin got him for 61 with one that bounced, top-edged up to Vaughan who was waiting round the corner. Vaughan then ran Martyn out, almost balletically, and the Bin, who had taken two international wickets for 305 runs so far this summer, had Clarke caught behind off a quicker ball. Possibly the best moment of all came when Flintoff was running up to bowl to Gillespie. 'Right,' said Tony Greig. 'He needs a yorker right up there in the blockhole.' Amazingly that's exactly what Flintoff bowled. Gillespie missed and was lbw. Langer gritted it out for 82, and Gilchrist was stranded on 49 not out, but Australia conceded 99 on the first innings. It looked decisive.

And against anyone other than the best team in the world, it might have been. Shane Warne removed Andrew Strauss on Friday evening with his famous silly ball: the one that turns so much the batsman looks a complete idiot. The following morning Brett Lee took three quick wickets: 31 for four. Warne then worked through the batting order, aaahing and oofing and reeling them in with sheer force of personality. When Harmison was out for 0, the score was 131 for nine, the lead 230. 'Boy, this is now trouble for England,' said Tony Greig. Flintoff was still there, but he had hurt his shoulder earlier trying to pull Warne, and had played so far within himself you wondered if it was actually him. A pain-killing injection at lunch seemed to perk him up. One over from Kasprowicz went for 20, one from Lee for 18. 'Oh! Hello! Massive!' cried Mark Nicholas as the ball disappeared into the stands. One six was fished out of the TV cables on the pavilion roof by Graham Gooch. The last wicket pair added 51 (Simon Jones 12 not out). Warne got Flintoff in the end, for 73. 'Freddie! Well played,' we could see him say as the giant walked off. It was Warne's sixth wicket in the innings, tenth in the match and 599th in Tests. And Australia needed 282 to win.

How much of this sticks in the memory. Flintoff's first over, for example. Langer and Hayden had started well, looking comfortable against Hoggard and Harmison. Flintoff was on a hat-trick first ball, as he had taken wickets with the last two balls of the first innings. Langer survived the first, played it out to point, no run. Second ball, a touch faster, Langer played on. The crowd went mad. 'That'll get 'em going,' said Mark Nicholas. In came Ponting. Third ball, an inswinger, and a good shout for lbw, but just outside the line and maybe a bit high. Fourth ball, Ponting edged well short of gully. 'Oh, I say,' said Mark Nicholas. 'Flintoff has changed the whole feeling of the occasion.' Fifth ball, another shout for lbw, outside the line again. Sixth ball, well outside off-stump, Ponting left it alone, but it was a no-ball. Seventh ball, a perfect fast leg-cutter, which Ponting edged to Geraint Jones. Flintoff had softened him up as a cook tenderises meat. 'Really, he's set the place alight,' said Mark Nicholas.

After this it just became easier to believe in an England victory. For every batsman England seemed to have a plan, and each plan seemed to work. When Gilchrist chipped the Bin to mid-on for one, the score was 136 for six. 'Gone,' said Richie, 'and so might be the match.' At 140 for seven, England claimed the extra half hour, hoping to polish them off with two days to spare. Michael Clarke and Shane Warne took umbrage. Warne clumped the Bin for two vast sixes, and Clarke played with great maturity. Until Harmison bowled his loopy slower ball, the one we didn't know he could bowl. Clarke missed it. It was the last ball of the day: Australia were 175 for eight. Down and out, we all thought.

That Australia came so close the following morning is a testament, I think, to their greatness. No other team could have done it. Warne and Lee clearly decided that while they were still in, the game could be won. For three days Australia had been the team under pressure, harried and pushed as never before by these England players. On Sunday morning, for the first time, England were the team under pressure. Suddenly their bowling looked anodyne. Everyone bowled too short. When Warne trod on his stumps with 62 still needed, it was a relief, but it was also a surprise. The last two men were now at the crease: Brett Lee and Michael Kasprowicz. And gradually, inexorably, the target came down. Run by run by run.

With fifteen needed, Kasprowicz flicked a ball from Flintoff up to Simon Jones at third man. It would have been a difficult catch even if it hadn't potentially meant the difference between victory and defeat, but Jones seemed to see it late and couldn't quite hold on. With three runs required, Harmison banged another one in short, it hit Kasprowicz's glove and Geraint Jones took a superb tumbling catch down the leg side. 'Jones!' said Richie. Cut to the umpire raising his crooked finger. 'Bowden!' said Richie.* England had won by two runs. 'It just got big quick,' Kasprowicz said afterwards, 'and I didn't see too much of it.'

But was he out? Several thousand TV replays showed that Kasprowicz had taken his glove off the bat nanoseconds before the ball hit it, so technically he was not out. But as Steven Lynch observed in *Wisden*, Billy Bowden 'would have needed superhuman vision to see this, and an armed escort involving several regiments to escape the crowd had he actually refused to give it out'.† As it is, four days later when the Old Trafford Test started, a DVD calling itself *The Greatest Test* was already on sale. And no one argued with that judgement. 'Test cricket usually gives you an hour or two for a snooze, or a read, or even a discussion of "great Test matches",' wrote Gideon Haigh in *Ashes 2005*. 'Not for a ball could you avert your eyes at Birmingham: if you missed

---

* This may be a deeply eccentric choice, but I think 'Jones! Bowden!' is my favourite cricket commentary moment of all time. Although Bill Lawry's 'Tufnell! Tufnell! YEAH! TUFNELL!' isn't far behind.
† Kasprowicz himself said, 'It would have been a very tough decision to make. If I was the fielding side and didn't get that one, I would have been devastated.'

something, it was bound to be a turning point.' The two-run margin of victory had been the closest in all England-Australia Tests, and the photograph of Andrew Flintoff consoling Brett Lee, a display of chivalry and sportsmanship we thought had gone from cricket for ever, had given the contest an extraordinary resonance. And there's a thing: it's a photograph. Everyone thinks they saw it on telly, but it wasn't shown live, and it's hidden in the Channel 4 DVD box set in one of the special features, a scene we think we have seen but we haven't until we see it. It's this gesture, I would suggest, more than any of his cricketing feats, that sealed Flintoff's status as national hero.

So to Manchester, where two fake umpires walked out of the pavilion at the start of play on the first day. They were nabbed before they reached the outfield and the two real umpires came out. England, unchanged, had won the toss and were batting. Australia had Glenn McGrath back (for Kasprowicz) but there were suspicions he wasn't fully fit. Almost immediately, Adam Gilchrist dropped Trescothick. 'Oo, that's a shocker,' said Boycott. Brett Lee clanged Strauss on the helmet, then yorked him, for his 150th Test wicket. The captain emerged from the pavilion. 'He knows it. We know it. Michael Vaughan needs runs,' said Mark Nicholas. On 41 he slashed outside off stump. The ball was going straight for Warne at first slip but Gilchrist leaped in front of him and dropped it. If you listen carefully to the DVD you can hear Boycott at the back of the commentary box laughing fit to bust. Next ball, McGrath bowled him. 'Out!' said Boycott. 'Whoa! No-ball! Bad luck! Bad luck, you Aussies!' Huge cackles off-mike. 'Settle down there, Boycs,' said Michael Slater, trying not to sound nettled.

'All you need is to wait and wait on a pitch as true as this,' said Mark Nicholas. Trescothick and Vaughan put on 137 for the second wicket, and Vaughan got better and better. He was helped by Gillespie's lack of 'nip', which is to put it kindly: Gideon Haigh noticed the last three letters of his surname and suggested that that was what he was bowling. (He described him as 'the ideal helpmate for any batsman trying to play themselves back into form'.) One swivel-pulled six off Gillespie recalled the Vaughan of 2002/03. Several cover drives elicited that purring 'Aaah' you get from a crowd when they have seen something really special, as though they have just been stroked. After Trescothick edged behind on 63 to give Warne his 600th Test wicket, Ian Bell joined Vaughan for a stand of 127. The skipper was finally out for 166. 'A timely return to form,' said Athers. 'The whole ground rises to him, to appreciate his fluent stroke-play and his mental strength as well.' Wickets fell a little carelessly after he went, but Flintoff and Geraint Jones had another pro-ductive partnership to bring the total to 444 on the second morning. Time to 'put them under some pressure'.

Again, England's bowling was accurate and probing. Hoggy might have had Hayden lbw early on, might have taken him c & b. Bell caught Langer off the full face of the bat at short leg, a catch that looks amazing in slow motion because at normal speed it's just incomprehensible. Giles was lucky to have Hayden lbw – it was just outside the line – but his ball to dismiss Martyn was a beauty. 'Pitched outside, turned, defensive shot, hit the top of off-stump,' said Boycott. 'Eat your heart out, Shane Warne.' Flintoff and Simon Jones were soon reversing it at speed, as Simon Katich found out to his embarrassment, when he was bowled by Flintoff not playing a shot. Australia were 129 for five. Gilchrist and Warne started going for everything. Bell dropped Gilchrist at gully, Pietersen dropped him at short cover. Simon Jones finally got him, yet again off the first ball of a spell. Michael Clarke had hurt his back and, said Haigh, was 'moving with the freedom of Boris Karloff'. At the end of a wonderful day, Australia were 210 for seven, with Shane Warne 45 not out.

On Saturday it rained and rained, for this was Old Trafford. Play began at 4.10 p.m. Geraint Jones dropped Warne and missed a stumping. The Sunday papers would roast him. By the time everyone gave up, Australia had saved the follow-on and reached 264 for seven.

On Sunday Warne holed out for 90. We wouldn't have begrudged him the hundred, much. Simon Jones had taken six for 53 and Ashley Giles three of the other four. England led by 142 and sought quick runs. Strauss hit Lee for six. 'That's a lovely shot,' said Tony Greig. 'I tell you what, it's a lovely feeling as well. Fast bowlers running in bowling short deliveries, and despatching 'em for six. There's no better feeling for a batsman.'* Strauss's 106, scored with a piece of white plaster on his ear (from the first innings helmet-clang), 'fleshed out the generally good impression he had left this series,' said Haigh. Bell made his second fifty of the match, Geraint Jones hit 27 off 12 balls, Vaughan declared on 280 for six and Australia had 422 runs to win, or more pertinently, a day to bat out for the draw.

'Here we go,' said Mark Nicholas. Harmison's first ball to Justin Langer was short and fast. 'Just a little throat ball to say hi.' Langer went early, and Hayden was worked over by Flintoff in that way of his, eventually being bowled behind his legs. At lunch Australia were 121 for two, with Ponting 41 not out. Martyn was out to Harmison, lbw, off a thick inside edge. 'I'm not sure that's a good decision, that,' said Boycott. Ponting, though, was looking invulnerable. 'You do not become the best team in the world unless you fight to the very end,' said Mark Nicholas. It wasn't just a defensive innings, though: the loose stuff was picked off, and very marginally short balls from Giles were pulled with ferocity to the mid-wicket boundary. At tea Australia were 216 for five, with Ponting on 90. Michael Clarke, his back irritatingly improved, stayed with him for 73 minutes, before

---

* It had taken 28 years, but we all loved Greig again now, especially his predilection for terms like 'telecast' and 'crash helmet' that no one else ever used.

neglecting to offer a stroke to Simon Jones's reverse swing. Shane Warne, 'the ultimate competitor' as someone had called him, dug in for an hour and a half, and survived another drop by Kevin Pietersen at short mid-wicket. But with nine overs to go, he edged to Andrew Strauss at second slip. Strauss missed it completely, it bounced high off his thigh, and Geraint Jones took it one-handed, down to his right, just off the ground. Australia 340 for eight, with Lee coming in, and only McGrath to follow.

Simon Jones to bowl. Sixth ball of the next over, he shapes one away from Lee, who edges just short of fourth slip. Ponting survives the next over from Flintoff, playing and missing once. Seven overs left. Simon Jones pulls up with cramp, has to go off. Harmison takes over. First ball he hits Lee on the arm. 'Brett Lee is back where he was about a week ago,' says Mark Nicholas, 'taking a horrendous pounding.' (Again you can hear Boycott cackling in the background.) Second ball, big shout for lbw. Billy Bowden says no. Sixth ball, Lee digs out a yorker and it goes through square leg for four. Six overs to go. Ponting plays and misses at Flintoff's first ball, but survives the next five. Five overs left: Harmison bowling to Lee. Gets a single second ball. Fourth ball, another lbw shout against Ponting. Very close, but not out. Last ball is short, Ponting gloves it down the leg side, Geraint Jones catches it. Astonishing. Ponting is furious with himself, almost distraught. He has batted all day (for 156) and given it away with four overs to go. 'What an innings,' says Mark Nicholas. 'The applause should last for ever. The Australian captain has stood up and played one of the great rearguards.'

In steams Flintoff with seven slips. Lee plays and misses the first, fourth and fifth balls. As we bite our nails and chew our clothes watching televisions around the country, Lee and McGrath somehow hang on. The last ball of the 108th and last over is a full toss from Harmison – he is looking for the yorker – which Lee cracks to the square leg boundary. The game is drawn, the two not-out batsmen dance a jolly jig and we all wonder, was that it? Was that the chance? Have we utterly screwed it up? Gideon Haigh puts it in perspective: 'With the Old Trafford pitch in excellent order, the task of taking ten Australian wickets on the last day was a tall one.'

At Trent Bridge, ten days later, the two fake umpires again walked out before the real umpires. This time they reached the middle before being taken away for interrogation and, maybe, cakes. Each was fined £70 under the Public Order Act. England, still unchanged, again won a useful toss. Australia made two changes. McGrath's elbow was inconveniencing him, and Gillespie was a broken reed, so Kasprowicz came back and a first cap was given to 22-year-old Shaun Tait, a slingy young speed-ster from South Australia. It hardly seemed to matter. They still bowled it outside off stump, and Trescothick still hit it for four. 'This is exactly what England need,' said Tony Greig. Trescothick played on to Lee, but it was a no-ball. 'Lee doesn't know it yet,' said Richie, 'but he's going to in a moment.'

Andrew N: I was there with my son. England put on a hundred for the first wicket, and Warne came on ten or fifteen minutes before lunch. And immediately there was silence. I said to my son, watch this, it's a great moment, because you're seeing Warne come on, but you're also seeing the effect he has. And of course he took the first wicket.

At lunch England were 129 for one. Then it rained, and thumbs were twiddled until 3.50 p.m. Shaun Tait bowled Trescothick for 65 with an inswinging yorker. 'I'm here to tell you that that was an absolute cracker,' said Richie. Ian Bell didn't last long – another tentative shot – but Australians were dropping catches again: Kasprowicz missing a c & b off Pietersen, and Hayden shelling one at backward point off Vaughan. Boycott wasn't impressed: 'It's just a straightforward catch, that, isn't it?' Ponting brought himself on and had Vaughan caught behind for 58. The Australian captain looked like a small boy who had just found a fiver on the pavement. His teammates were quite pleased too.

On Friday morning Pietersen edged Lee behind for 45. The score was 241 for five and underachievement loomed. Flintoff scythed a ball from Lee over gully. 'There were all sorts of shouts of "Catch it!"' said Richie, 'but it would have needed Joel Garner, standing on Joel Garner's shoulders.' When he was hitting the spinners, Flintoff sometimes looked as though he was winding himself up, like a huge blond clockwork toy. One straight drive off Lee elicited gasps of delight from Boycott. 'That's battin'. That's not hittin'. That's battin'.' Within a trice Flintoff and Geraint Jones had put on a hundred. 'This is exactly what England needed,' said Tony Greig. The Australians thought they had Jones caught behind straight after lunch. Steve Bucknor obviously didn't hear the woody noise, although the stump mic did. With the Barmy Army in full voice and Shaun Tait's Monica Seles-like grunts every time he bowled, it's amazing he could hear anything. Flintoff reached his fifth Test hundred off 121 balls, and was instantly lbw to Tait for 102. Jones was eighth out for 85 and England's 477 was their third consecutive first innings score over 400. The Australians were beginning to wilt.

The most extraordinary thing about all this, for those of us who had endured his batting before, was this thrilling new sense that Hayden could get out at almost any moment. This time Hoggy swung it in to his front pad. 'You've got to give that out,' said Boycott. 'A blind man would give that out. What a fantastic delivery.' Simon Jones had Ponting lbw, although he might have hit it. Martyn definitely hit his. Langer gave a bat-pad catch to Ian Bell at short leg and Australia were 58 for four, which became 99 for five when Harmison beat Clarke for pace. Could Australia avoid the follow-on? The following morning Gilchrist whacked one past gully, or at least, we thought he did, for suddenly Strauss was flying through the air to catch it one-handed at full stretch. 'The catch of the summer – actually many summers,' wrote Gideon Haigh. 'Time seemed to stand still for half a heartbeat while the impossibility of this catch was mentally converted into certainty.' On my own mental hard drive I have a distinct memory of the catch from at least three different angles.

By this time the obdurate Katich had also gone, for 45, and even Brett Lee's agricultural 47 could not save Australia from a wholly novel humiliation. Not since Karachi in 1988/89, 191 Tests ago, and long before any of the current team had started playing, had they been asked to follow on. Simon Jones was the man who had done it, with five for 44. No player on either side had come on so far, so quickly: his knack of picking up a wicket with the first or second ball of a spell was uncanny (and also made Vaughan look good for changing the bowling). What a great future he had before him. Just as long as he didn't get injured, that was the main thing.

Like most teams following on, Australia batted better second time round, although they were helped by Simon Jones hobbling off the field after four overs with an ankle injury. At 155 for two the game was beginning to slip away. Ponting was on 48 not out, looking invulnerable again. Martyn called his skipper for a short single. At extra cover was a substitute fielder, 23-year-old Gary Pratt of Durham, who swooped down on the ball, flung it at the stumps, and ran out Punter by a foot. 'That is a gigantic moment,' said Mark Nicholas. 'Not just in the day, or in the game, but maybe in the series.' Nicholas can oversell a point, but I don't think he was wrong here. Ponting was incandescent. He had been complaining all summer about England's tactical use of substitutes (allegedly to give their fast bowlers a rest). As he stomped off the field, he looked up and saw Duncan Fletcher in the England dressing room, having a laugh. It was too much for him. He was later fined 75 per cent of his match fee for the outburst but, more significantly, he had also made a complete tit of himself.

Andrew N: The Ponting run-out was quite sweet.
Nick N: Yes, I watch that regularly on my DVD.
Andrew N: And the aftermath. Him swearing on the balcony.

Nick N: It's the swearing that makes it. World-class swearing.

Pratt, of course, became an instant cult hero. He was only at Old Trafford because he couldn't get a game for Durham. Stephen Moss in the following year's *Wisden* talked of 'the hand that won the Ashes'. Supposing Ponting had scored another of his 156s? As it is, after his departure and that of Martyn two overs later, Katich and Clarke knuckled down. They made a contrasting pair: Clarke the latest young blade, all graceful off-drives and badly highlighted hair, Katich the side-on accumulator, shovelling his drives with a strong bottom hand. Both made fifties, but Clarke nibbled fatally at the second new ball and Katich, after 262 minutes, was sawn off by Aleem Dar. The ball had pitched outside leg stump and would have gone over. 'That was a bit of a shocker for Simon Katich,' said Athers, who clearly sympathised with his fellow limpet. 'He's worked so hard . . . and he's not happy.' Warne (45), Lee (27 not out) and Kasprowicz (19) again resisted longer than a few of their fellows, and England were set 129 to win.

That day I was playing cricket in Surrey. It was a new fixture, in a beautiful village, with a terrific pub, against nice people. Unfortunately they hadn't believed me when I had told them we weren't any good. They had pulled in ringers from outlying parts of the Commonwealth, just to be sure. We were all out for very little and they won by nine wickets fifteen minutes after tea. And thank heaven they did, because it enabled us all to settle back in the pavilion and watch England stagger like drunk men towards the victory target. Warne – who else – extracted Trescothick, Vaughan and Strauss, and Bell hooked Lee straight to long leg. England were 57 for four. Ponting then made another mistake. Lee had bowled eight overs straight, so he turned to Shaun Tait. Pietersen and Flintoff added 46 with admirable certainty, milking Tait at a run a ball for his four overs. We started to breathe again. Lee came back on, had Pietersen caught behind and bowled Flintoff with reverse swing: 111 for six. Five runs later Geraint Jones tried to hit Warne over the top and got no further than extra cover. Thirteen still required. Hoggard came out to join Giles. 'He's reversing it at 95 miles an hour,' Giles told him. But Hoggard was unfazed. 'Bizarrely, I was very confident,' he said later. With eight runs needed, Lee bowled a full toss outside off-stump. Hoggard cracked it for four through extra cover. For all Flintoff's crashing sixes, Pietersen's flamingo shots, Vaughan's elegant caresses, Ponting's pulls and straight drives and even Warne's inside-out clumps over backward point, this was for me the shot of the summer. Had anyone seen Hoggy hit a boundary before, other than by accident? Moments later the Wheely Bin hit the winning runs. England were 2–1 up with one Test to go.

Robin W: Hoggard's cover drive. Because it was so unexpected and it was just such a release of tension. I tell you why it was so fantastic. It's because it encapsulates why cricket is such a fantastic game. People who are bowlers may not be very good at batting, but they have to bat as well. People who are not very good at something having to do it as well. And it's how well they do it that may make all the difference.

For the Oval England were finally forced to make a change, when Simon Jones's ankle injury did not improve.* Instead of going with Hampshire's Chris Tremlett, who had been 12th man for most of the summer, the selectors chose an extra batsman, Paul Collingwood, in what was widely considered a defensive move. (Probably because it was.) Glenn McGrath's elbow was better, though, and he supplanted Kasprowicz. Shaun Tait, who had taken three top-order wickets in England's first innings at Trent Bridge, retained his place. 'Men Will Be Made, Men Will Be Broken, All We Are Required to Do is Watch,' said one newspaper headline. Vaughan won the toss once again on another

* His only consolation, in the desolate years of injury that would follow, was a 2006 poll in *New Woman* magazine that voted him the ninth sexiest man in the world. George Clooney came tenth.

glorious sunny day. 'We're going to have a bat . . . We're going to try and get a good total in the first innings and put Australia under some pressure.' Almost unable to bear it any more, we held our breath. A few of us were starting to turn blue.

Trescothick and Strauss went off again at five an over, the two left-handers now looking a match for their eminent counterparts in the Australian side. After an hour Ponting introduced Warne, who didn't turn it much, didn't get a lot of bounce, but nonetheless took the first four wickets to fall. From 83 for no wicket to 131 for four: time to hide your eyes behind your hand. The fourth was Pietersen, bowled through the gate. 'That's it!' shouted Slater. 'The battle's over!' 'That's big, big, big for Australia,' said Boycott. Strauss and Flintoff calmed us all down. Playing utterly sensibly, with the confidence of men who had already scored a few runs against this attack, they added 143 for the fifth wicket. Flintoff went first for 72. 'Can't complain about that,' said Boycott. 'He's played superbly under pressure.' Collingwood was lbw to a Tait yorker that hit him several inches outside the line of off stump. Strauss's 129 was his seventh century in Tests. Geraint Jones, Giles and Harmison all passed 20, and we were all out for 373. It felt like a vulnerable total. In the circumstances, 573 would have felt like a vulnerable total. If anyone had crept up behind any of us and gone 'Boo!', they might well have found themselves stabbed.

Langer and Hayden now settled down to put together the partnership we had been dreading all summer. Hayden, playing for his place among other things, had downgraded his aspirations and was concentrating purely on survival. Langer, his resemblance to C3P0 never more pronounced, became the aggressor, hitting Giles over the top as soon as he came on. 'He hasn't got that properly,' said Richie. The ball flew high into the pavilion. 'Otherwise it would have gone for nine.' Langer reached 50 in the 20th over out of 66 for no wicket. Trescothick dropped him at slip, a high, difficult chance off Collingwood. At 96, Giles had a good shout for lbw. Billy Bowden shook his head. Hawkeye suggested middle stump, two thirds of the way up. On 112, just after tea on the second day, the umpires offered the batsmen the light, and everyone trooped off. It was bewildering. Australia needed to win the game, and they weren't going to do that in the dressing room. At four o'clock the rains came, and at 5.40 p.m. play was called off for the day. A nation rejoiced.*

On the third day, Hayden reached his first fifty of the summer and maybe the scratchiest one of his career. As Langer passed 100 for the 22nd time in Tests, Harmison suddenly found an extra yard of pace and made him play on. After more stoppages for rain and bad light – vast cheers from the crowd – Ponting was surprised by a ball from Flintoff that bounced and gave a catch to gully. Australia were 277 for two by close of play. Their gameplan was clear: bat on all day Sunday, then bowl out England on Monday. Job done; Ashes retained.

England's task was to resist and, ideally, to conquer. On Sunday Flintoff got the old ball to bounce and Martyn played an ungainly semi-hook, spooning an easy catch to square leg. Fifteen minutes later the new ball was taken. Clouds gathered. The umpires offered the batsmen the light. No, said the batsmen. Clarke slashed Hoggy to Flintoff at second slip. Dropped! 'He normally swallows those, doesn't he?' said Slater. Hayden was now playing very well, and hit a couple of crunching drives off Hoggy. Flintoff finally got him lbw for 138. 'A fightback knock,' said Tony Greig. The new ball was swinging all over the place. Clarke slapped Hoggy high to deep backward point, but Bell didn't see it in time. Poor Hoggy! Flintoff had Katich lbw. 'This is a huge performance by Andrew Flintoff,' said Mark Nicholas.

---

* To this end a couple of men called Gav and Mike had set up a website, raindancefortheashes.co.uk. Among their suggestions were leaving the car sunroof open, planning a barbecue, hanging out the washing, going for a day out at the seaside, and dressing in tissue paper.

Gilchrist slashed Hoggy through the slips for four. 'Safe,' said
Richie. 'Not sound, but safe.' Hoggy swung one in to him:
another lbw. The Oval went bananas. At lunch Australia were
356 for six. Flintoff had bowled unchanged, and carried on after
lunch. For once the tail didn't wag, didn't move a muscle. Shane
Warne mis-hooked to mid-on, where Michael Vaughan took a
juggling catch. 'It's just out-and-out aggression from England,'
said Boycott, with satisfaction. How long had we been waiting
for this? Almost best of all was Ashley Giles's running catch in
semi-darkness at cow corner to dismiss Brett Lee. Australia were
all out for 367, conceding a lead of six. Flintoff had taken five for
34 in 17 overs, bowling unchanged, and Hoggard had four for
four in his last 19 balls.

The bad light now was in England's favour. McGrath, who
might now have tired of the '5–0' taunts from crowds, barmen
and taxi-drivers, had a rush of blood and bowled a bouncer. The
umpires offered the batsmen the light and they accepted, trying
not to laugh. When the gloom had cleared a little, the Australian
fielders walked back on the field wearing shades. England supporters countered by unfurling umbrellas, although it wasn't
raining. Australian supporters took off their shirts to bask in
imaginary sunshine. It got darker again and everyone trooped off.
The cheers were deafening.

And so day five dawned, the last of the summer.

*Richard B: Someone who I know has only the slightest passing inter-
est in cricket went to both the last day of the Headingley Test in 1981
and the last day of the Oval in 2005. It's infuriating.*

Strauss had gone the previous evening, deceived by now
extravagant turn from Warne. On 67, McGrath had Vaughan
caught behind for 45, and next ball Bell clipped to slip for a pair.
'Surely, surely, we can't have another finish like those that have
gone before,' said Tony Greig. The hat-trick ball hit Pietersen's
shoulder and popped up to Ponting at second slip. All eyes on
umpire Bowden, who said no. (What a good series he had.) In the

next over, still on 0, Pietersen edged Warne to Gilchrist, who parried it to Hayden, who could not hold on. When he reached 10, he would have been run out if Clarke's throw from mid-on had hit the stumps. On 15, he edged to Warne at first slip, who dropped it. But Warne didn't drop Flintoff, when he offered a tricky low caught-and-bowled. Warne didn't so much celebrate as issue a great primal scream.

Andy R: There was silence. Everyone thinking the same thing. We're going to lose this, aren't we.

In 2006/07 a pitch announcer in Australia would refer to 'Paul Collingwood MBE', to mock the award of a gong to a man who played just one Test in 2005, took no wickets and scored just seven and 10. To which my response would be: fuck him. The crucial stand on that last day was the one between Pietersen and Collingwood. When Flintoff was out, we thought it was all over. When Collingwood was out, caught bat-and-pad, having survived 51 balls and 72 minutes, Pietersen had scored another fifty or so runs and the match, if not safe, was certainly saveable.

Andy R: That first hour after lunch . . . it was like Atherton vs Allan Donald in 1998. Brilliant cricket, could only have happened in cricket, because nothing happened, but everything happened in that little spell. It was the same with KP and Brett Lee. He could have been out any ball, and yet he hit him for how many sixes?

Alan W: It was the most amazing counter-attack, and probably the best bit of batting, I'll ever see.

Crucially, also, Warne was tiring. Shaun Tait bowled Geraint Jones, but the only reason he was bowling in the first place was that Ponting was running out of options. At tea England were 227 ahead, with three wickets left, and 49 overs to go, if the light did not fade. (It was 12 September: the evenings were drawing in.) By the time Pietersen was out, for 158, the draw was certain and the Ashes were ours. At the other end, another cricketer whose stature had grown through the summer, Ashley Giles, was calmly recording his highest Test score, 59.

Darrien B: Watching the very end of the series in the pub next to work. No one was talking – even though we'd won by that point, that was clear. But we're all sitting in silence, watching every ball. And Giles was batting, and he hit the most amazing shot, straight past McGrath.

As Warne stood at third man, no doubt contemplating what might have been, the crowd alternated between three chants: 'There's only one Shane Warne' (true), 'Warnie's dropped the Ashes' (a little harsh, maybe) and 'We wish you were English' (the greatest of all compliments). He had taken six for 122 in the first innings, six for 124 in the second, and 40 in the series overall. Terry Alderman had taken 42 wickets in 1981 and 41 in 1989, and Rodney Hogg 41 in 1978/79, but each of those were six-match series. Warne had done it in five. He had also scored 255 runs at 27. 'Warne, for long a great player in a grand side,' wrote Haigh, 'was here seen in a new guise: Australia's best, last and sometimes only hope.'

Andy R: He was fielding near us on the boundary edge, and somebody obviously said something. And he didn't ignore them or anything, he just turned round and did a sort of butterfingers mime. Couldn't catch anything, me. They were still up for winning the game at this stage. But he could make a joke of it. We all loved that.

And afterwards, the whole vibe was amazing. We were sat there for an hour in the dark. Have we finished? Is that it then? Have we won?

Reliving this series again, often crying and laughing at the wonder of it all, I have to admit to a feeling of mild mystification. We won 2–1 and, a lot of the time, we completely outplayed them. And yet, if things had gone even slightly differently, Australia could have won 4–0. Think of it another way: if they had won at Edgbaston, would we have dominated Old Trafford as we did? McGrath might have been right: it could have been 5–0. But if we had dismissed the last pair at Old Trafford, and won at Trent Bridge, would we have played so well at the Oval? Dead-rubber syndrome would suggest not, which would have meant a 3–2 victory – and that wouldn't have been quite the same somehow. This extraordinary summer, in other words, could only have been exactly what it was: anything else that happened could only have made it different, and not as good. Fortunately that's the essence of cricket: we can speculate all we like over what might have been, but the narrative is so complex that *everything* depends on what has happened before, and *everything* that is yet to happen will depend on what happens now. Great sport, as 2005 was, demands that we live in the present. And thanks to the magic of DVD, we can happily go on living in that present for the rest of our natural lives.

Interlude
2005

Tom H: The wonderful quality of the cricket was perfectly comple-
mented by the sensational quality of the commentary team. I thought it
was the dream commentary team. Perfect balance. And the sense of slight
disappointment that has shadowed England ever since is mirrored by the
fact that I really don't like Sky at all.

Alan W: I was at Lord's for the last of the ODIs, the one we tied. There
was an amazingly drunk man in my stand, who was conducting all the
chants. He stood up and saw an Australian girl in the front row. I think
we needed nine to win off the final over at that stage and of course every-
one's hammered. Anyway, he screams at her, 'Who's going to win?' and
she screams back, 'We are, of course.' And he turns to the whole stand
and bawls, 'YOU SEE? THAT'S WHY SHE'S AUSTRAL-
IAN . . . BECAUSE SHE BELIEVES!' Which made no sense,
except it did, and all these quietly smashed people came out of their shells
and started shouting, 'YEAH, WE BELIEVE!'

Chris D: I persuaded my girlfriend to move in after the Lord's Test. And
she moved in, whereupon Trescothick and Strauss made more than a
hundred before lunch. It was quite strange, the whole of that series, really
quite life-changing. When she moved in she knew nothing about cricket

at all. At the end of the series I was having to review eight Ashes books, and I got so tired, I had so many to do, that she had to do Thorpey. So within a few weeks she went from not knowing anything about cricket to being able to review Thorpey's book.

Andy R: We were at Edgbaston on the Saturday, when Freddie took two wickets in the same over and turned the game round in the evening. What was amazing was the sheer level of concentration from both sides in that game. I don't remember any period when nothing was happening, even though on paper it doesn't look that spectacular. But the bowling seemed to be totally in their face all the time, and they batted really solidly, until the end.

And the atmosphere from the Hollis Stand . . . So often I sit in a stand and think, god, I wish I was over there. Because they got louder and louder and louder. We were in the members' bit, and all I could hear around me was members going, I wish those people would be quiet, I'm trying to watch the cricket. And I'm sitting thinking, actually mate, if it weren't for them we'd probably have lost this game already. It was stunning. Absolutely amazing atmosphere. Every time Freddie ran in to bowl, waaaaaa-aaaayyy! Every ball.

Bren S: I was at the Big Chill. Big alternative music festival, twenty, thirty thousand people. Tent city. And on the Sunday morning, every fourth or fifth tent had the wireless on. Everybody sitting in groups listening to the cricket, all morning, and when every time a wicket fell, a huge roar. And I thought, this is a music festival. But nobody's listening to any music.

Robin W: Edgbaston, the last day. I turned up at your flat, a lot earlier than I would have done usually, to get a bit of the Test in. And we watched a bit and it got worse and worse. From nailed-on certainty the day before, to probably, to even-stevens, to probably not, to almost definitely not. And we had to go to play a cricket match ourselves. I'd thought of this eventuality, so I had my radio and my headphones. Sitting in Polly's car, between Martha and James . . .

Me: In their car-seats.

Robin W: Yeah, and I remember that you were just too scared . . .
you wouldn't have it on the car radio, would you?

Me: I just couldn't bear it.

Robin W: And I thought, That's probably wise. For as sure as eggs
is eggs, we're not going to win. And you said, I've been in this situation
so many times before. It's not going to happen. You hope and you hope,
and hope is dashed. So I must have had hope to keep listening. I only
had one headphone working. I always buy really cheap headphones.
They needed three runs to win. There was complete and utter gloom in
the car. You were in your private hell, and I was in mine, squeezed in the
back seat between two small children. And Polly driving, no real inter-
est whatsoever.

Me: And then you yelped.

Robin W: I think I must have stifled my yelp. Because Polly was
driving. It could just have been an embarrassing squeaky noise. But the
most amazing thing had happened.

Andrew N: Boxing Day 2004, I was pretty bored, so I went online to the
Oval website, and it said £10 for the last day, 12 September, and I
thought, Well, this is a losing bet. But I bought a couple of tickets anyway.

Chris D: And you gave me the ticket in January, didn't you, a bit
reluctantly. And I lost it. At first I didn't tell you that I had lost it. But
about a week beforehand, I had to 'fess up. And you said, oh god, why
did I give it to you? I knew I shouldn't have given it to you.

Andrew N: I remember it somewhat differently.

Chris D: And then the day before, Nicola my girlfriend found the
ticket.

Nick N: That's good. You're stuck with her for ever now.

Andrew N: I remember I got there about nine-thirty, and just sur-
veyed this day, and thought, This is a wonderful thing to have done. And
everyone seemed more interested in the fact that I'd only spent £10 on it,
instead of buying it for hundreds on eBay.

★

Robin W: I was doing jury service in Snaresbrook. I was watching it in a holding bay for all the different jurors. It was up on a fuzzy screen, and Pietersen was batting, and my number came up for court number two and I was saying, no! It's so unfair! I don't want to be here!

Ben D: I was obviously thrilled by 2005. And ecstatic, and absorbed. But I felt it very personally, and it really annoyed me, the general excitement of the nation. Because I thought, Where were you in 1989 when I was watching Jack Russell saving us from a humiliating innings defeat? All these people with corporate tickets watching Kevin Pietersen. I thought, You bastards! You're not real fans and you weren't there for the bad times. Because there were a lot of bad times.

Alan W: You know that thing about your favourite band becoming popular and how the magic goes? Well, actually I felt that a bit, round the time the open-top bus tour was going round. You sort of resented all the Johnny Come Latelies who were out on the street celebrating and who didn't spend the entire 1990s praying that Steve Waugh would get out, in vain.

Neal R: I was on the Strand when the victory parade went by, and I was more than a little worried that Kevin Pietersen might be about to throw up on top of me.

David J: I thought the whole thing we made of that was ridiculous. The way we behaved, the way Tony Blair behaved, and the press behaved, in making it some enormously important enterprise . . . it's the Ashes, it's a big thing but it's not that big. Trafalgar Square I thought was disgraceful. Completely over the top. Pomp and circumstance, jingoism at its worst. And of course it came back to haunt us eighteen months later, and quite right.

Tristan H-A: All Ashes series between 1987 and now, except 2005, were faked on a Californian sound stage. They never happened.

*

Chris P: From the moment Glenn McGrath trod on that ball at Edgbaston, I started to feel uncomfortable about it. I don't know why. I watched the Edgbaston Test and loved it. The bit where Brett Lee put two sixes over the stand and on to the bonnet of the chairman of Warwickshire's car: that was spectacular, and I loved that. But then other little things started to happen. Shane Warne treading on his stumps. I listened to or watched every minute of that series, but I couldn't get excited about it, because I had this nagging feeling at the back of my mind that something was not quite right about it. Bear in mind that the person who profited most, financially, out of that series would have been Rupert Murdoch. The interest in cricket that series generated led to an enormous number of people subscribing to Sky, as the ECB had sold English cricket down the river, which was outrageous. And I just think it was almost scripted. Keep the excitement going right up to the final day of the final Test match. I hope I'm wrong. But I have this awful feeling that, in thirty years' time, someone will write an autobiography saying, they fixed that series.

David T: My dad loved cricket, and if there was an exciting Test match going on in some far-flung corner of the world, you could be sure that he would be listening to it at two o'clock in the morning. And it was a sign, a symbolic mark, that he was on the way out, that for his 85th birthday, in summer 2006, we bought him the DVD of the 2005 series. Although he had six months to live, he never even put it in the machine. We knew then. The year before he had been really excited about it. A year later he just wasn't bothered.

Twenty

2006/07

I just thought, Well, they're only out on loan.
Ricky Ponting, after the Oval, 2005

On 23 November 2006, at the Gabba in Brisbane, Stephen Harmison prepared to deliver the first ball of the 2006/07 Ashes series. Here we all were again. The suffering never ended. It could never end. We will die, and know nothing more of this, but our descendants will squirm in their seats as we have done, will drink too many tinnies, and eat too many crisps, and wish they were somewhere else, able to think about something else. It is a form of mental imprisonment from which there is no escape: a life sentence. Such thoughts may have floated through our minds as Harmison ran in, his mouth at least as dry as ours, and bowled the ball straight at his captain, Andrew Flintoff, standing at second slip. Steve Bucknor called a wide.

Nick N: I was so tense before the first ball was bowled. My hands were literally shaking. But as soon as he bowled it, I thought, Ah, that's a relief, I don't have to go through all that mental anguish again about can-we-do-it? Because we're not going to. We're going to lose.

And we did, five-nil.

ACKNOWLEDGEMENTS

Thanks to everyone who agreed to be interviewed, offered advice, ideas and support, or listened to me bang on when it turned out to be twice the amount of work I had thought it was going to be, including: Cliff Allen, Maxie Allen, Stephen Arkell, Peter Bently, Darrien Bold, Jon Buck, David Burnage, Ross Clark, Tim Cooper, Thomas and Georgia Coops, Richard Corden, Sam Craft, Amanda Craig, Tim de Lisle, Alan and Selena Doggett-Jones, Christopher Douglas, Ben Dowell, Sally Ann Fitt, Richard Foreman, David Freedman, Petrina Good, Tristan Haddow-Allen, Peter Hall, John Haydon, Sarah Hesketh, Ian and Victoria Hislop, Tom Holland, Patrick Howarth, Iain Hunt, Sarah Jackson, Andy James, David Jaques, Bob Jones, Andy Leonard, Oliver Lewis-Barclay, Steven Lynch, Mark McCallum, Leo McKinstry, Howard McMinn, Mark Mason, Bill Matthews, Nick Newman, Andrew Nickolds, Peter Noble, Matt Odwell, Simon O'Hagan, Julian Parker, Matthew Parker, Chris Pollikett, Fred Ponsonby, Susy Pote, Neal Ransome, Lucy Reese, Sir Tim Rice, Tom Rice, Andy Robson, Simon Rose, Patrick Routley, Ken Runciman, Terence Russoff, Kate Saunders, Louisa Saunders, Rose Smith, John Stern, Bren Suhr, Mitchell Symons, David Taylor, Russell Taylor, David Thomas, Hilary Todd, Robin Welch, Francis Wheen, Alan White, Helen White and Ceili Williams. And also to super-agent Patrick Walsh; to my friend and publisher Richard Beswick (who said, can you do it by Christmas, and I said, yeah); and to the blond(e)s at home, Paula, Martha and James, as always.

ACKNOWLEDGEMENTS

BIBLIOGRAPHY

Adamson, Mike, Dart, James, Ingle, Sean, and Smyth, Rob • *Is It Cowardly to Pray for Rain?* (Abacus/Guardian Books, 2005)

Arlott, John • *The Ashes 1972* (Pelham Books, 1972)

Arlott, John • *Arlott on Cricket: His Writings on the Game* (William Collins, 1984)

Arnold, Peter, and Wynne-Thomas, Peter • *An Ashes Anthology* (Christopher Helm, 1989)

Baldwin, Mark • *The Ashes' Strangest Moments* (Robson Books, 2005)

Batty, Clive • *The Ashes Miscellany* (VSP, 2006)

Brearley, Mike • *Phoenix from the Ashes* (Hodder and Stoughton, 1982)

Chappell, Greg, and Frith, David • *The Ashes '77* (Angus and Robertson, 1977)

The Daily Telegraph: Battle for the Ashes '89 (Pan, 1989)

Frith, David • *England versus Australia* (Macdonald/Queen Anne Press, 1989)

Gatting, Mike • *Triumph in Australia* (Macdonald/Queen Anne Press, 1987)

Haigh, Gideon • *Ashes 2005: The Greatest Test Series* (Aurum, 2005)

Hoult, Nick (ed.) • *The Daily Telegraph Book of Cricket* (Aurum, 2007)

Knox, Malcolm • *Adult Book* (Bloomsbury, 2004)

Lewis, Tony • *A Summer of Cricket* (Pelham Books, 1976)

Marlar, Robin • *Decision Against England: The Centenary Tests 1982–3* (Methuen, 1983)

Martin-Jenkins, Christopher • *Assault on the Ashes: MCC in Australia and New Zealand 1974/75* (Macdonald and Jane's, 1975)

Martin-Jenkins, Christopher • *The Jubilee Tests: England v Australia 1977 and the Packer Revolution* (Macdonald and Jane's, 1977)

Martin-Jenkins, Christopher • *In Defence of the Ashes: England's Victory, Packer's Progress* (Macdonald and Jane's, 1979)

Martin-Jenkins, Christopher • *Cricket Contest 1979–80: The Post-Packer Tests* (Queen Anne Press, 1980)

Martin-Jenkins, Christopher • *Grand Slam: England in Australia 1986/87* (Simon and Schuster, 1987)

Martin-Jenkins, Christopher, and de Lisle, Charles • *An Australian Summer: The Story of the 1998/99 Ashes Series* (Faber and Faber, 1999)

Rae, Simon • *It's Not Cricket* (Faber and Faber, 2001)

Rayvern Allen, David (ed.) • *The Punch Book of Cricket* (Granada, 1985)

Rice, Jonathan • *The Fight for the Ashes 2001* (Methuen, 2001)

Ross, Alan (ed.) • *The Penguin Cricketer's Companion* (Penguin, second edition, 1979)

Selvey, Mike • *The Ashes Surrendered* (Macdonald/Queen Anne Press, 1989)

Synge, Allan • *Sins of Omission: The Story of the Test Selectors 1899–1990* (Pelham Books, 1990)

Williams, Marcus (ed.) • *The Way to Lord's: Cricketing Letters to the Times* (William Collins, 1983)

Willis, Bob, with Murphy, Patrick • *The Cricket Revolution: Test Cricket in the 1970s* (Sidgwick and Jackson, 1981)

Willis, Bob, with Lee, Alan • *The Captain's Diary: England in Australia and New Zealand 1982–83* (Willow Books, 1983)

The Wisden Cricketer: Flying Stumps and Metal Bats (Aurum, 2008)

Wynne-Thomas, Peter, and Griffiths, Peter • *The Australian Tour to England 1993* (Limlow Books, 1993)

And, of course, *Wisden Cricketers' Almanack* (1979–2008).

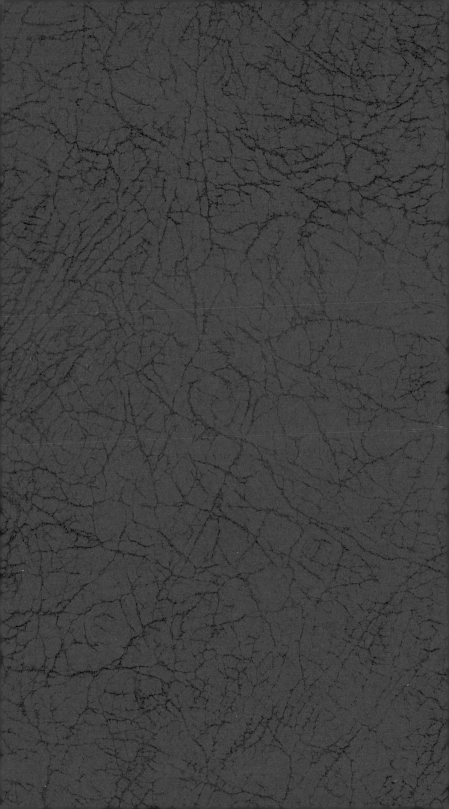